How to Write Best-Selling Fiction

by Dean R. Koontz

Writer's
Digest
Books

Cincinnati, Ohio

Second printing, April, 1982
Third printing, May, 1984

Library of Congress Cataloging in Publication Data

Koontz, Dean.
    How to write best-selling fiction.

    Includes index.
    1. Fiction—Authorship. I. Title.
PN3365.K63   808'.025   81-2083
ISBN 0-89879-045-X   AACR2

Design by Barron Krody.

This book is dedicated to

my fellow worker, my toughest critic,

my greatest fan, my inspiration,

my best friend, and my wife

—who are all the same person:

Gerda Ann Koontz

I wish to thank my editors, Carol Cartaino and Howard I. Wells III, for their contributions to *How to Write Best-Selling Fiction*. Even before I began writing, they helped design a solid structure for the book. In later stages, they persuaded me to include material that proved to be vital, persuaded me to cut other material that was extraneous, and managed to do all of that without getting any of us bruised or ruffled!

Contents

1.

A Brief Explanation of the Author's Purpose
Why has Koontz done another book about writing after he swore he told us everything he knew in his first book?

2.

Writing the Great American Novel
Why do so many perfectly nice people make pompous asses of themselves when they sit down at a typewriter?

3.

The Changing Marketplace
I'm sorry, but we're no longer buying epistolary Gothic espionage novels set on the planet Mars in the seventeenth century. Readers seem to be tiring of that genre.

4.

Creating and Structuring a Story Line 55

A novel without a strong plot is like a beautiful blonde all dressed up and ready for excitement—but with no place to go.

5.

Action, Action, Action 129

A plot without action is like pasta without garlic, like Dolly Parton without cleavage, and like a writer without his similes.

6.

Heroes and Heroines 139

Your lead character doesn't have to leap tall buildings in a single bound, and he doesn't have to stop speeding bullets with his bare hands, but he darn well better know the difference between right and wrong, and he better be kind to animals, and it sure wouldn't hurt any if he brushed his teeth regularly.

7.

Creating Believable Characters 147

If your heroine is a beautiful actress, a fine painter, an engineer, a cabinetmaker, a superb cook, a daring test pilot, a whiz at electronics, a doctor, a lawyer, and an Indian chief, don't you think you ought to humanize her at least to the extent of giving her a zit on the end of her nose?

8.

Achieving Plausibility through Believable Character Motivation 157

If your villain guns down sixty people, blows up an airport terminal, hijacks a jet and then crashes it into the White House—all because his Social Security check arrived one day late, you're going to have trouble selling your novel.

9.

Background 167

If your hero is eating dinner in Moscow, you better know that steak is thirty bucks a pound; if he is drinking *sake* in Tokyo, you better know which hand he should use to hold the cup; and when he is sunning on the beach at Cape Cod, remember that there won't be palm trees.

10.

Grammar and Syntax

If you think grammar is just a small child's mispronunciation of "grandmother," and if you think syntax is a tax that the church levies on sin, maybe you should consider becoming a nuclear physicist or a neurosurgeon or just about anything at all except a novelist.

11.

Style

You can paint like Rembrandt or Grandma Moses and be acclaimed in either case; but if you paint by the numbers like my Aunt Matilda, no museum is going to hang your pictures of flowers and sailing ships.

12.

Two Genres: Science Fiction and Mysteries

If you absolutely insist on confining yourself to a literary ghetto for the rest of your life, here are a few tips about how to get along well in a couple of those neighborhoods.

13.

Just when you thought it was safe to go into the literary waters, here are a few more sharks no one's told you about.

14.

Money is freedom; money is time; money is fame; money is respect; money is a yardstick of many things, but most of all, money is money.

15.

It is the writer's privilege to help man endure by lifting his heart.
—William Faulkner, 1897-1962

To the man with an ear for verbal delicacies—the man who searches painfully for the perfect word, and puts the way of saying a thing above the thing said—there is in writing the constant joy of sudden discovery, of happy accident.
—H.L. Mencken, 1880-1956

Against the disease of writing one must take special precautions, since it is a dangerous and contagious disease.
—Peter Abelard, 1091-1153

1.

**A brief explanation of the author's purpose
or
Why has Koontz done another book about writing after he swore he told us everything he knew in his first book?**

In 1972, *Writer's Digest* published my book *Writing Popular Fiction*, in which I attempted to show new writers how to build successful careers as category novelists. By "category," I meant those books to which publishers—in their ceaseless and determined effort to pigeonhole every writer—could affix comfortable labels. The categories I discussed in *Writing Popular Fiction* were science fiction, fantasy, suspense, mysteries, Gothic romance, Westerns, and erotica.

I am happy to report that *Writing Popular Fiction* was a success in its field. It went through several printings, sold rather well, and was well reviewed. Over the years, I received a considerable amount of mail about the book, and every one of those correspondents was kind enough to say that my advice had been of value. In a number of cases, readers of the book went on to write and sell their own fiction, much of it quite good, and when they sent me complimentary copies of their first published works, I was almost as delighted as I was when *Writer's Digest* sent my royalty checks. (Please note the most crucial word in that last sentence—"almost"!)

Writing Popular Fiction was a good book for its time. But times have changed. They always do.

I have three primary reasons for wanting to replace that old text with the book you now hold in your hands:

1. *The marketplace has changed drastically.* During the past decade, most major publishing companies have been acquired by conglomerates, and this development has had profound effects upon the book industry. In Chapter 3, I will discuss those effects and the changes (both for the better and for the worse) they have wrought.

2. *Readers' tastes have changed.* For instance, Gothic romance novels were once eagerly sought by readers and, therefore, by most publishers as well; in the early 1970s, that was the hottest fiction category of them all, and some paperback houses released five, six, or even seven new Gothics every month, for a cumulative yearly total in the hundreds of titles. Today, I am not aware of a single major house that regularly—or even sporadically—publishes Gothic romances. For reasons which I will discuss later in this book, huge numbers of previously faithful readers suddenly abandoned the genre; the number of copies sold fell below the level of profitability; Gothic lists were slashed and then canceled at virtually every publishing house; and those authors who had been producing books exclusively in that extremely formula-bound category were no longer able to sell their manuscripts at any price. Many of them had been receiving good or even excellent advances; but abruptly they were unable to give their books away. Only the well-established, bestselling ladies of the genre—such as Victoria Holt—survived that mini-Armageddon unwounded. The average Gothic writer either disappeared from the bookstore shelves or began writing different kinds of books. Admittedly, the fate of the Gothic is the most extreme example of how readers' tastes have changed over the past ten years; no other genre was so completely wiped out as that one. Most categories of fiction rise and fall and rise again in popularity, but they have floors of profitability through which sales never crash, not even at the lowest point of the deepest down-cycle. Nevertheless, it is essential that I update the market advice I gave in 1972.

3. *I have grown and changed as a novelist.* My knowledge of both the art and the craft of fiction is greater than it was in 1972. That doesn't mean I'm terrifically bright and clever. Any greater understanding that I've acquired has come about because I've remained open-minded and self-critical about my work and because I've labored hard since 1972—an average of seventy hours a week, year after year.

I've written, rewritten, and re-rewritten, polished, sanded, buffed, and repolished quite a few books in a variety of categories and styles. I'd have to be exceptionally thick-headed not to have learned *something* from all those hours at the typewriter.

Besides, when *Writing Popular Fiction* was published, I was only twenty-six years old. Although I had sold two dozen novels by that time, my writing skills and experiences were nevertheless limited. Understand—at that time I didn't realize I was still a neophyte. Like every twenty-six-year-old, I thought I knew all the tricks. These days, when I need cheering up, I just think of myself as I was back then, and the recollection of my old beliefs and opinions never fails to give me a good belly laugh.

Now I am an old man of thirty-five (sarcasm intended). I am entering my twelfth year as a full-time freelancer. My books have more than twenty-five million copies in print, and that figure continues to grow more rapidly every year. I have had both short and lasting relationships with editors—of whom several were excellent, many indifferent, and a few downright incompetent. I have dealt with copyeditors who knew little or nothing about grammar and syntax, but who felt they had a *moral obligation* to revise my prose; I have also dealt with good copyeditors. I have endured larcenous publishers, honest but slow-paying publishers, good critics, bad critics, and the vicissitudes of the strange book distribution system that operates in this country. I feel as if I am a battle-scarred but happy-to-be-alive veteran with a treasure of survival tips to pass along to the new recruits.

That is why I'm writing this new book, even though I swore I told you everything I knew when I wrote the first one.

I have quite a few friends who are writers, and most of them believe that the creation of well-crafted fiction cannot be taught. They are convinced that no one can learn to be a polished professional novelist by attending creative writing classes or by reading textbooks on the subject. In the opinion of these friends of mine, writing fiction is not in any way a mathematical or scientific—therefore not a teachable—process; good prose is not produced merely by faithfully following a set of rules or guidelines. Fiction (they argue) is a product not only of the conscious mind, but of the subconscious as well, and textbooks do not allow for input from the artist's heart and soul. My friends insist that each writer is unique, that each must achieve enlightenment and find his own special voice in his own way, in his own time.

I agree. To a certain extent, a novel can be dissected, its musculature revealed, its skeleton uncovered for study. But a pathologist cannot find a man's soul while doing an autopsy on his corpse, and a critic can never hope to pin down and dissect the *spirit* of a novel. Primarily, one learns to write fiction by writing it, then by writing more of it and more of it and more. . . .

Creative writing teachers and classroom situations often give the new writer the mistaken notion that the creation of novels and short stories is a communal art form. Not so. While there is some benefit to be derived from the feedback that a beginning writer receives from other students and from his instructor, by far the greatest portion of his artistic maturation will take place when he is in a room by himself, confronted only by blank pages.

A creative writing teacher *can* be of significant value to a student in the early stages of his growth. By being an inspiration. By offering encouragement. By explaining the basic fictional structures. By providing a fresh, unbiased reaction to work in progress and to finished material. But the teacher should never be an absolute arbiter of taste and style; unfortunately, that is what often happens.

Most students compose stories with the intention, first and foremost, of pleasing the teacher and, perhaps secondarily, with the desire to impress other students. In a classroom situation, the fiction upon which the new writer models his own stories will most often be the work of authors recommended by the teacher. If the teacher's favorite novelists happen to be the student's favorites too, such imitation can be a worthwhile exercise. Both the student's mind and soul will be involved in creating those imitations, and he will learn something about style while he gradually evolves his own voice and (eventually) forsakes mimicry. But if the student's favorite authors are not the same as those admired by the teacher (which is usually the case), and if the student nevertheless models his fiction on them, in a cynical effort to get good grades, his mind will be involved but not his soul. He will learn a lot about deception but little about prose style. That is an unhealthy start for anyone who seriously intends to pursue a career as a novelist. First and foremost, you must write to please yourself; *your heart must be in it.*

In college I took three creative writing courses in which students were expected to produce several pieces of their own fiction. At that time, my favorite reading material was science fiction and suspense novels. Both of those genres were looked upon with disdain in the academic community. (Since then, science fiction has gained a modicum of respectability on university campuses, though for all the wrong reasons. I'll discuss that development in a later chapter.) When I wrote science fiction and suspense short stories to fulfill the requirements of those creative writing courses, my professors generally reacted negatively, even condescendingly. The best grades usually went to those who slavishly imitated the work of Willa Cather, John Barth, Philip Roth, Virginia Woolf, Henry James, and other darlings of the literati.

Then, in my junior year, everyone in my creative writing class was required to submit a piece of fiction to the annual, nationwide college writing competition sponsored by the *Atlantic Monthly*. I sent in one of my suspense stories, "The Kittens," which had a real shocker ending. It was definitely not the sort of thing one was expected to enter in such a prestigious contest. When the winners were announced, all the Barth-Roth-James imitations were passed over by the judges, and much to my surprise (and to the surprise of my instructor) "The Kittens" was awarded one of the five fiction prizes. A few months later, at the start of my senior year, "The Kittens" did something better than win an award; the story sold to *another* national magazine and earned the first money of my career.

The point? Just this: For the most part, each writer of

fiction must find his own way. Fiction isn't a communal art form. It cannot be learned in a classroom or from a textbook to the same extent that math, physics, or even journalism can be learned. A good teacher can be valuable as an explainer of form and structural function. But fiction is more than form; it must have heart and the distinct stamp of an individual personality. In many ways the life of a novelist is lonely, for this profession requires its practitioner to spend long, long periods of time alone in intense, uninterrupted concentration. In a laborious, stumbling, fumbling, sometimes frustrating, trial-and-error fashion, each writer searches for and gradually finds his own handle on the process, his own method and style.

I know you're all asking yourselves the same question: If Koontz believes that the writing of fiction can't be taught, why did he bother to write the book I now hold in my hands? Earlier in this chapter, I listed three reasons why I wanted to replace my first writing text with a new and better book, but that list in no way explaiꞏed why I wanted to bother with the subject in the first place. I have three other reasons for thinking that a text of this sort is worth your time and mine.

1. I am going to point out a couple of hundred pitfalls into which new writers always fall. I fell into every one of them, and I still have a few bruises to prove it. If my warnings help you avoid just a few of those traps, or if I am able to help you climb out of them more quickly than you otherwise might, you will probably save weeks, months, even years in your struggle to attain the goals you have set for yourself.

2. This book will be more blunt and more honest about the hows and whys of marketing fiction than any book has ever been before. I will tell you about the strengths, weaknesses, successes, and failures of editors and publishers. I will tell you about the strengths that make a writer succeed, and I will warn you about the weaknesses and self-delusions that cause some writers to fail. I will lead you through the maze of book contracts and explain some of the more insidious and odious clauses that publishers try to slip past unwary authors. In the process, some myths will be shattered, including the one which would have you believe publishing is a refined, sensitive, gentlemanly business.

3. One of the most valuable things to be obtained from a book of this sort is the knowledge that you are not alone in your madness, that your obsession with words and *stories* is not as rare as you think. There are others of us who share your burning if somewhat irrational need to write and publish fiction. Bankers, lawyers, bakers, plumbers, and other ordinary citizens find us a bit odd. In the early days of our careers, when we're working without much in the way of financial rewards, our relatives look askance at us and—quite ignorant of the hard work involved in novel-making—ask us when we intend to get honest jobs. For the new writer, this negative input from the people close to him can be depressing and debilitating; it is helpful for him to know that many other writers have faced the same subtle hostility, have persevered, and have gone on to financial as well as artistic success. I'm going to offer you ample encouragement along those lines.

Rest assured, dear reader, I didn't take on this job just to make a fast buck at your expense. Money was *not* a contributing factor in my decision to write this book. Even if it sells as well as *Writing Popular Fiction* sold, it will earn me only about 2 or 3 percent of the money I would make if I put the same time and effort into another novel. Writing this text is an act of financial idiocy on my part.

But I don't write just for money; no one does. I write to entertain. In a world that encompasses so much pain and fear and cruelty, it is noble to provide a few hours of escape, moments of delight and forgetfulness. I write for ego-gratification, and any writer who says he doesn't is a liar. I write because writing demands discipline and therefore becomes a framework for my life. I write because I'm afraid of dying, and maybe there's a chance, if only a very small one, that some scattered bits of my work will live on after me and thereby frustrate Death. I write in order to communicate my ideas, feelings, hopes, and dreams; it is the author's function to reach out to all the lonely, frightened people and let them know that, at the core, we are all alike, every one of us. Not that we have to love one another without reservation, or even *like* one another without exception; after all, there are bores and jackasses and downright evil people among us. But even the bores and the jackasses and the evil ones are lonely and frightened, and they share the same anxieties and joys that the rest of us share; we have a common destiny. If you're reading this and saying, "*I'm* not lonely. *I'm* not frightened of anything," then you're deluding yourself, my friend. We are *all* lonely and frightened, even the most macho of us, even those of us lucky enough to be married and in love; deep down, on that level where we subconsciously acknowledge the vastness and indifference of the universe, we are *terrified*. Generally, we keep our terror well hidden from ourselves. Extended contemplation of our role in the scheme of things—in which we are smaller and more powerless than grains of sand on a vast beach—would be simply intolerable, suicidal. So we make jokes, and we laugh, and we busy ourselves with temporal concerns. We read *stories* because they bring us together in a gestalt of readership, and they allow us to live more lives than just the brief one that God (or a biochemical accident) allotted us. Some of us live other lives by *writing* those fictions. It is another way of pretending we live forever, while in our secret hearts we know that each of us dies alone.

So. If this book encourages even one or two of you to become good, polished, full-time yarn spinners with respect for solid craftsmanship, the time I've put into it will be time well spent.

Throughout this book, whenever I have needed an example of a specific writing technique, I have either invented a simple scene on the spot or I have quoted from my own published novels. Lest it appear that I am an egomaniac, quoting from my own work because maybe I think it's the only good work around, let me assure you that I am painfully aware of my faults as a writer. I have not chosen to quote exclusively from my books in order to glorify them or to send you out to buy them. I have used my own work because I am more familiar with it than I am with the work of anyone else, and when I tell you what the author was intending to do, I can be absolutely certain that those *were* his intentions because I am he.

I have tried to keep all examples short. However, at one point it was necessary to use three rather long excerpts from three novels, one right after the other, for I was discussing the qualities necessary in an opening chapter, and it was necessary to show you how those elements are coordinated over several pages.

2.

**Writing the Great
American Novel
or
Why do so many perfectly
nice people make
pompous asses of
themselves when they sit
down at a typewriter?**

Recently, I received a letter from a woman who taught me high school English eighteen years ago. In it, she gently scolded me about my books. I was disturbed because I didn't think I deserved to be scolded.

Let me make one thing clear: She is a fine teacher and a good person; she has a quick and intriguing mind. I will always owe her for the encouragement she gave me in my youth. She *knew* I should be a writer even when I was only fourteen years old; I was writing humor pieces and drawing cartoons for a class newspaper in my freshman year, and she spotted some crude talent, did what she could to nurture it, nudged me along.

In her most recent letter, she was still nudging me. She said, "You know, you really write rather well. There's a high degree of polish to your prose. What I don't understand is why on earth you keep producing these thrillers and adventure stories when you have the potential to do something better. I wish you would at least take one stab at writing the Great American Novel."

For the first time in the course of our relationship, I thought I detected a note of naivete in this venerable lady. As I mulled over what she had to say, I was struck by the realization that many new writers—and many not-so-new writers—share her misconception about the artistic process by which lasting fiction is created. This is a very dangerous and destructive misconception that slows the development of—and even aborts—the careers of countless authors. When I answered my friend's letter, I attempted to present an effective argument in favor of those authors who write *for* the masses—as opposed to those who, like Marge Piercy and John Barth and a host of others, seem to write *at* and *down to* the masses.

Young writers must learn the difference between ambition and pretention. I am convinced that the very best writing is born of humility; the truly great stuff comes to life in those agonizing yet exhilarating moments when the artist is acutely aware of the limitations of his skills and the poverty of his philosophies, for it is then that he strains the hardest to make the most he can from the imperfect materials and tools with which he must work.

This is how I put it in my letter to the woman who taught me high school English so many years ago:

> The idea of sitting down to create "important and lasting literature," the idea of sitting down with just that express intent, strikes me as pretentious and self-defeating.
>
> For one thing, what *is* the Great American Novel? *Moby Dick? The Deerslayer? The Scarlet Letter?* Those books are seldom read nowadays. *The Sun Also Rises? For Whom the Bell Tolls?* Hemingway will always remain readable because of the simplicity of his style. It seems to me, however, that he is slowly but surely passing out of fashion on university campuses, which are the very institutions that have kept him alive. He may eventually occupy a position like that which Henry James now fills: That is, he will be widely admired by people who have never read him. Fitzgerald? The body of his work is small, and like Hemingway he seems to be slowly drifting out of favor with the university crowd that has kept his flame burning these past few decades.
>
> The short lives of American literary reputations are partly the result of the ever-enlarging wave of hungry degree-seekers. Several generations of scholars industriously mine the body of an author's work, digging out every possible theme for doctoral dissertations, until the literary corpus is utterly hollow; whereupon new generations of would-be Ph.D.s, in

need of hot new areas of inquiry, have nothing to gain and everything to lose by helping to perpetuate the reputations of previously acclaimed literary giants. If an author turns his back on the masses and refuses to write novels with popular appeal, if he chooses to live solely or primarily by the grace of academe, then he surely will die by the *whim* of academe.

What I did not say in that letter to my teacher friend, but what now occurs to me is this:

If one believes that being read is not necessarily a criterion of greatness, then what I have said so far and what I am about to say next will all seem to be beside the point. I feel, however, that being read is *the* fundamental test of greatness in literature. The purpose of fiction is communication, and if the work is not read, the purpose is not fulfilled. More to the heart of the matter—if the author's efforts at communication are worthwhile, if what he has to say and the way he chooses to say it are truly of deep and lasting significance, then he *will* be read by the masses, for he will have touched the common cord that binds us all, will have plucked it and will have compelled large numbers of his fellow creatures to pay attention to him.

In short, not all popular novelists are good, but all good novelists are, sooner or later, popular. There is no merit in writing for a like-minded clique and selling two thousand copies of your book.

Now that I've gotten *that* off my chest, I'll return to the letter from which I was quoting and to my argument in favor of those novelists who are sometimes disparagingly referred to as "commercial writers," which is a meaningless term coined by those writers who feel the need to inflate the value of their own work by belittling the work of others.

I believe that some writers shape their work to please the academic elite because that is considerably easier than writing for the masses. The average reader demands eight things of a novel: 1) a strong plot; 2) a great deal of action; 3) a hero or a heroine or both;

4) colorful, imaginative, and convincing characterizations; 5) clear, believable character motivations; 6) well-drawn backgrounds; 7) at least some familiarity with the rules of English grammar and syntax—the more familiarity the better, of course; 8) a style which embodies at least a trace of lyrical language and as many striking images as possible, for good writing is always vivid and visual. [I will discuss each of these eight points in detail in later chapters.]

The standards of academe, on the other hand, are considerably less stringent than those listed above. For one thing, the academic generally has little or no use for plot in a novel; he feels that plot is a constraint upon the artist's imagination, and he refers to it as "artificial" or worse. I believe that to take such a position is akin to insisting that a sonnet should not be limited to fourteen lines and that it need have no special rhythm, rhyme, or plan. Plot is the skeleton of the novel, the bare bones that keep everything else from collapsing in a formless heap. If a plot is properly shaped, it not only supports but also dramatizes and enlarges upon the *thematic* structure of a book; it reinforces and strengthens all characterizations as well. In many ways, putting together a well-crafted plot—one without holes and without misfitted joints—is the most difficult, demanding task that a novelist must face; it is the supreme test of self-discipline, craftsmanship, and art.

Furthermore, plotting is not the only chore from which the academically oriented novelist is freed. He does not need to worry about pace, about filling his story with action. The university-trained critic disdains action; it is said to be the tool of hacks.

Likewise, so-called "literary" novels seldom have genuine heroes or heroines. The characters in such fiction are nearly always weak, flawed, and often downright unlikeable. This convention of the academic novel makes the author's task much simpler than it otherwise would be. As any writer will attest, it is usually more fun to write about villains and weaklings than it is to write about heroes; and it's easier, too.

Departing from the text of that letter to my ex-teacher, I'll tell you why writing about villains is easier than writing about heroes. Basically, there are three reasons: 1) A villainous character's possible courses of action are virtually unlimited; he is capable of *anything.* An admirable, heroic character, however, must conduct himself in such a fashion as to keep the reader's respect and sympathy, and this limits *his* courses of action. 2) Villains are often more fun to write about (and read about) because they provide vehicles for the vicarious release of the less-than-admirable impulses that exist in all of us. Recently, the entire country has been captivated by a television program—*Dallas*—in which the most popular character is the chief villain. Ninety-nine percent of the time, the mass audience prefers to cheer for the good guys, but now and then they find it amusing to work off their own frustrations by cheering for the *bad* guys. 3) I am sorry to say that it is easier to write about villains because we live in a world in which villainy is observed more clearly and more frequently than is virtue; we are achingly familiar with the ugliness of human nature—murder, rape, lying, cheating, stealing, betrayal, prejudice, ignorance, fanaticism—all of which compose three-fourths of the evening news on TV.

Although some authors find it taxing to write *convincing* heroic characters, and although the academic community has long supported the contention that admirable characters are not an essential part of fine fiction, I believe with all my heart that a heroic figure is a vital element of any good novel. Earlier, I said that the primary purpose of fiction was to communicate ideas, feelings, hopes, and dreams, but I believe it is *also* the purpose of fiction to inspire, to champion that which is good and right in man, and to condemn that which is evil. I am not saying that fiction must be solely inspirational, nor am I saying that a novel should espouse religious principles of any kind; certainly not! But what use is art if it is not humane? What use is art if it does not give us hope, if it does not lift our spirits?

What value does art have if it does not make our years on this earth better, happier, and easier to bear than they otherwise would have been? I'll answer my own question: If it doesn't do those very things, then art is of no use whatsoever. (I strongly recommend John Gardner's *On Moral Fiction,* a book-length essay on this very subject.)

Now let's return to that letter I wrote to my teacher friend and to the subject of the Great American Novel, academic fiction versus popular fiction:

> Finally, I suppose that some writers curry the favor of the academic establishment because they actually think it *is* the university-trained critic who confers immortality on a novelist and his work. It is difficult for me to take such an idea seriously, but I guess the "literary" writer seriously believes that academe's approval automatically assures that his work will be read a hundred or two hundred years from now.
>
> In fact, one could more easily justify the opposing point of view: that academe's kiss is the kiss of death, that its embrace is an assurance of eventual, total, lasting obscurity. Historically, the works of *story-tellers* are those which last through the ages, yet academics are, almost to a man, scornful of storytellers.
>
> Charles Dickens was not favored by the intellectuals of his day. The critics wrote him off as a hack who ground out vast reams of material, who was paid by the word to thrill the masses with melodrama. But what other British novelist of the 1800s has lived on as long as Charles Dickens? Are any of the critically acclaimed authors of that era so widely read today as Dickens still is? Of course not. His stories are unfailingly entertaining. The masses kept Dickens alive for such a long time that the academic community gradually accepted the fact that he was a great writer in spite of the melodrama and the flamboyant prose that they disparaged.

In that letter I did not mention the career of Feodor Dostoevsky, but that is another piece of evidence in support of my argument. As John D. MacDonald put it in a letter to me: "Keep Dostoevsky in mind. The Russian Lit'ry Establishment sneered at this grubby commercial writer whose work was actually serialized in newspapers, a fellow (they said) of meager talent and too much energy for his own good. When 50,000 people came to his Moscow funeral, that merely confirmed their evaluation. Today we think him pretty classy."

What other writers are still widely and enthusiastically read long after their deaths? Mark Twain. Poe. Robert Louis Stevenson. Defoe. Jules Verne. There are a number of others, all quite different from one another, but all sharing that one quality: They are storytellers.

The masses read storytellers; they don't read the works of academically oriented novelists. And it is the masses, millions upon millions of men and women, through generation after generation after generation, who ultimately confer immortality (of a sort) on a writer and his books. But they only wield their awesome power in favor of those stories that speak to them, to their interests and needs and experiences.

I have told you that I will point out the pitfalls into which most new writers tumble, and I have observed that I cannot keep you from plunging willfully into those pits; it seems that most of us have to learn from our own mistakes and from the resultant suffering. I know, therefore, that some of you will flirt with academe; some of you will write the kind of prose favored in academe, and you will eagerly seek an ivy-covered blessing upon your fiction—regardless of what I say. All I can do is warn you of the folly of that approach to a writing career. Of all the dangers awaiting a new writer, disdain for popularity—combined with too great a reverence for the opinions of the literary elite—is in many ways the worst of the lot; it seems to be the hangup that destroys more careers than any other. If I thought it would do any good, I would arrange to have this section of the book printed in red to make you aware of how serious a warning I mean it to be.

Just remember this: When you write to please yourself (as you always should), you are writing to please an individual. When you write to please a large audience, you are writing to please *many* individuals. When you write to please the academic crowd, however, you are writing to please an institution, crafting your fiction to satisfy doctrinal guidelines; such fiction can never have the energy and joy and *value* that is so evident in the best of popular fiction.

(I *do* think there are American novelists of this century who will live as long as people read books. But for the most part they are not the writers whose works are currently being taught in university courses. They are included in a long reading list in Chapter 15, and their names are James M. Cain, Raymond Chandler, John D. MacDonald, Robert Heinlein, and Theodore Sturgeon.)

After reading *that* diatribe, you must be wondering what I think of my own career to date. Since I'm playing the critic in portions of this book, it's only fair that I look at my own work with a jaundiced eye.

There are basically three things about my career which do not entirely please me. And I do believe new writers will find some value in a discussion of those three things:

1. During my first six years as a full-time novelist, before I had achieved solid financial success, when I was struggling to help put food on the table and to help keep a roof over our heads (with my wife doing her share of the helping), I wrote a lot of ephemeral stuff, anything that would pay some bills and gain me a bit of worry-free time for more serious, more ambitious fiction aimed at untested markets. I did Gothic romance novels under a pen name, even though I had no interest whatsoever in *reading* that genre; each of the Gothics was written in a week or so, and each bought me a few weeks in which to labor on those more demanding, more ambitious novels that I couldn't be sure would earn me anything. Like many writers, I did some pornography, too, and a variety of other things, none of which required me to commit my heart or my soul to the task. (This is not to say I didn't bother to do a good job; on the contrary, I never wrote down to any market, and I always tried to give my editors and readers their money's worth. However, the requirements of the Gothic romance, for example, are such that I could produce perfectly adequate product without straining, which wasn't good for me because an author should always strain and push himself to the limits of his talent.) As a result of that massive output of novels during those first six years, I wasted a staggering amount of time writing utterly disposable fiction, and my publishing record was forever marred by a number of, shall we say, less than dazzling books, some of which were under my own name.

Of course, that coin has another side. At least I was *writing* all those years, even if much of what I was producing left me dissatisfied with my direction and with myself. I've known young authors who, having published a few books but still needing money to pay the rent, haughtily refused to write anything they felt was beneath them. "I won't prostitute my talent" is the usual, self-righteous, defiant challenge to the universe, delivered with chin thrust forward and eyes set in a steely, uncompromising glare, as if the universe really cared. To avoid this alleged prostitution, they take jobs as clerks, door-to-door salesmen, rain gutter installers, and donut shop waiters—even though they could support themselves entirely by writing if they simply bent just slightly. Unfortunately, when writers take these mundane jobs rather than "prostitute" themselves, they often earn just enough money to pay the bills, but not enough to build up a bank account that will allow them to plunge into full-time writing. The temporary job becomes increasingly permanent with each passing month; the author writes on the weekends and sometimes in the evening, after he gets home from work, but his energy level is low, and he isn't able to put his best into the small amount of fiction he *is* able to write. In every case of this sort of which I am personally aware, once the author had a chance to make it strictly as a full-time wordsmith but backed away from the opportunity because of a fear of somehow prostituting himself, he *never* went on to build a solid, full-time writing career.

I also learned discipline during those six years, an iron discipline that few people ever develop or need. Writing large amounts of material in a wide variety of fiction categories, including some categories in which I would have preferred *not* to write, I had to train myself to sit at the typewriter hour after hour after hour, day after day, seven days a week, in order to meet all of the deadlines. Once learned, such rigid discipline stays with a person. It has served me well over the past twelve years.

Still, if I had had another choice, I wouldn't have written so much fluff in my early days. When I no longer needed to write for quick money, when I was finally able to concentrate on my serious work, it took me much longer to gain the notice and the interest of important editors than it would have if I had started out writing only carefully crafted, major novels. I regret that I wasn't able to make a cleaner, more ambitious start. However, having come from a poor family, having been denied the cushion of a trust fund check every month, having no parental support to fall back on, I had to do what I had to do.

Other writers have been faced with this same dilemma, of course. Jack Higgins (whose real name is Harry Patterson) wrote twenty-some books before finally breaking through to the big time with *The Eagle Has Landed*. Although many of those early Higgins novels were excellent examples of their kind, others were clearly written in haste, with an eye toward the rent. John Jakes wrote reams of material, mostly science fiction, before hitting the best-seller lists with his ambitious American Bicentennial series. Harlan Ellison, an award-winning science fiction writer, kept the proverbial wolf from the door by grinding out television scripts for programs (and producers) of which (and of whom) he was often a *very* vocal and scathing critic.

Although I don't see eye-to-eye with Harlan Ellison on every issue—in fact I am certain that Harlan and I disagree on *most* subjects—I believe that his approach to establishing a sound financial base under himself was a clever one. Old, hastily written books and short stories have a distinctly unpleasant way of coming back to haunt their creators years after they were originally published, but although old, trashy television programs *also* come back via network reruns and subsequent syndication, they are not nearly as embarrassing to their authors, for no one really pays attention to the brief screenwriter's credit that flashes on the tube at the start of the show.

However, I don't recommend that a serious writer should consider working *primarily* in television. In my opinion, with but rare exception, television writing is not genuinely an art, for it is not exclusively or even primarily the work of a single mind, a single sensitivity. In addition to the original author, countless other people tinker with or even totally rewrite the script: the producer, the assistant producer, the director, the program's story editor, a flock of studio executives, another flock of network executives, the network's in-house censor, and (more often than not) other screenwriters who are hired to "fix" the original story, whether or not it *needs* any fixing. Television writing is writing by committee, and no committee has ever had the vision, the single-mindedness of purpose, or the *soul* required for the creation of art.

When considering whether to strive for a long-term, full-time career in television, rather than seeking a career as a novelist, the new writer would do well to remember this oft-quoted line from an anonymous wit: "A camel is a horse designed by a committee."

Currently, I write substantially fewer words per year than I once did, although I spend just as much time at the typewriter. Now that my books are earning pleasantly large royalty checks, I am able to take time to extensively rewrite, polish, repolish, and re-repolish each manuscript. For instance, *Whispers,* my most recent novel (published in 1980), was eight hundred pages long in manuscript, but I used more than fifty-one reams of paper while writing it; that works out to an average of thirty-one discarded versions for each finished page. I would be the first to admit that thirty-two drafts is silly, excessive, even a bit mad; it's self-delusional, too, for *nothing* would benefit from that many reworkings. Nevertheless, it was gratifying to be able to afford to put that much time and energy into a project.

In addition to publishing books under my own name, I

write under a couple of pen names as well. My original intention was to drop those pen names once the books published under my real name achieved a comfortable level of success, but two of my pseudonyms became best-selling novelists while I wasn't looking, and now it would be financially irresponsible for me to cut their careers short. Besides, a subtly different style of writing has evolved for each of my alter egos, which makes it challenging, refreshing, and even fun to write those novels.

Now that I am writing fewer books than I once did, each book I *do* write is meeting with substantially more success than my novels used to achieve. One of my most recent books has sold more copies than the first *twelve* novels I wrote back in the late 1960s. There is nothing mysterious about this. With more time to spend on each manuscript, I'm producing better books, and better books really do sell more copies than bad books. Generally speaking, though some truly awful novels do reach the bestseller lists, the reading public doesn't want poorly conceived, hastily written trash, and it will reward the author who tries hard to deliver a tightly plotted, well-written story. That's why my chief regret is that I couldn't afford to spend a lot of time on any one script in my early days.

2. The second thing about my career that displeases me is the fact that I began as a science fiction writer. This may sound odd to the new writer who is working hard to become an established science fiction writer himself, but I *do* have good reasons for wishing I'd begun my career in another fashion, and there *is* something for a new writer to learn from my problems.

Throughout my childhood, adolescence, and college years, 80 percent of my reading material was science fiction; my heroes were science fiction writers; therefore, it was natural that the first pieces I wrote were in that genre. I published a couple of dozen science fiction short stories and twenty-two science fiction novels in six years. A couple of those books were very good, a few were atrocious, and most were neither horrid nor exquisite, just professional. I was as financially successful as anyone in that genre, more so than most.

So why was I unhappy?

For one thing, although I was publishing at least six short stories and four science fiction novels each year, and although I was a financial success by the standards of the genre, I was earning only an average wage by the standards of society at large—perhaps even below average. In order to support a moderately comfortable lifestyle, I found it necessary to write Gothic romances and other books on the side. In the late 1960s and early 1970s, there just wasn't a lot of money to be made in science fiction—which is such a ludicrous understatement that it's like saying Hitler was occasionally capable of unpleasant behavior. Most full-time writers in the SF field were living hand-to-mouth in those days. I'm talking here about *good* writers, hard-working writers, *famous names* who had to worry about where next month's rent would come from and whether or not they could afford a new typewriter ribbon.

(Today, of course, science fiction is a substantially more lucrative genre for authors than it once was. Many science fiction writers now manage to make a decent, though un-spectacular living out of one or two books a year. More than a few make better than average money, and a tiny, select group—including Frank Herbert, author of *Dune* and its sequels—even hit the national bestseller lists and earn hundreds of thousands of dollars from a single title. Never-theless, being a science fiction writer is *still* not the best of all possible worlds. Many authors in that field, perhaps even the majority, still receive advances against royalties of $5,000 or less. Although the recessionary floor in sales is higher than it once was, the genre still goes through booms and busts as it always has, and in the bad times, financial survival eludes some science fiction writers.)

Money wasn't the only thing about my science fiction career that displeased me. I was also disturbed by the fact that, when I *did* have time to do my best work, the books pretty much sank into oblivion; science fiction received no intelligent critical notice. Science fiction was, is, and ap-parently will continue to be looked upon as a bastard child of mainstream fiction by those publications that seriously review, evaluate, and thereby help to promote literature.

But most important of all, I wanted to escape from the science fiction ghetto when I began to realize that I had started writing SF primarily because it was the category with which I was most familiar—and also because I desired, in a rather childish way, to be a member of a group of authors I admired so enormously. My interest in the science fiction field went no deeper than that; my commitment to it was sentimental, shallow rather than gut-deep, based largely upon my limited choice of reading material. I had started to sell my short stories and novels at such a tender age that I hadn't had the opportunity (or the wit) to make a careful, mature decision as to the direction I preferred my career to take.

By the time I was struck by that realization, however, I had already been typecast by publishers, editors, and critics. Editors are usually reluctant to buy a manuscript from an author who is writing outside of the genre in which he is an established name, for they are worried about confusing book buyers. Many people in the publishing industry underestimate the reading public's intelligence and catholicity. Anyway, after being stuck with the SCIENCE FICTION WRITER label, I knew I faced an exhausting, protracted battle to be recognized simply as a WRITER, period.

The only way I could make publishing people forget my science fiction career was to erase it as completely as possible. To this end, I bought back or otherwise reacquired the publishing rights to fifteen of the eighteen novels I produced in that genre; publishers of the other three could not be persuaded to let loose of them. I repurchased good books as well as bad, everything I could get my hands on. I could sell those novels right now for many thousands of dollars apiece, but I don't intend to let any of them return to print in my lifetime—at least not without substantial rewriting in an effort to lift them out of the genre pit. In spite of this extreme and expensive plan to remake my image, some critics still occasionally refer to me as "Dean Koontz, the science fiction writer." It happens only two or three times a year, but that is sufficiently often to make me despair of ever entirely escaping from the cage in which I began my life as a novelist.

Perhaps now you can understand why I wish I had begun as something other than a *science* fiction writer. Allowing oneself to be typecast is a deep and dangerous pitfall that every writer must avoid at any cost.

Read the previous paragraph again.

And again.

Dismiss it or forget it only at your peril.

3. The third thing that displeases me about my own career is the fact that, because I started writing as young as I did, my early work was founded upon and infused with naive insights; it was passionately sincere in propounding shallow philosophies that can now be justified only with the I-was-too-young-to-know-better excuse, one upon which a host of authors have fallen back. The realization that, even in those early days, my books were fast paced and entertaining does not compensate for the faults I can see in them. It's a bit like taking a new girl home to meet the folks and having to sit in embarrassed silence while your mother shows off your bare-bottom baby pictures.

Yet, if I had it all to do over again, I wouldn't wait for complete emotional and intellectual maturity before writing my first novel. I would do again what I did the first time: take the plunge as soon as possible. If I hadn't spent those years earning a living as a novelist, I would have been forced to make my way as a schoolteacher (a job I held for two years before becoming a full-time freelancer). If I had unnecessarily spent extra years in a nine-to-five job, at the mercy of bosses I did not respect, that would have been worse than having to suffer a bit of embarrassment over the all-too-visible naivete in my early novels.

With *Whispers* and other recent novels, I believe I'm writing books with the sinews and guts that make them more than just ephemeral entertainments—even while they remain (I hope) suspenseful page-turners. But am I writing Great American Novels? No. If I ever started to think of a book in those terms, I'd tear it up and begin again. Perhaps my recent fiction will form a solid base upon which I can build a body of work that will last after I'm gone, even if just for a short while. I don't know. I think it's foolish to worry about that. Expert craftsmanship requires meticulous, conscious, and conscientious attention to the task at hand, and I give that to all my books. Fine art, however, is not entirely a matter of conscious intent; it is an unconscious, emotional outpouring rather than a carefully gauged and mapped-out plan to bedazzle the world with one's supposed literary genius. I am looking ahead to several projects that I think have great potential. Perhaps they will have the substance to gain them a lasting place on library shelves. Maybe not. *Probably* not. So little of anything—fiction, music, painting—really lasts. But if I sat down to write the Great American Novel, I would end up with a self-conscious, pedantic mess. Therefore, I work hard at being a humble storyteller, and that is the approach that I recommend to new writers.

Thought.

Care.

Craftsmanship.

Storytelling.

If you never forget those four words, and if you have at least *some* talent, you can't go too far wrong.

3.

The changing marketplace
or
I'm sorry, but we're no longer buying epistolary Gothic espionage novels set on the planet Mars in the seventeenth century. Readers seem to be tiring of that genre.

"Books have gotten too expensive, and the publishing industry is dying fast."

"No one wants to read fiction any more."

"Everyone is watching television, and books are dead."

Don't you believe any of that. Books are selling better than ever. In spite of the gloom and doom stories you often hear, building a long and profitable career as a novelist is still very much an attainable dream.

I did it, and many of you can do it, too, so long as you are willing to work very hard at your craft and art.

This chapter is going to tell you considerably more than you probably think you want to know about the business side of a writer's career. Some of you have surely said to yourselves, "I don't need to know anything about the business of publishing because I'm an artist, not a businessman, and I'm above that sort of thing." If that's what you really believe, then you're setting yourself up for a very bad fall. You absolutely *must* understand the business structure that feeds on your art, for it is only when armored with complete understanding that you can protect the integrity of your work and lobby intelligently for such things as advertising budgets and publicity campaigns. Every failed and floundering writer I know is abysmally ignorant of the publishing business; many of them think they understand it, but they're operating on little more than hearsay; they've made no conscientious, intelligent effort to search out the facts. On the other hand, nearly every successful writer I know is acutely aware of the politics and theories and mechanics, the creative as well as the mundane aspects of the business side of publishing. Ignorance in this matter can seriously affect the size of your bank account.

If the word "money" offends your delicate artistic sensibilities, if you feel that money should not concern the writer, then you are living in a fantasy world. Money is important to the serious artist for three excellent reasons. First of all, in the early years of a new writer's career, the money he makes is often his only way of knowing whether or not his work is being accepted by the reading public. New writers seldom get reviewed and do not generate large amounts of fan mail. Fat advance checks and royalty payments are valuable indications of your popularity among readers (the only ones who count, when all is said and done), and they give you the positive mental attitude necessary to continue in what must be one of the loneliest occupations a person can choose. Second, the freedom bestowed by a comfortable, steady income is perhaps the single most important factor bearing upon a new writer's— or *any* writer's—productivity. With all the bills paid and savings stored up against a run of bad luck, you can devote yourself full time to your craft and dispense with the need to hold another job. Finally, financial success is important because, in a publisher's eyes, it is the best credential you can have when you want to sell him a new book. If your work enjoys large sales and earns top dollar in your field, your publisher will treat your books with more concern and more respect than the books of a writer whose sales barely cover printing costs.

Must you write for money? No. But neither should you write in ignorance of what money and success can mean to the quantity and quality of your creative output. Naivete is an invitation to victimization; but more importantly, it prevents the author from clearly perceiving the needs and changing currents of the marketplace.

It is not only the new writer who is naive in business matters; most writers require years of regular publication in order to gain the experience and insight that allow them to deal comfortably (sometimes cynically) with publishers. In this chapter, I have boiled down my own observations and those of writer-friends into a stew meant to nourish new writers *and* writers who have been publishing for some time but have not yet gotten a firm grasp on the slippery *business* details of their careers. Before we get on to the how-to-write part of this book, let's dispel some of the myths and delve into the mechanics and psychology of the marketplace. After all, even if you know how to write well, your work is all for naught if you can't *sell* what you write.

I opened this chapter with three disheartening quotations. The book business, according to many so-called experts, is going down the drain. That's the first myth I want to dispel.

Ever since I sold my first short story in 1965, and my first novel in 1967, I have been hearing that the book industry is on its deathbed. When inflation forced paperback book prices from seventy-five cents and ninety-five cents to $1.25 and $1.50, I listened to editors who were convinced that the public would cease to buy books. "No one will pay a dollar and a half for a paperback," one experienced and widely respected editor told me. "No one. It's crazy. A year from now, we're all going to be on the street, selling apples and pencils." In spite of his pessimistic view, books continued to sell better each year than they had the year before. When inflation pushed cover prices past the two-dollar ceiling, the industry panicked again. But books continued to sell well. As I write this, paperbacks are commonly priced at $2.95 and $3.50 and occasionally even higher, and again one hears editors and publishers talking about selling apples for a living.

What some of these doomsayers seem to forget is that the inflationary pressures that have caused higher book prices have also driven up the prices of everything else. A loaf of bread doesn't sell for what it did ten years ago. Neither does an automobile. Neither does *anything*. I contend that a paperback book is still an excellent value. Even at $3.50, it is a dollar or a dollar and a half cheaper than a ticket to a movie theater, yet a movie provides two hours or less of entertainment, while a good book might well fill several empty evenings for the average reader, in addition to which, both a husband and a wife—or several friends— can read the same copy of a book, thus sharing the cost, instantly reducing the expense to each. Although I am not much of a drinker, I think one of the best methods of judging the fairness of a book's price is to compare it with the price of cocktails. A $3.50 novel is still cheaper than two martinis in a nice cocktail lounge. As Albert Einstein said, it's all relative.

The proclamations of disaster and ruin generally come from five types of people. Type One knows little or nothing about the publishing industry, its history, or its economics, and he is speaking out of ignorance; this group includes journalists who do a bit of quick research to write a short piece for the lifestyle and business sections of their newspapers. Type Two knows the publishing industry fairly well, usually works in it in one capacity or another, but seems not to have the desire (or maybe, in some cases, the wit) to study and properly interpret the ongoing developments in his own trade; he suffers from the well-known Chicken Little Syndrome—panic based on misinformation or a misreading of events. Type Three is an editor or a publisher who intentionally downplays every publishing industry success and exaggerates every failure in a relentless attempt to frighten authors into accepting lower advances and lower royalty rates than they deserve. Understand, I have nothing against Type Threes, for they are only doing their jobs—maximizing profits for their employers; however, all writers should be aware that Type Three is the source of much (probably most) of the doomsday talk that periodically sweeps through the book business. Type Four works in the trade as an editor, agent, writer, or whatnot; Type Fours know, like, and trust Type Threes and, lacking the time and inclination to research the facts about book sales, simply accept as gospel everything that is said by Type Threes. Finally, Type Five is a writer, either lazy or incompetent or both, who refuses to accept any responsibility for his own failure to sell his work; he takes refuge in the vociferously expressed opinion that the entire publishing trade is going to Hell in a handbasket.

During 1979 and 1980, the agonized wailing of the oracles of doom—especially the Type Threes—was worse than anyone had ever heard it before. This extended spate of teeth-gnashing was primarily occasioned by these three things:

1. An unusually high number of stridently touted books, for which publishers had paid fortunes in advances, bombed at the bookstore box office. Now, highly touted books are *always* bombing at the box office, but during 1979-80, the level of poor editorial judgment was astoundingly high. These devastating failures were widely interpreted as evidence that people were turning away from books as a form of entertainment. Actually, the books failed solely because most of them were bad—worse than bad, unreadable. No publishing house can sell the public lots of copies of a bad occult novel merely because readers are hungering for occult novels; likewise, no publishing house can sell a poorly written family saga just because the public is crying for involving, multi-generational novels. This should be obvious, but it is a lesson the book business never seems to learn.

2. The most profitable genre in paperback publishing began to fade in popularity, a turn of events that panicked many editors and publishers. For years, the romantic (and racy) historical saga, exemplified by the work of Rosemary Rogers, had enjoyed constantly, rapidly increasing sales. Each year, scores of these sagas—cynically referred to as "bodice rippers" or "historical rape novels" by many people in the book trade—sold between 200,000 and 300,000 copies each. Dozens more sold 500,000 each, and a surprising number passed the million-copy mark each year. The floor under the genre—that is, the minimal sales expectations based on prior experience—was profitably high. Every paperback house released a couple of historical sagas every month . . . then three a month . . . then four . . . until some houses were publishing five or six sagas a month, contributing to the phenomenal number of titles in the genre.

There is a law of economics which describes the insidious nature of currency inflation: "Bad money always drives out good." This same law could be applied to publishing. When the number of badly written books far outnumbers the good books within any category of fiction, then that category will suffer a decline in popularity. For a time, it seemed that half the shelf space in bookstores was given over to bodice rippers. Of the scores of new titles that appeared every month, 90 percent were wretched beyond description. Readers of the genre, confronted by this bewildering array of titles, which were all identically packaged, were so often burned by amateurish or cynically written books that they kept their money in their pockets or went looking for something new and different to read. The bodice ripper is still a profitable category of fiction, but the sales floor beneath it is substantially lower than was once the case, and the number of titles being published in that previously dominant genre has declined dramatically in the past two years.

(It is encouraging to note that most of the best authors of romantic historical sagas survived the purge with their sales figures undiminished, and a couple of good new writers in that category actually managed to launch successful careers in spite of the fact that countless second- and third-rate novelists were going down in flames at the same time. This is just one more indication that readers can tell the difference between the work of uncommitted hack writers and the work of those who sincerely care about what they're doing. They can also tell the difference between the fine craftsman and the inept amateur, and when the crunch comes, they actively support the former at the expense of the latter.)

3. The third reason for the publishing panic of 1979-80 was the stunning price that Bantam Books paid for Judith Krantz's novel, *Princess Daisy.* In a subsidiary rights auction marked by near hysteria on the part of many reprinters, Crown (Mrs. Krantz's hardcover publisher) and Morton Janklow (her agent) obtained the astonishing price of 3.2 million dollars for the paperback rights to her second novel. (The first was the bestselling *Scruples.*) This figure topped the previous record for the sale of reprint rights by almost one million dollars. In the cold light of the days that followed that buying frenzy, many publishers began to wonder where the rapidly escalating cost of reprint rights would end. They started to think about costs—including the cost of *financing* such huge advances—and they made a lot of noise about vanishing profit margins. These worries, compounded by the failure of an unusually large number of other big money books and by the collapse of the romantic historical saga exacerbated the incipient panic that already existed in the industry. Some publishing executives genuinely believed that authors' advances had to be cut in order for the book business to survive; others were more sanguine about the future of publishing, but they took advantage of the situation to squeeze cash out of the pockets of writers, into the treasuries of publishing houses, thus widening profit margins and pleasing their employers.

Throughout the panic of 1979-80, publishers talked of wildly plunging unit sales and devastating losses. *Publishers Weekly,* the *New York Times, The New Yorker,* and a host of other publications dutifully reported the grim predictions of disaster issuing from the offices of virtually every major publishing house. Curiously, a number of bookstore chains and several of the largest book wholesalers in the nation reported *increased* unit sales. Furthermore, statistics to be found in the quarterly reports that the federal government makes on U.S. industry indicate that, overall, publishing suffered nothing worse than a couple of no-growth quarters in those years, stagnant periods that were balanced by other quarters in which growth was very good indeed. During the recent recession publishing suffered less than virtually any other business in the nation. Certainly, some segments of the book trade have had to cinch in their belts; the sales of *some* kinds of hardcover fiction have been infected by the economic illness that plagues the rest of the country. By and large, however, these few disquieting symptoms are signs of change, not portents of total ruin. Those who wildly exaggerate the seriousness of these symptoms are either ill-informed—or they are Type Threes who are intent upon improving the figures on the bottom lines of the profit and loss sheets—at the expense of the authors who create their product.

However, I do not see the publisher-author relationship as a *violently* antagonistic one, and I would be the last to claim that publishing is a safe and worry-free business. The book trade *does* have serious problems. In the decade to come, it will face more than one crisis. For the most part, however, the industry's difficulties are of its own making, a result of short-sightedness and wishful thinking. In Chapter 14 of this book, I'll outline the nature of those problems and upcoming crises.

So listen, my friends. When you hear the doomcriers, when you read newspaper articles about the death of the book, don't pay any attention. Don't let it get you down. If you're a new writer, as yet unpublished, don't let the doomsayers dissuade you from pursuing your own career as a storyteller.

What you must keep in mind is this: *Books are selling better than ever.*

Furthermore, there is every indication that books will continue to sell steadily and well for as long as civilization survives to produce them.

We are *not* working in a dying industry. We are *not* the modern equivalent of buggywhip manufacturers. Millions and millions of people out there truly *love* books; they know that no other form of art or entertainment can be so totally involving as a good book. No movie or concert or stage play or painting or television mini-series can possibly have the complexity, breadth, depth, richness, and emotional impact of a well-wrought novel, and that is why novels will always prosper.

Yes, the marketplace for fiction has changed. It is continuing to change even as I write this. But change is not to be feared; it is healthy. If an author understands the changes that are sweeping the publishing business, he can flow with them and find tremendous opportunities in the days ahead. In the next section of this chapter, we'll explore the stunning changes that have swept through the business in the past decade.

The publishing industry underwent an incredible and exciting transformation during the 1970s. In the late 1960s, a hardcover bestseller seldom sold more than 75,000 to 100,000 copies. A Herman Wouk novel, a James Michener extravaganza, or a national sensation like Mario Puzo's *The Godfather* might sell as many as 200,000 copies exclusive of book clubs, but this level of performance was the exception, not the rule. Today, many bestsellers soar past the 200,000-copy mark. Indeed, as I write this book, nine out of the fifteen titles on the fiction side of the bestseller list have at least 200,000 copies in print; a couple of those have reached the 300,000-copy level, and one is even approaching half a million. It is extremely unlikely that a novel could have a satisfyingly lengthy run on today's bestseller lists with less than 75,000 to 100,000 in sales, which used to be the upper limits of commercial success.

The same explosion in sales has taken place in the paperback world as well. In the 1960s, when I first became a published author, a million-copy bestseller in paperback was considered a peak of popularity, and it was rare. Some monster bestsellers like *Peyton Place* and, again, the books of Wouk and Michener and Harold Robbins and their like might sell two or three million. Last year, more than forty books topped a million in paperback sales. Two million is common. Three million is becoming a regular achievement by certain novelists: Stephen King, Sidney Sheldon, John Jakes, and others. A really *big* bestseller these days will reach far more people than did the most popular books of other generations: *The Godfather* has sold fifteen million in paperback; *The Exorcist*—twelve million; *The Thorn Birds*—nine million; *Coma*—four and a half million; *Trinity*—five million; *Valley of the Dolls*—twelve million or more. I could go on and on listing supersellers.

Why is the market for books so much larger today than it was just ten or twelve years ago?

One reason is vastly improved distribution. The number of places where people can buy books has increased enormously over the past decade. Major retailing chains like B. Dalton-Pickwick and Waldenbooks have expanded into hundreds of outlets in shopping malls, smaller cities, and suburban neighborhoods where bookstores were once few and far between. In addition, computerized, super-efficient national distribution companies like Ingram have made it possible for any bookstore, no matter how small, to supply its customers with virtually any current title. Huge rack-jobbers like Levy & Company have opened literally thousands upon thousands of new points of sale for paper-backs in airports, department stores, drug stores, conven-ience markets like 7-11, supermarkets, and other primarily non-book businesses. Many supermarkets consider books to be impulse purchases (at least within their stores), and they display and sell books the same way they sell chewing gum, candy bars, Bic pens, and novelty items—right beside the cash register at each checkout counter. These days, a top bestseller often finds hundreds of thousands of buyers in supermarkets alone! The effect on authors' royalties is amazing and gratifying.

Chains like Dalton and Walden have helped the book business not merely by bringing its product into virgin territory, but also by making that product more accessible and less threatening to people who used to be slightly or even profoundly intimidated by bookstores. Prior to the tremendous growth enjoyed by Walden and Dalton, many studies of the public's attitudes toward books indicated that nonreaders and those who read books only occasion-ally were often uncomfortable, uneasy, apprehensive, and even downright frightened of entering a bookstore. By operating spacious and well-lighted stores, by using color-ful display material, by aggressively employing all manner of modern marketing techniques, and by creating a supermarket-like atmosphere, chains like Dalton and Walden have done a great deal to make bookstores more inviting and have generated thousands upon thousands of new book lovers, to the benefit of everyone in the publish-ing business.

Another factor has contributed to soaring book sales over the past decade: most publishing houses, both hard-cover and softcover, have been acquired by enormous cor-porations, and those conglomerates have brought their financial resources and their sophisticated marketing skills to the book business. For example, my current hardcover publisher, G.P. Putnam's Sons, is owned by Music Corporation of America (MCA), one of the largest entertainment-oriented conglomerates in the world. In addition to Putnam's, the MCA publishing empire includes Coward, McCann, and Geoghegan; Jove paperback books; and Berkley Publishing Corporation, another major paperback house. Simon & Schuster and its paperback arm, Pocket Books, are owned by another entertainment giant, Gulf & Western. New American Library and its various imprints belong to the Times-Mirror Company, while Avon paperbacks is a division of the Hearst Corporation. Bantam, the biggest paperback publisher in the world, has been owned by several different big corporations over the past fifteen years. Until recently, RCA owned Random House and Ballantine Books. The list of acquisitions goes on and on.

(One conglomerate actually grew up within the publishing industry itself: Doubleday & Company. In addition to the hardcover books it publishes under its own famous imprint, Doubleday now owns an astonishing array of publishing businesses: Dell Publishing, one of the three largest paperback houses in the world; Dial books, which issues hardcover editions; Delacorte books, the hardcover arm of Dell; some of the biggest printing and binding facilities in the nation; some of the largest book clubs in the country, including the Doubleday Book Club, the Literary Guild, the Mystery Guild, the Science Fiction Book Club, the Occult Book Club and many others. These days, Doubleday is expanding out of publishing, into other endeavors; the company now co-finances motion pictures and even owns a major league baseball team.)

In the 1960s, when I began my career, when publishing houses were not associated with huge conglomerates, books were seldom advertised extensively. Only the biggest of the big-name authors were given promotion and publicity budgets of any size, and even those were not large by today's standards; furthermore, most if not all of that money was spent on display ads in *Publishers*

Weekly, the *New York Times Book Review,* and a very short list of other book-oriented publications. Publishers made no attempt to reach casual readers or nonreaders; all advertising was geared toward those who already knew that books offered excellent and comparatively inexpensive entertainment.

In those days, common wisdom held that advertising did not sell books. Publishers insisted that the marketing techniques used so successfully with other kinds of products were utterly useless when applied to books. According to common wisdom, the only thing that sold books was good word-of-mouth, one satisfied reader recommending a title to another reader. Good word-of-mouth *is* vitally important; however, if a publisher does not advertise a book, if he does not print it in large quantity, good word-of-mouth doesn't even have a chance to begin. If the reading public doesn't know that a particular book exists, if people can't find that book in the stores, then there will never be enough early readers for good word-of-mouth to have any impact whatsoever. Common wisdom is sometimes really common ignorance or self-delusion.

Prior to the conglomerate takeover of the book industry, no publisher would have seriously considered advertising a novel on television or radio. Any such suggestion from an author would have been greeted with surprise and scorn. Everyone *knew* that advertising had to be directed at the readers of book-oriented publications, at people who were already converted, already book lovers. Everyone *knew* that no book could ever sell sufficient copies to justify the enormous expense of radio and television ads. And everyone *knew* that advertising a book on radio or television would only make it appear cheap and sleazy, thereby alienating all the *true* book lovers who might otherwise have purchased it. No one had ever done even the most cursory market study to determine if any of these bits of common knowledge made sense; no one felt the need to do research because, after all, these were things that everyone simply *knew.*

As large corporations began acquiring publishing houses, that long-nurtured common "wisdom" was discarded, much to the benefit of all writers. Enormous sums were pumped into advertising and promotion. Predictably, modern marketing techniques radically and rapidly expanded the market for books. In their "unseemly" rush to generate greater and greater profits, these conglomerates did more in one decade to bring the book to the common man than did all the self-styled "gentlemanly" publishers who had controlled the business since the first book had been put on sale in the first bookshop.

My own career has benefited from the salesmanship and the business savvy of the new-style publishers. For example, while I was writing this text in the autumn of 1980, one of my novels was released with the support of a massive advertising campaign. It was a horror novel, the first of three paperback originals which I contracted to write under a new pen name. It was the lead title of the month at the house that handled it, and the ad budget was $300,000, which paid for print ads, giveaway bookmarks, bookstore bags imprinted with the title, and saturation television spots on local stations in major cities all over the country. Partly because of this extensive promotion, the book did quite well and made most of the nation's paperback bestseller lists.

Two more examples: In February, 1981, another paperback house released a novel under another of my pen names; again, it was their lead title of the month, with a promotional budget of approximately $150,000, most of which was spent on network and local radio commercials. Shortly thereafter, in April, 1981, the paperback edition of Whispers, which was published under my own name (hardcover: G.P. Putnam's Sons, 1980), was released by Berkley Books, and it, too, received a major advertising and promotion push—at least $250,000, which paid for bookmarks, print ads, subway and bus ads in major cities, two weeks of nationwide radio commercials, and two weeks of nationwide TV advertising.

During a period of just six months, publishers spent $700,000 to promote my books. That is most definitely not old-style publishing.

Admittedly, this is an unusually large amount of promotion to be given to one writer in such a short time. It is a result of basically four things: 1) having an agent who believes in my work; 2) finding three publishers who believe in my work; 3) finding four editors who believe in my work—an astonishing thing, when you know how indifferent this business usually is; and, last but not least, 4) having agent, editors, and publishers come together in their enthusiasm at the same time that positive reader reaction to my books is growing. Still, even though I find myself in an unusual situation, it is nonetheless representative of the changes that have transformed publishing from a cottage industry into a major twentieth century business.

Even though the book industry has grown rapidly in the past ten or fifteen years, there is evidence that a few conglomerates are still dissatisfied with the profits to be made, and it is likely that a few of those huge corporations will even divest themselves of their publishing interests during the coming decade; but that doesn't mean publishing will shrink back into a cottage industry with less emphasis on blockbuster books. The efficacy of market research, product advertising, and other big-business techniques has been deeply impressed upon everyone who works with books. There is no going back.

Don't misunderstand me and get the idea that *any* book can be a bestseller if it is extensively advertised and promoted. If it were that easy, every writer would be a multimillionaire. Many heavily advertised books die at the box office each year. First of all, to succeed, you must have a well-written story, not a hastily scribbled piece of dreck; second, your novel must be about something that will interest large numbers of people; third, your story must be told with breadth and scope and style and verve that lift it out of all category classifications and make it at least *appear* to be something special; fourth, it must be sufficiently entertaining to generate favorable word-of-mouth once the initial advertising blitz comes to an end; and, finally, you must have a bit of good luck, so that you hit the marketplace with the right book at the right time.

The blockbusters, the million- and multi-million-copy hits, are the bedrock upon which the new-style publishing is built; those books give publishers the money to experiment on other things and keep the stockholders happy as well. Editors will buy every blockbuster-type book they can get their hands on.

One of this text's primary purposes is to show you the difference between promotable and unpromotable books, which is essentially the difference between genre and mainstream. Editors are desperately looking for novels that can be used as lead titles, with large ad budgets, for it is from these bestsellers that publishers make the highest profits; one big bestseller can support literally dozens of money-losing titles farther down on a house's list. But there simply aren't enough books suitable for major promotion because very few writers are willing to take the time and make the effort needed to produce such tales. Writing an ordinary category novel—a simple mystery, a quick little thriller, a romance—is a great deal easier than writing one of the complex, extensively researched, thematically ambitious stories that editors need for the top of their monthly list of releases. If the new writer is willing to put in the requisite hard work, and if he has some talent, and if he understands the difference between a genre novel and the kind of book that transcends genres even while borrowing from them, then editors will fight to get their hands on his manuscripts.

Because I believe that a writer should try to reach the largest audience within his power, because I believe a writer should stretch himself further with every book, and because I believe that a financially successful writer is the most productive and happy writer, I will repeatedly recommend throughout this text that you eschew the temptation to write unambitious little genre novels; I will recommend that you write the kind of complex, ambitious, mainstream fiction that publishers are able to promote. Rise above the genres, just as James M. Cain did, just as Raymond Chandler did, just as John D. MacDonald does. I am convinced that this career strategy will be the most rewarding one you could follow for at least the rest of this century.

Those of you who have read *Writing Popular Fiction* know that I am now giving advice that is almost diametrically opposed to the advice I gave in that text. In 1971, when I was working on *Writing Popular Fiction,* the publishing industry had only just quietly begun its transformation; few people had noticed those first, small changes in the way things were being done, and no one had looked ahead to see where those changes would put the publishing business by 1980. At that time, it was quite reasonable of me to advise the new writer to concentrate his work in his favorite genre—whether it be mystery, science fiction, or Gothic romance—because it seemed that, given the limited number of opportunities outside the genre, the best chance for success lay within those formulized categories. Now, a decade later, the opportunities beyond the genres have become so numerous and enormous, the need for good writers of popular *mainstream* fiction has become so great that I must advise every new author to think of himself not as a SCIENCE FICTION WRITER, not as a MYSTERY WRITER, not as a ROMANCE WRITER, not as a WESTERN WRITER, but simply as a WRITER, period.

If you're in love with a particular genre, and you don't mind settling for a smaller income, a smaller audience, and a smaller forum for the presentation of your thoughts and ideas, then by all means write whatever form of fiction you find most appealing. If you absolutely love science fiction, write it and don't worry whether it is accessible to those who are unfamiliar with science fiction. Please yourself first. If you don't please yourself, there's no chance whatsoever that you'll ever please anyone else. In Chapter 12, I will give you a lot of suggestions about how to write successful fiction in several genres. However, if it *is* your goal to be a category writer, if you're intent upon writing for one small segment of the reading public, for one specialized interest group, be certain you are aware of the problems and the limitations of that choice before you launch your career.

But if you don't mind my asking: Why *not* shoot for the top?

Not every writer is as enthusiastic as I am about the recent changes in publishing. Following are ten objections I frequently hear, along with my responses.

1. *Conglomerate-owned publishing houses favor a few blockbusters at the expense of all other books.* Phooey. No publisher can survive without a complete, well-rounded list, and today's publishers are acutely aware of that. Yes, they put a lot of effort into finding and promoting the blockbusters because that is where they make their highest profits, but that has *always* been true, even before conglomerate ownership became a factor in the business. Yes, they favor the lead titles on their lists, but not at the expense of all other books; they will continue to publish anything that readers will buy in sufficient quantities to make publication worthwhile. No publisher will walk away from genre profits merely because those profits are smaller than the money to be made from the mainstream blockbusters; it's *still* profit, after all; it still pays salaries and buys stationery. After being told for years that publishers will soon be printing *only* blockbuster-type books, I'm not aware of any house at which the big-buck, highly promoted books at the top of the list constitute more than 10 or 15 percent of the publishing schedule. Maybe publishers would *like* to publish only books that can reach a million-copy audience; but the cold, hard truth is that there aren't many writers who are willing or able to regularly deliver books with that broad appeal.

2. *The mystery novel is a perfect example of a genre being destroyed by the concentration on blockbuster fiction.* Baloney. This is an example you hear all the time. Recently, *The Third Degree,* a publication of Mystery Writers of America, gave voice to hysterical warnings about evil, conglomerate-owned publishing companies that were refusing to print mysteries because they were too busy printing and promoting million-copy blockbusters. This is cheap rationalization.

Yes, for several years now, the traditional mystery novel has suffered a collapse in popularity. But that has nothing to do with the way the new, conglomerate-owned publishers are treating the genre. The mystery has been in trouble because most of the current crop of mystery writers have failed to engage and entertain their readers. I am a mystery lover; I am disposed in favor of such a book even before I read the first page of it, but for several years, even I have been disappointed by 98 percent of what I've read. There has been a dismaying trend toward syntactical and grammatical sloppiness in many, many of the mysteries I've been reading. Worse, the genre has become stale, imitative. The book racks are stuffed full of too many weak imitations of Raymond Chandler, too many tough-guy detectives who are indistinguishable from the legion of tough-guy detectives who came before them. There are too many genteel Agatha Christie imitations. If I have to read one more locked room murder mystery, one more tale of a lost Nazi treasure, one more story about a private eye with a criminal's tough exterior and the good heart of a priest . . . well, I just may put on my fedora and trenchcoat, get in my dark sedan, and go looking for some of the mugs who grind out this stuff on their battered Remingtons. For far too long, the mystery has existed without innovation. No one seems to be sitting down with the idea of shaking up the genre, with the intention of pumping it full of new ideas and modes. Too often, the Edgar Awards (a yearly honor presented by the Mystery Writers of America) have singled out mysteries that do nothing more than smoothly recapitulate the styles and stories of favorite authors of the past. No category of fiction has a guarantee of immortality, and any category that fails to grow deserves to die.

If conglomerates were purposefully killing off mysteries in order to be able to concentrate solely on million-copy sellers, then they would be purposefully killing off *all* genres. But some fiction categories are actually flourishing. Science fiction is a good example. More science fiction novels are being published than ever before, and a lot of SF novelists are making more money now than they ever dreamed of making. The average sales of a science fiction title are a long, long way below a million copies, but the figure is much higher than the average sales for a mystery novel because science fiction still delivers fresh, innovative, entertaining stories to its readership. While there are a lot of science fiction writers who endlessly imitate favorite authors and books, they are not in the majority in SF— as they seem to be in the mystery field. For this reason, SF is a vigorous form that continues to attract sufficient numbers of book buyers to remain a profitable enterprise for both hardcover and softcover publishers. (**WARNING!** The rosy things I've just said about science fiction do not in any way ameliorate the negative picture I painted of that genre earlier in this book. Here, we are comparing SF to the mystery, and it is only in this comparison that science fiction seems to offer its writers greater creative and financial opportunities. Compared to *mainstream* fiction, SF clearly provides the author with a much smaller chance of creative and financial satisfaction.)

In short, the ultimate fate of any book or any genre is in the hands of the readers. The faceless executives of conglomerate-owned publishing houses do not have the final word. Writers who insist differently are simply failing to accept responsibility for the shortcomings of their own work. If you keep cheating the readers, if you keep delivering the same old formula stuff, sooner or later they'll stop coming back for more.

3. *The books the conglomerate-owned publishers favor for big promotion are uniformly trash; they prefer formulized "products," not real novels.* Bosh. What about James Clavell? He writes *real* novels. What about Lawrence Sanders? What about Stephen King? Are you seriously saying that Stephen King, one of the most ambitious novelists to rise out of popular fiction, is cynically grinding out "product" to some conglomerate's rigid specifications? What about John Le Carré? His books make it to the top, and I dare say you would get a lot of argument from a lot of people if you tried to call Le Carré a hack. *Of course* there is trash that gets promoted into blockbuster status; there has always been trash that makes it big. But there are dozens and dozens of fine novelists whose works are exactly what publishers are looking for when they talk about blockbusters. My own books began to make big money and receive large promotional budgets only after I began to stretch myself as a writer; the more ambitious I've become, the better my books have sold, and the happier my publishers have been. What the devil is so sinister about publishers pushing writers into more ambitious projects? Isn't that exactly the kind of encouragement a serious writer should be delighted to receive? Those who raise objection number three are rationalizing away their own shortcomings, just as some mystery writers have done: "Well, if they won't promote *my* books and sell tens of millions of copies of *my* novels, then it's because they're only willing to promote trash." How sad that so many writers have wasted so much energy and time convincing themselves of this ego-soothing rationalization.

4. *When conglomerates took over the business, they ceased to support those uncommercial "literary" writers who are keeping alive the sacred flame of American LIT-ERATURE.* If you've read Chapters 1 and 2 of this text, you know my opinion of self-appointed "literary" novelists. Only the masses decide who is writing lasting literature; and the masses have always favored the storytellers. Besides, nearly as many "literary" novels are being published today as were published in the 1950s or the 1960s; in fact, some studies show that publishers are turning out even more of them than ever before.

In reality, the academic crowd is complaining about the fact that the advances for "literary" novels have been substantially reduced. At one time, many academically oriented novelists were receiving $50,000 and more for books that routinely sold only three thousand copies in hardcover and twenty-five to fifty thousand in paper. Publishers were taking a financial bath in the name of supporting literature. Now those same writers are paid advances more in line with what their books actually earn. I see nothing wrong with that. It's about time they had to face reality and give some thought to the interests of the book-buying public.

5. *The new-style publishers have no commitment to developing new writers.* According to industry statistics, there were more than one hundred first novels released in hardcover last year. There are no statistics available for paperback first novels, but I would be willing to bet that that figure would be close to two hundred. Publishers are engaged in a continuing, earnest search for new authors because they are the very life and breath of the business.

6. *Conglomerate-owned publishing houses are big*

business, and big business is always out to rip people off.
More baloney. This country has been laboring too long
under the misconception that a business gets big by cheating people. Never. A business becomes big by giving people what they want, at a price they're willing to pay. Certainly, now and then, one runs across a genuine con artist
in a businessman's clothes, a thief looking to make a fast
buck. But these are the exceptions. Customers who have
been ripped off do not return to do business with the thief
who took their money; they go to a more reputable company the next time, and it is *that* company which becomes
huge. I have dealt with small, family-owned publishing
companies of the old style, and I have dealt with the new
conglomerate-owned businesses, and there is little difference between them so far as integrity is concerned; both
old and new-style publishers are tough negotiators and
both handle royalties, subsidiary rights, and other financial matters in the same manner.

7. *Conglomerate-owned publishing houses will censor
all writing that has an anti-business slant.* Nonsense.
Many publishing houses have been owned by conglomerates for as long as a decade, and they are publishing just as
many books from an anti-business point of view as they
ever did; in fact, some of the most virulent, anti-business,
pro-left books ever to see print in this country have been
put between covers by those very conglomerate-owned
publishing houses that the left-leaning writers have de-
nounced. The executives in charge of publishing companies do not have the time or the inclination to comb
through manuscripts with the intent of excising all
thoughts that fail to conform with their own positions on
the issues. Publishing executives are busy struggling to
protect their jobs by insuring profits for their companies,
and that is very much a full-time occupation; if those
profits can be made by publishing left-wing books (or
right-wing books) or by books that advocate an end to the
printed word, publishers will market them. Lenin said,
"Capitalists will sell us the rope with which we will hang
them." Although I despair of capitalists and capitalism at
times, I am a capitalist myself, and I'm pretty sure Lenin

was dead wrong. I have a hunch that, once having sold the rope for their own hanging, capitalists would then quickly invent something new and better than rope, something that made rope obsolete. It is this ability to adapt, this willingness to cater to all points of view in pursuit of profits that makes capitalist publishers indestructible, and it is this flexibility that makes it counterproductive for them to act as censors.

8. *The big bookstore chains like Dalton and Walden handle only bestsellers and have no interest in stocking valuable, well-written books with smaller sales potential.* That's bunkum. Do you really expect me to believe that my local B. Dalton outlet, which stocks twenty thousand titles, is stocking *only* bestsellers? *Twenty thousand bestsellers?* If there were twenty thousand bestsellers at any one time, the book industry would be larger than all other American businesses combined! In reality, I can go to a Walden or Dalton shop and buy anything from Dickens to Max Brand to Joyce Carol Oates to Edgar Rice Burroughs to Barbara Cartland to Stephen King to Stanley Elkin. The incredible diversity of the stock in these chain stores is one thing that has contributed to their tremendous success.

9. *The big chain bookstores squeeze out good, full-service, neighborhood bookshops and thereby limit competition.* Ninety percent of the chains' growth has come from the opening of outlets in neighborhoods which have never before had a bookstore of any kind. In those comparatively few cases when an independent merchant has been crushed by a nearby chain store's marketing muscle, the independent was often running a poorly managed store that did little or nothing to promote the cause of books or to serve the book-buying public. I know of independent bookshops that have actually *benefited* by proximity to a chain outlet, for the chain has drawn in new customers that have spilled over to the independent. Finally, government-compiled statistics prove there are no grounds to support this fear of reduced competition, for in spite of the phenomenal growth of the bookstore chains over the past decade, the number of other kinds of book outlets has *also* increased. The broadening of the book marketplace, engendered by conglomerate-owned publishing houses and chain bookstores, seems to have had a salutary effect on business for everyone working in the world of books.

10. *Conglomerate-owned publishers and chain bookstores have led to a homogenization of subject matter, styles, and viewpoints in the books that are being published.* I don't even want to dignify this one with a response. If you really believe that individuality has vanished from the American book scene, if you truly see a drab similarity in the work of Stephen King and Kurt Vonnegut and Evan Hunter and Dick Francis and Erica Jong and Norman Spinrad and Richard Laymon and Saul Bellow . . . well, then there's no sense in trying to reason with you; you belong in a padded room somewhere, and you shouldn't be permitted to handle anything sharper than a banana.

These days, too many writers waste too much time fretting about and protesting against the changes that are sweeping through the publishing business. Change is inevitable. Railing against it is pointless and stupid.

A few years ago I canceled my membership in the Authors' Guild. I did so for more reasons than I have space to list here, but one of the main reasons I disassociated myself from that group was that I believed its resistance to change was damaging to the welfare of all authors. The Guild seemed (to me at least) to be governed by a clique of writers infected by a kind of literary Luddism; they feared anything big—big business, big publishing, big success—and wanted to force conglomerates to divest themselves of their publishing enterprises; they wanted to stop the growth of chain bookstores, in spite of the fact that chains have contributed huge sums to innumerable authors' royalty statements; in my opinion, they wanted to reverse the course of the publishing revolution that has brought the book to the common man. I suspect that many people in the Guild think of books as the special province of the intellectual elite, and they have a subconscious distaste for the common man that conglomerate publishers and bookstore chains serve. What wonderful books might those anti-change Guild authors have written if they'd not spent those hundreds and thousands of hours in a futile and wrong-headed battle against change?

Change is nearly always beneficial. If you think our world has changed for the worse from what it once was, you should have the opportunity to travel back in time and live with the pox-ridden, disease-scarred, lice-plagued residents of "romantic" eighteenth-century London (or Philadelphia or Rome). Certainly, some changes are for the worse, but bad developments are eventually erased by more change; new developments succumb to newer developments; that is the fascinating nature of the process.

Embrace change. Flow with it.

Become a faithful reader of *Publishers Weekly, Daily Variety, The Hollywood Reporter, Marketing Bestsellers,* and any other trade publications that have a direct or indirect relationship to the book industry. Learn how the publishing business operates; learn about the brains and the bowels of it. If you love books, this education won't be painful; you'll find the technical side of their production and marketing every bit as interesting as the artistic aspects of their creation. If you care about your art, you should care about how that art will be brought to the public. If you keep in touch with the changing nature of publishing, and if you teach yourself how to take advantage of the changes, you will have a better chance of becoming both a successful businessman *and* a successful artist.

Earlier in this chapter, I said, ". . . I would be the last to claim that publishing is a safe and worry-free business. The book trade does have serious problems." In the interests of fair play, I promised that I would outline some of these problems. Because a publisher's problems are always a writer's problems, too, it is vitally important that a new writer learn about such industry headaches as book returns, excessively high authors' advances, and so forth. At this point, however, I believe we need to take a break from all this business talk and move on to the how-to section of this book. Therefore, the business problems that plague publishers—and, by extension, authors—will be gone into at length in Chapter 14: Selling What You Write, where the material is also pertinent.

4.

**Creating and structuring
a story line
or
A novel without a strong
plot is like a beautiful
blonde all dressed up and
ready for excitement—but
with no place to go.**

There is no such thing as a novel without a plot, for plot is one of the classic requirements of the form. In the hands of a truly brilliant (or truly crazed) author, a book-length, unplotted story might be a viable form of experimental fiction, and it might be a valuable sort of therapy for certain authors, and in some rare cases it might even be worth reading, but it can *never* be a novel because it does not conform to the classic definition of a novel any more than a limerick conforms to the definition of a sonnet, any more than a horse conforms to the definition of an elephant.

Occasionally I encounter a critic or a would-be writer who believes that an author should let his characters create the entire plot *as they act it out.* According to this theory, any pre-planned plot line is hopelessly artificial, and it is supposedly preferable for the writer to discover the direction of the story only as the characters discover it. In some arcane fashion, this is supposed to lead to a more "natural" plot.

Balderdash.

When a master furniture maker crafts a splendid Queen Anne-style table, is he being "artificial" merely because he follows an established pattern?

Are the paintings of Andrew Wyeth "artificial" because the artist limits himself to a painstakingly realistic rendition of our world?

The answers to both of those questions are, of course, the same: *No!*

It is true that fictional characters *do* frequently become so vivid, so intriguing, so alive, that the author finds it worthwhile to alter his previously planned plot and some thematic threads in the overall weave of the book in order to accommodate the growth and change of his story people. However, while every professional novelist has had this exhilarating experience, most will tell you that there are nearly always disastrous consequences when an author permits his characters to control the *entire* course and intent and meaning of a novel. One of the things that fiction does so well is to squeeze and process real-life experiences into a pungent essence; the pressure applied by plot structure is one of the things that helps reduce the chaos of real life to a manageable and meaningful moment of observed truth. If a writer allows his characters to seize total control, he is actually allowing his subconscious mind to write the book without benefit of the more sober and steady guidance of his conscious intellect, and the result is fiction as formless and purposeless as much of what takes place in the real world, precisely the kind of fiction that frustrates most readers.

Another view of novel writing insists that plot comes *third,* characters second, and theme first. I have heard new writers argue that every twist and turn of the story line should be a device to support the message of the book. A unifying theme *is* a requirement of good fiction, but when it becomes the primary purpose, then the author is writing either an essay or a sermon, but not a piece of fiction. This approach leads to pedantic, preachy prose that is about as popular in the bookstores as the Edsel was in the automobile showrooms.

You cannot pretend that plot is less important than other elements of a novel's construction.

You cannot let your characters create your story any more than an automobile designer can allow the assembly line workmen to design a new car as they build it.

You cannot subordinate entertainment values to some lofty message.

If you are to have any chance at all of succeeding as a popular novelist, you must have the proper respect for plot. You must have at least as much respect for it as readers do.

As I told you earlier, I cannot give you a magic formula that will guarantee you success as a novelist. I can only make suggestions and observations based on my own experience and on the experiences of my friends who are writers and who have been pulverized by the same mill. I can point out the pitfalls, but it is up to you to avoid falling into them. Here are some things that should help you with the problems of plotting fiction.

Finding story ideas

Plot wheels, plot cards, and story construction lists, all of those strange devices that were once for sale to help writers get ideas—some of which are still for sale, in fact— are utterly without value to the serious novelist. After all, writing is an art as well as a craft, and it requires emotional involvement on the artist's part, a deep commitment you cannot buy and cannot find in a mechanical system of story construction. By "emotional involvement," I mean that an author should write about things which concern him, about subjects in which he is vitally interested, about stories and characters that appeal to him. Although the *idea* for a story, the initial spark, nearly always comes from an external source—a newspaper article, a nonfiction book, another author's novel, a chance remark by a friend—that spark should be the *only* thing about the plot that comes from outside the writer himself. The rest of the story line must develop *within* the novelist; every twist and turn and complication of the plot should be formed by the author's unique personality, filtered through his point of view, so that it becomes a reflection of his character and his interests. Plots taken entirely or even primarily from external sources are flat, cold, and uninvolving because the author is not intimately involved in their creation.

I mentioned newspaper articles as a source of ideas for plots. Let me stress that I mean exactly that: a source for *ideas,* not for plots themselves. If you believe that you can establish a respectable body of work by borrowing entire stories in complete detail from newspaper (or magazine) clippings, you are chin-deep in self-delusion. Some writers *have* sold fiction that evolved from human interest stories in newspapers; indeed, I know of one writer who has sold a couple of novels and at least a dozen short stories that originated in this fashion, and he swears by the method—even though none of those stories or novels has achieved any notable critical or financial success. Fiction raised up from seeds of this sort *can* be good fiction, as long as the newspaper article remains only the *seed* of the plot and does not become the plot itself. It is dangerous to base all of your plot developments on the actual twists and turns of a real-life incident because the most engaging human interest stories in the newspapers usually revolve around a quirk of Fate, a fascinating coincidence; therefore, the final plot of the novel or short story based entirely on this material is forced or outright implausible, for coincidence in fiction always looks like author manipulation.

You also run the risk of using a clipping that is simultaneously being developed by another writer, one who—if the idea *is* viable as fiction—may hit the proper market before you and thereby render your work dated and imitative. Several years ago, magazines and newspapers reported on the deaths of two New York City physicians, twins, who died in a particularly eerie fashion; subsequent to their deaths, it was discovered that their brotherly relationship and their home lives were singularly strange, sick, and terrifying. A number of writers were sufficiently fascinated with the case to attempt to mold it into fiction, but only one of those novels was a success, the first one to see print, *Twins* by Bari Wood and Jack Geasland. In another instance, Judith Rossner's *Looking for Mr. Goodbar* was based on a shocking, sensational, and tragic real-life murder case, and it was an enormous success; a few other writers were intrigued by the same case, produced books based on it, but met with no success at all, at least in part because their efforts reached the marketplace after Ms. Rossner's novel.

My own novel *Whispers* was centered around the tracking down of a unique, bizarre, and entirely fictional psychopathic killer. To the best of my knowledge, the psychosis—as well as the supporting background and causes—that I created for my villain had never been reported in the annals of psychology. Nevertheless, it seemed to me that I had theorized a psychosis that could conceivably arise in the mind of a person subjected to the hideous childhood which I had imagined for my villain, so I went ahead and wrote the book. Seven months after Putnam's published *Whispers,* newspapers all over the world carried a story about two women in Britain who had been discovered suffering from very much the same kind of psychological illness that I had created for the character in my book. The British case was stunning, fascinating, and except for the fictional case in *Whispers,* it was the very first time any doctor had encountered a patient plagued by such an odd psychological malady. (I have deliberately avoided describing that malady here, for *Whispers* generates much of its suspense and mystery from the gradual unfolding of its villain's mental condition, and I have no desire to spoil the effect of my own book for you if you have not as yet read it.) Naturally, I was disconcerted, even chilled, by the way reality imitated my fiction, but that is not the point I want to make. The point is this: If the true story of the women in Britain had appeared in the press before I wrote *Whispers,* I never would have done the book; I would have expected half a dozen other novelists to seize upon such an intriguingly weird case, and I would have looked elsewhere for my next plot rather than risk being trampled in the stampede.

It is also unwise to construct a plot with the *sole* intent of exploiting the public's interest in a currently hot topic. For one thing, in this age of media overkill, the public quickly tires of each new sensation, and by the time an author finishes a novel that exploits the latest hot topic, the public is hopelessly bored with it. Immediately after the Three Mile Island nuclear accident near Harrisburg, Pennsylvania, a couple of dozen novelists churned out books about nuclear power plant catastrophes; by the time these tales began to appear in bookstores, authors not only had to compete with a flood of similar fictions, but they also had to try to sell their wares to a reading public that had been saturated with and bored half to death by endless news reports, TV specials, and slick magazine investigations of the subject. None of those books was successful. The only project that managed to ride on the coattails of Three Mile Island was a rather dumb, inaccurate film, *The China Syndrome,* which happened to be in the theaters already when the Harrisburg crisis developed.

Plot wheels and newspaper clippings cannot provide you with a genuine concern for your characters and their situation; that concern must arise from your own personal emotional and intellectual view of life and its meaning. A newspaper article is only a bare collection of facts and hearsay; the events it reports do not have any fictional structure, theme, *meaning.* Good fiction must grow from your own feelings and experiences, from lessons and truths that you have personally learned.

This does not mean you must write only about what you have done yourself. Obviously, that would severely limit your choices. "Personal experience" may include things that have happened to you, to your friends, to your enemies, to strangers that you have heard about; it may include things you've learned from books, movies, television, radio, school, and from other sources. Everyone is a witches' cauldron of bubbling facts, ideas, images, and memories. You must learn to tap your own magical brew of rich but amorphous material and build orderly structures to contain the unconscious plots within it.

There are several things an author can do to strain out good story ideas from the boiling soup of his subconscious mind.

1. Read, read, read. Read everything you can get your hands on. A writer should read while he is relaxed because that is when the stuff he is reading sinks most deeply into his mind; furthermore, reading should be his *primary* form of relaxation, not skiing or tap dancing or fishing or building model trains or watching television, but *reading.* No novelist can expect to reap harvest after harvest of fresh, golden ideas from his subconscious if he is not constantly fertilizing his subconscious with reams of other writers' fiction and nonfiction. With every novel you read, thousands of facts, characters, images, narrative techniques, and plot twists are stored in your subconscious, thereafter constantly interacting below the level of awareness. When bits of this input jell and surface, they are usually in an original arrangement that bears no resemblance whatsoever to the books from which they came. Also, you will often find a concept in another writer's work which intrigues you, something he tossed away in one line or one paragraph but which *you* see as the entire center of your own novel. If you develop this idea into a book that does not resemble his, you are not guilty of plagiarism; you have only benefited by literary feedback, which is a source of story ideas for all writers.

Do not limit your reading to one type of book. Even if you want to become a science fiction writer, you will not serve yourself well by reading *only* science fiction. Your input must have as much variety as possible if your output is to be fresh and interesting. In Chapter 15, I will provide you with a reading list that ought to keep you well occupied for years to come.

2. Write, write, write. Many new authors operate under the mistaken impression that they should not sit down at the typewriter until they have thought of an absolutely *perfect* idea, something to make Robert Ludlum or Lawrence Sanders or Helen MacInnes weep with envy. Nonsense. As soon as you have come up with a story line that makes any sense at all, even if it is not something that is likely to make you rich and famous and loved, park your back-end on a typing chair and *write* the thing. The very act of writing fiction keeps the mind focused, limber, and creative. Perhaps you will write stacks of unpublishable material at the start of your career, but while you're writing that throwaway stuff, you will be generating better and better ideas, until at last you will be turning out the real thing. Sometimes, during the writing of one story you will conceive the plot line for another story, or even for *two* others. While I was working on a pseudonymous novel—an odd sort of romantic thriller set in Kyoto—the pieces of *Whispers* gradually fell into place; by the time I finished the Kyoto novel, *Whispers* was entirely plotted in my mind, even though the two books had absolutely nothing in common. Writing, especially in sessions lasting six hours or more, is exactly what's needed to prime the idea pump that lies deep in the subconscious.

I can almost hear the screams of protest from those of you who are not yet full-time writers and who hold down mundane jobs in the "real" world. You're saying, "I don't get home from the stirrup buckle factory until six-thirty, and by the time I freshen up and eat dinner, it's seven-thirty or even later, and I've got to get up at six-thirty in the morning to go *back* to the stirrup buckle factory, so how can I possibly squeeze in regular six-hour-long sessions at the typewriter?"

Well, if you want to become a full-time writer badly enough, if you positively *ache* for it, you can find two six- or eight-hour blocks of time every weekend. Then there are holidays, vacations. . . . For a couple of years prior to becoming a full-time novelist, and for many years *after* I broke through that barrier, I spent 90 percent of my weekends at a typewriter. I *still* work an average of six days a week, though I anticipate cutting down to five when I get an IBM word-processing system and can escape from the drudgery of typing and retyping my manuscripts as they pass through their endless drafts. During my first eight years as a full-time freelancer, my wife and I took exactly *one* vacation. Today, the financial rewards and a creative satisfaction gained from all that sacrifice have grown quite large and are growing even larger with each passing year—but getting this far sure wasn't a piece of cake. I never told you that writing bestselling fiction would be *easy*. *Tanstaafl:* There ain't no such thing as a free lunch.

3. Tickle your imagination and generate story ideas by playing around with exotic titles. A story title is not always dictated by the finished work. Indeed, by spending an hour playing with title possibilities, with arrangements of odd or interesting words, you might gradually tease your subconscious into revealing an entire plot line.

Begin by choosing a dramatic or colorful word that will catch a book buyer's interest. This will be the central word of the title upon which you finally settle. Man, horse, winter, rain, coat—those and similar words would not be good choices for this experiment because they are too common and lacking in drama. Death, blood, fear, witch, thief, darkness, prisoner, love, sword, fire, rage—those are the kinds of words that catch a potential reader's eye. With a key word in mind, you're ready to begin winging it.

In *Writing Popular Fiction,* I recounted the process by which I generated a title and, simultaneously, a plot for the first science fiction short story I ever wrote. I believe it might be valuable, by way of example, to include that same information here. I began with the central word "dragon," because it was rich with fantastic, fearful implications. At first I played at adjectival amplification of that single word, jotting each idea down in a list:

The Cold Dragon
The Warm Dragon
The Dancing Dragon
The Black Dragon
The Eternal Dragon
The Waiting Dragon
The Dead Dragon
Steel Dragon
The Crying Dragon

When that seemed to be leading nowhere, I tried following the word "dragon" with various prepositional phrases:

Dragon in the Darkness
Dragons on My Mind
Dragon in Amber
Dragon in the Sky
Dragon by the Tail
Dragon for the King
Dragon in the Land

Several of those attempts were good titles but didn't spark my imagination at that time. Next, I tried using a series of verbs with the key word:

The Dragon Stalks
The Dragon Watches

The Dragon Creeps
The Dragon Feasts at Midnight
The Dragon Fled

None of those titles was particularly intriguing. I moved on, trying to amplify the title by adding another noun:

The Dragon and the Sea
The Dragon and the Night
The Dragon and the Knight
The Dragon and the Key of Gold

Finally, when I tried coupling the key word with other words that seemed at odds with it, I hit upon the right track:

The Weak Dragon
The Sad Dragon
The Timid Dragon
The Tiny Dragon
The Soft Dragon

The contrast in the last of those five titles somehow appealed to me. I began toying with different applications of it:

The Soft Dragon
The Dragon Who Screamed Softly
The Dragon Who Walked Softly
The Dragon Came Softly
Soft Come the Dragons

Abruptly, with that last one, I had a title that came alive for me, that made me wonder about the tale that would go with it. Scenes began to float up from my subconscious. I had primed the idea pump. In another few minutes, I had an entire story in mind. It concerned an alien world where flying dragons, as insubstantial as tissue paper, are inexplicably able to kill with their gaze. Working up a set of characters and character motivations was also easy, and the story was finished in two days."Soft Come the Dragons" was published in *The Magazine of Fantasy and Science Fiction*, the best magazine in its field; the piece received a modest amount of acclaim, brought me a couple of dozen fan letters in the years after its publication, became the title story of a paperback collection of some of my science fiction short stories, and has been translated into Spanish, French, and Japanese. The muse had been reluctant at first, but I had tickled her feet with a mental feather, and she had gotten to work!

4. The fourth way to goose a somnolent imagination is to sit at a typewriter and tap out a bunch of narrative hooks until you find one of them so intriguing that you simply *must* find out what happens next. Since it's *your* narrative hook, only you can say what happens next—and suddenly your idea pump is working at a frenetic pace. In case you aren't familiar with the term "narrative hook," let me explain that it is used to describe an opening sentence, paragraph, or scene designed to be so shocking or surprising or eerie or curious or controversial or puzzling or scary or in some other way so intriguing that the reader is instantly hooked by it and dragged into the book almost against his will. Most popular novels begin with narrative hooks, some of them blatant and some of them subtle.

Here's how you play this idea-generating game. Sit at your typewriter and, without a great deal of cerebral exercise, pound out a gripping opening sentence or paragraph. It is not necessary or even desirable to think about where the story will go or what it will be about before you type that opening. Just *do* it. The less planning you put into this exercise, the more freely you allow these narrative hooks to just roll off the top of your head, the greater the likelihood that the experiment will succeed. The theory behind it is not complicated: If you present yourself with interesting and challenging beginnings, one of them might provide a spark of inspiration; free-floating, subconscious associations might begin to be set off by that spark, and you might quickly construct an entire story line. Write one narrative hook after another, regardless of how crazy some of them sound, regardless of how unlikely it seems that any of them could be developed into worthwhile pieces of fiction. Sooner or later, after you've written a bunch of these hooks, you will find yourself so drawn to one of them that you won't rest until you've carried on with it.

The first piece I wrote in this fashion was a science fiction novelette titled "Where the Beast Runs." After its magazine publication, I incorporated it into the middle section of a SF novel. It was not one of the best things I wrote in the science fiction field, far from it, but it was competent and professional, and it paid a few bills, and it provided me with one more in an endless series of learning experiences of the kind that refine an author's craftsmanship. The story begins:

> Long ago, shortly after my mother's blood was sluiced from the streets of Changeover and her body burned upon a pyre outside of town, I suffered what the psychologists call a trauma. That seems like a very inadequate word to me.

The bizarre events and the somewhat flippant tone of that off-the-top-of-the-head opening spurred my imagination into a gallop, and I rapidly worked up a story to explain them.

Years later, when I had become a considerably more polished and controlled writer than the man who wrote "Where the Beast Runs," I used the narrative hook game to launch a novel, *The Voice of the Night*, which was published under my "Brian Coffey" pen name, an identity I reserve for those occasional books that fit nowhere else in my publishing program. I think *The Voice of the Night* is one of the best things I've ever done, and a number of other writers and more than a few critics have responded extremely well to it. This is how *The Voice of the Night* begins:

> "You ever killed anything?" Roy asked.

I typed those six words without really thinking about them, just playing around, looking for something that would set my imagination afire. After I batted out the line, I stared at it for a minute, and for reasons I cannot explain, I decided that Roy was a boy of about fourteen. Obviously, that decision came out of my subconscious mind; my idea pump was already laboring in my behalf, and when it supplied me with Roy's age, the course of the novel was irrevocably set. Within ten minutes I had expanded those six words into almost two pages of material:

"You ever killed anything?" Roy asked.

Colin frowned. "Like what?"

The two boys were on a high hill at the north end of town. The ocean lay beyond.

"Anything," Roy said. "You ever killed anything at all?"

"I don't know what you mean," Colin said.

Far out on the sun-dappled water, a large ship moved northward, toward distant San Francisco. Nearer shore stood an oil-drilling platform. On the deserted beach, a flock of birds relentlessly worked the damp sand for their lunch.

"You must've killed something," Roy said impatiently. "What about bugs?"

Colin shrugged. "Sure. Mosquitoes. Ants. Flies. So what?"

"How'd you like it?"

"Like what?"

"Killing 'em."

Colin stared at him, finally shook his head. "Roy sometimes you're pretty weird."

Roy grinned.

"You like killing bugs?" Colin asked uneasily.

"Sometimes."

"Why?"

"It's a real popper."

Anything that Roy thought was fun, anything that thrilled him, he called a "popper."

"What's to like?" Colin asked.

"The way they squish."

"Yech."

"Ever pull the legs off a praying mantis and watch it try to walk?" Roy asked.

"Weird. Really weird."

Roy turned to the insistently crashing sea and stood defiantly with his hands on his hips, as if he were challenging the incoming tide. It was a natural pose for him; he was a born fighter.

Colin was fourteen years old, the same age as Roy, and he never challenged anything or anyone. He rolled with life, floated where it took him, offering no resistance. Long ago he had learned that resistance caused pain.

Colin sat on the crown of the hill, in the sparse dry grass. He looked up admiringly at Roy.

Without turning from the sea, Roy said, "Ever kill anything bigger than bugs?"

"No."

"I did."

"Yeah?"

"Lots of times."

"What'd you kill?" Colin asked.

By this point I was thoroughly hooked, and I figured most readers would be hooked, too. There were many questions to which I wanted answers. What bigger things has Roy killed? People? Could a fourteen-year-old boy be a cold-blooded killer? Roy seems to be creepy, and Colin seems to be normal, so why is Colin hanging around this weird kid? What is Roy leading up to with this eerie interrogation?

Within minutes I knew I was writing a novel about the frightening duality of human nature, about the capacity for good and the capacity for evil, both of which exist in every man and woman. I knew the story was about a good, likeable boy (Colin) who, in order to preserve his own life, must suddenly and prematurely cast off childish things and become an adult. I knew that by the end of the book he would have to confront and successfully come to terms with the capacity for evil within himself. I knew Roy was the villain. And, finally, I knew the book would be fast-paced and suspenseful; I liked the brisk style of the narrative hook, and I intended to stick with it in order to maintain the flavor that it gave to the opening pages.

An hour later, I had jotted down a rough outline of the

plot, no more than a page of cryptic notes to myself. Here's what it looked like.

Roy is the first close friend that shy Colin has ever had.

Roy keeps talking about killing, and Colin thinks it's a test or joke.

Roy and Colin become "blood brothers" through a pricking-of-the-thumbs ceremony.

Roy tries to enlist Colin in the rape and murder of a neighbor woman. Colin doesn't take him seriously but makes a game of listing reasons why Roy's plan would fail and land them in prison. Roy drops it.

Relationship gets weirder.

Colin becomes afraid of Roy at the same time that he's drawn to him.

Roy tries to enlist Colin in a plot to wreck a passenger train, and when Colin finally realizes Roy is serious, it is almost too late to save the people on the train.

Colin stops the train wreck at the last second.

Roy feels Colin has broken their blood brother oath. He tries to kill Colin.

Colin turns to mother for help. She doesn't believe that sweet Roy is a killer.

(Much in book about Colin's alienation from mother and father, about lack of communication in many modern families.)

Colin realizes he is utterly alone.

He also discovers Roy has killed other friends and playmates in the past, though each death has appeared to be an accident.

Colin, a weak and shy boy, must find the strength to defend himself against Roy and find a way to prove that Roy is a killer.

He starts by researching Roy's past, trying to learn what lies behind Roy's violent nature. He uncovers a family tragedy (work out later) that has twisted Roy's psychology. At this point, he realizes that Roy is as much to be pitied as feared.

Through this section of the book, Colin is stalked

through his small town, day after day, as Roy tries to kill him. While this incredibly tense little war is going on, the adult world is utterly oblivious to it, and the contrast between the small town's peacefulness and Colin's desperate, protracted fight for his life will give the book a curious power and a moodiness not unlike that in a horror novel.

In the end, Colin and Roy confront each other in a deserted, dilapidated old building of some sort, which will be, in a way, a symbol of the decay that seems always to infect and eventually destroy too many human relationships.

This was a crude plot line. There were many changes along the way. A great many additions, other characters, more action; nevertheless, by the time I finished the novel, it was still basically as I envisioned it that first day, when I teased it out of my subconscious by playing the narrative hook game.

It is worth noting that I had long wanted to write a book about a child with Colin's poor self-image, for he is exactly like *I* was as a boy. I believe I needed to write about the pain of being a social outcast at fourteen, and the narrative hook game provided me with an idea that allowed me to use just such a character as the lead in a novel.

And by the way, if you think that a narrative hook isn't all that important, if you prefer to open your own books with a leisurely two-page description of a place, or with a quiet character essay, pick up any twenty bestsellers and read the first sentence of each, the first paragraph, then the first page. If you don't find good narrative hooks in at least seventeen or eighteen of those twenty, then either you have picked up twenty ordinary books rather than twenty bestsellers or you have stumbled into the Twilight Zone, into another dimension where readers' preferences in popular fiction are very different from what they are in *this* world. Readers have *always* wanted the same story qualities. Consider these opening scenes from three classics:

On the first Monday of the month of April, 1626, the market town of Meung, in which the author of *Ro-*

mance of the Rose was born, appeared to be in as perfect a state of revolution as if the Huguenots had just made a second Rochelle of it. Many citizens, seeing the women flying toward the High Street and leaving their children crying at the open doors, hastened to don the cuirass, and supporting their somewhat uncertain courage with a musket or a partisan, directed their steps toward the hostelry of the Jolly Miller, before which was gathered, increasing every minute, a compact group, vociferous and full of curiosity.

> —*The Three Musketeers,* Alexandre Dumas

Although the style and language of Dumas's book might seem somewhat antiquated to the modern reader, one responds nonetheless to the scene of panic with which Dumas opens his story. Even the modern reader wonders what is happening in the town of Meung and wants to know what comes next—and Dumas makes very sure that, paragraph by paragraph, the reader keeps on wanting to know what comes next.

"Christmas won't be Christmas without any presents," grumbled Jo, lying on the rug.

"It's so dreadful to be poor!" sighed Meg, looking down at her dress.

"I don't think it's fair for some girls to have plenty of pretty things, and other girls nothing at all," added little Amy with an injured sniff.

"We've got father and mother and each other," said Beth contentedly from her corner.

The four young faces on which the firelight shone brightened at the cheerful words, but darkened again as Jo said sadly.

"We haven't got father, and shall not have him for a long time." She didn't say "perhaps never," but each silently added it, thinking of father far away, where the fighting was.

> —*Little Women,* Louisa May Alcott

What an opening for a novel! The first narrative hook is very low-key, just sufficient to make the reader go on for a few more sentences, but it rapidly leads to a second hook that is very powerful indeed. That opening sentence has two functions: 1) It makes the reader wonder why there will be no Christmas presents; 2) It generates sympathy for the young ladies we are about to meet. After several lines of brisk dialogue, we quickly learn that the father of these girls is away at war. At any moment they might become orphans. Within a remarkably few lines of prose, we are dealing with several fundamental human issues: sisterly companionship, family love, fear of poverty, the tragedy of war. That's a lot of heavy stuff to be laid down in those deceptively simple, highly readable one hundred and twenty words! Furthermore, Louisa May Alcott laces this opening with a liberal measure of pathos, unashamedly tugging at our heartstrings before we've even properly gotten to know the girls with whom we're supposed to sympathize. Any reader who can put down *Little Women* at this point and never return to it is a reader with a cold, cold heart indeed.

The third classic to which I direct your attention is *Oliver Twist* by Charles Dickens, in which the narrative hook is too long to quote word for word. I urge you to read it, but I will tell you here that in the space of just three pages, Oliver Twist enters the world in miserable circumstances, fights desperately for his life, and is orphaned before he is five minutes old. One need only read that opening scene to fully understand why the work of Charles Dickens has lasted for more than a hundred years and will continue to last as long as civilization exists.

I am not saying that Dumas, Alcott, and Dickens conceived the story lines of their books by playing around with narrative hooks; in fact, it is extremely unlikely that they did so. But the narrative hook as I have defined it is vital to the success of any piece of popular fiction, and playing games with it is certainly not the worst way to tease your imagination when you begin the search for a new idea for a novel.

5. You might also prime your idea pump by building up

a couple of characters in enormous detail, without the slightest thought about the story of which they will eventually be a part. Work up several pages of character details. (For an idea of what such a list ought to include, refer to Chapter 7.) When you have dreamed up two thoroughly realized, reasonably consistent, interesting, and *likeable* characters, put them together in a conversation, a conversation about anything, just so long as it is of some substance. Topics such as death, religion, war, chastity, honor, and love are just what you need for this exercise. While writing this conversation between your two imaginary people, work very hard at keeping each of them in character; force yourself to think of how each of them would really respond to the many aspects of the topic you've chosen for their dialogue; learn their opinions—don't just use them as mouthpieces for your own point of view on the issues. When you've done this, you ought to have a strong feeling for your characters; you ought to know how their minds work. *Now,* ask yourself these questions: What does each character fear more than anything else in the world? What would be the very worst thing that could happen to him? What event would throw his life into complete turmoil? For example, if one of your characters is a widow whose life centers around her only child, if she is totally devoted to that child and if the child is also devoted to her, the loss of the child would probably be the worst thing that could happen to her. There, you've answered those three questions. Now you start to wonder *how* she might lose the child. Would it die? Would it be kidnapped? Would it run away from home? When you have answered this question, a dozen others will pop up. Your idea pump will have been primed, and there's a good chance you'll put together a workable story line.

Without questioning the authors, it is impossible to say what famous novels might have begun with the creation of a couple of very vivid characters and *then* with the development of a plot. However, I would be willing to wager a tidy sum that Margaret Mitchell knew all about Scarlett O'Hara and Rhett Butler before she knew what was going to happen to them. But you see, once she had those two larger-than-life people in mind, once she *knew* them intimately, the events of *Gone with the Wind* were inevitable. I'm sure that more than a few other books have evolved in this fashion.

Please note: This method of generating a story line is not at all the same as letting your characters take over total control of the novel *as it is being written*. If you employ this method of plot creation, you will know virtually every major event of the novel before you type the words "Chapter One." Your characters will be as thoroughly planned as your plot, and there will be no opportunity for them to seize control and run the book into uncharted territory. It is only when you start a book with unexplored characters that you run the risk of losing control of them.

The classic plot

The vast majority of successful novels share the same story pattern. I have boiled this pattern down to four steps, and although this is somewhat simplistic, it is essentially accurate. 1) The author introduces a hero (or heroine) who has just been or is about to be plunged into terrible trouble. 2) The hero attempts to solve his problem but only slips into deeper trouble. 3) As the hero works to climb out of the hole he's in, complications arise, each more terrible than the one before, until it seems as if his situation could not possibly be blacker or more hopeless than it is—and then one final, unthinkable complication makes matters even worse. In most cases, these complications arise from mistakes or misjudgments the hero makes while struggling to solve his problems, mistakes and misjudgments which result from the interaction of the faults and virtues that make him a unique character. 4) At last, deeply affected and *changed* by his awful experiences and by his intolerable circumstances, the hero learns something about himself or about the human condition in general, a Truth of which he was previously ignorant, and having learned this lesson, he understands what he must do to get out of the dangerous situation in which he has wound up. He takes the necessary actions and either succeeds or fails, though he succeeds more often than not, for readers tend to greatly prefer fiction that has an uplifting conclusion.

Perhaps you feel that what I have just done is provide you with a story *formula*, and the word "formula" has a bad image because it sounds like the refuge of the hack writer. But I don't think these four steps constitute a formula; rather, they provide a pattern that has proven, through generations of novelists, to be the most satisfying, flexible, and least constricting structure by which to order and give meaning to a long piece of fiction. Robert Ludlum uses the pattern to write his contemporary thrillers. John MacDonald uses it, and James Clavell, Stephen King. . . . Dickens used this pattern for all his novels. Read *Great Expectations* if you believe that such a simple pattern must inevitably lead to hack fiction. Or read Hemingway's *The Old Man and the Sea*.

Terrible trouble

Judging by the many manuscripts I have read over the years, ninety-nine out of one hundred new writers make the same mistake in the opening pages of their books, and it is one of the *worst* errors they could possibly commit: They do not begin their novels by plunging their hero or heroine into terrible trouble. If you fail to interest and entertain the reader *right from the start* you will surely lose him long before the end of the first chapter.

Do not forget that editors are readers, too; they are searching for the same thing that library patrons and bookstore customers are looking for—entertainment value. When an editor sits down with a manuscript from an unknown author, he expects to be gripped and held within three pages—at the *most!* If he is *not* gripped by those first thousand words, he will read no farther. I can almost hear some of you screaming again: "An editor should read the *whole thing* before he rejects it!" Why should he? It is not an editor's duty to struggle valiantly through chapter after chapter of turbid, turgid, and tedious prose just because the author took the time to write and submit it. By composing a novel and offering it for sale, an author is demanding time, attention, and money from his readers; it is only right that he give them something in return, and the something that readers want is *entertainment*.

It is even a mistake for a writer to begin a novel with the

idea that he has several pages to seize his readers; if he is wise, a novelist will approach each book with the intention of proving himself in just *one* page. After all, when a potential book buyer is browsing in a bookstore or at a newsstand, or when he is hurriedly selecting from the offerings on a paperback rack in an airport or drugstore or supermarket, he will usually choose his purchase on the basis of five things: 1) the author's name, if it is a known author he wants; 2) the subject matter of the novel; 3) the cover illustration; 4) the description of the book provided by the advertising copy on it; 5) *a quick reading of the first page.* If your book fails to win that reader in the first page, he will put it back on the shelf and buy somebody else's novel.

Those are some of the coldest, hardest facts of a writer's life. A three-page chance with the editor. A one-page chance with the average book buyer. Not *much* of a chance in either case. On the other hand, the situation is challenging, and such challenges are what make a writer's workday endlessly interesting.

Okay. Let's assume you're convinced that you must open your novel by plunging your hero or heroine (or both) into terrible trouble. Just how terrible should this trouble be?

It doesn't have to involve a life-or-death struggle. Avery Corman's enormously successful *Kramer vs Kramer* is about a man whose wife leaves him—and then later returns in an attempt to win exclusive custody of their only child. No one's life is ever in danger in *Kramer vs Kramer;* there are no gunshots fired, no car crashes, no chases. Nevertheless, the hero is in terrible trouble because the domestic-emotional foundation of his life is collapsing under him, and he gradually becomes afraid of winding up alone. The loss of a husband, wife, or child—even if death is not the cause of that loss—is an extremely powerful theme. At some dark and brooding moment in our lives, all of us have considered what it would be like to live without the person who is dearest to us; many readers have already known the agony of such a loss, and they respond strongly to fiction that deals with the subject.

Ayn Rand's *The Fountainhead* is another book that opens with less than a life-or-death situation, yet it is gripping. The hero has suffered some serious career setback, the nature of which we do not immediately learn; what fascinates us and involves us is the fact that he does not seem to be unduly depressed or worried about his terrible trouble. Indeed, he is standing naked at the edge of a granite cliff, ready to dive into the deep water below for a swim, and he is laughing happily, challenging the world. We are instantly drawn to this character who can face adversity in such a splendid fashion, and we want to know more about his problems and his plans for solving them.

Although a popular novel does not have to begin with a life-or-death struggle, probably 30 percent of them do, and at least 80 percent arrive at that level of dramatic conflict sooner or later. In the opening scenes of Stephen King's excellent *'Salem's Lot,* a man and a boy are traveling cross-country, on the run from something awful that happened in Jerusalem's Lot, Maine. We do not know exactly *what* they are running from; at first it seems as if they might be fleeing from the police or from some other body of authority, but we quickly realize that the situation is not an ordinary one involving anything so mundane as policemen. Still, in those initial scenes, we don't know that the man and boy are afraid for their lives, though the dark and moody tone of the prose leads us to suspect that they have been and *will* be in mortal danger sooner or later. Eventually, a long and incredibly violent series of life-or-death struggles becomes the central concern of *'Salem's Lot;* before long, the novel reeks of death, and the reader is firmly gripped, propelled through the story by an urgent need to know which of the many sympathetic characters will survive. *'Salem's Lot* has sold more than three million copies.

James Clavell's *Shogun,* a novel of medieval Japan, *does* begin with a life-or-death struggle. John Blackthorne, the hero, is guiding his ship through the worst storm he has ever encountered, and he has little hope of surviving. Most of the crew is already dead, gone before the storm even struck, victims of a trouble-plagued journey that has led them halfway around the world. Blackthorne lives through the storm and through the violent grounding of his ship, but thereafter his life is in almost constant jeopardy from one source or another. *Shogun* has sold more than seven million copies.

I feel so strongly about the importance of a suspenseful opening scene that I am going to reprint the first scenes from three of my own novels by way of example. After each scene, I will discuss the reactions I hoped to generate in readers, and I will explain the techniques by which I sought to elicit those reactions. It is also part of my purpose to show you how the life-or-death struggle can be used in radically different ways to create an endless variety of opening sequences.

Hanging On was the first mainstream novel I wrote. It was a comic-adventure-war novel, with emphasis on comedy. It was extremely well reviewed, but in terms of sales, it enjoyed only modest success in this country. Strangely, the novel was quite popular in Denmark. But considering how small Denmark is, I could hardly contemplate writing books primarily for that market. I learned that comic novels, even critically acclaimed comic novels, are not widely popular, and I never wrote another. Perhaps, subconsciously, I already knew that comic novels had limited appeal even as I was beginning *Hanging On,* for although the bulk of the book maintains a fifty-fifty balance between comedy and suspense, the first scene hooks the reader with a big dose of the latter and only a small seasoning of the former. Here's how it begins:

Major Kelly was in the latrine, sitting down, his pants around his ankles, when the Stuka dive bombers struck. With good weather, Kelly used the last stall in the narrow, clapboard building, because it was the only cubicle not covered by a roof and was, therefore, considerably less offensive than any of the others. Now, in the late afternoon sunshine, a fresh breeze pouring in over the top, the stall was actually pleasant, a precious retreat from the men, the war, the bridge. Content, patient with his bodily processes, he sat there watching a fat brown spider weave its web in the corner behind the door hinge. The spider, he felt, was an omen; it survived, even flourished, midst stench and decay; and if he, Kelly, only spun his webs as well as the spider did, were as tenacious, he would flourish too, would make it through this damn war in one piece. One *live* piece. He had no desire to make it through the war in one *dead* piece. And that meant spinning tight webs around himself. Shallow philosophy, perhaps, but shallow philosophy was Major Kelly's one great weakness, because it was the only thing that offered hope. Now, mesmerized by the spider, he did not hear the Stukas until they were almost over the latrine. When he *did* hear them, he looked up, shocked, in time to see them sweep by in perfect formation, framed by the four walls of the stall, shining prettily in the sunlight.

As usual, the trio of stubby dive bombers came without the proper Messerschmitt escort, flaunting their invulnerability. They came from the east, buzzing in low over the trees, climbing as they reached the center of the open encampment, getting altitude for a murderous run on the bridge.

The planes passed over in an instant, no longer framed in the open roof of the last stall. A turbulent wind followed them, as did a thunderclap that shook the latrine walls.

Kelly knew he was as safe in the latrine as anywhere else in camp, for the Stukas never attacked anything but the bridge. They never bombed the cheap tin-walled bunker that was shelved into the soft ground near the tree line, and they ignored the heavy machinery building as well as all the construction equipment parked behind it. They ignored the headquarters which was half corrugated sheet tin and half clapboard and would have made a dandy target; and they were oblivious of the hospital bunker cut into the hillside near the river—and of the latrines behind HQ. All they cared about was pulverizing the damn bridge. They passed over it again and again, spitting black eggs from their bellies, flames blossoming beneath them, until the bridge was down. Then they bombed it some more. They transformed the steel beams into twisted, smoldering lumps of slag, unrecognizable and unusable. Then they bombed it some more. It was almost as if the three pilots had been severely traumatized by the bridge during their childhoods, as if each of them had a personal stake in this business, some old grudge to settle.

If he avoided the bridge, then, he would be safe. Intellectually, he was quite aware of this; however, emotionally, Major Kelly was certain that each Stuka attack was directed against him, personally, and that it was only good luck that the pilots got the bridge instead. Somewhere deep in Nazi Germany, some fine old school chum of his had risen to a position of influence and power, some old chum who knew just where Kelly was, and he was running these Stuka flights to have him wiped out as fitting retribution for some slight or other that Kelly had done the old chum years and years ago. That was it. That had to be it. Yet, as often as he considered his school days back in the States, Major Kelly could not recall a single old chum of German extraction who might have returned to the fatherland for the war. He still would not give up on the theory, because it was the only one which made sense; he could not conceive of a war, or any battle in it, that was waged on a purely impersonal basis. At one time, he was sure, Churchill, Stalin, and Roosevelt must have snubbed Hitler at a cocktail party, thereby generating this whole mess.

Now, caught in the latrine at the start of the attack, Major Kelly stood and jerked up his trousers, catching them on an exposed nailhead and ripping out half the backside. He slammed through the dusty latrine door into the open area at the south side of the machinery shed. He was just in time to see the Stukas, four hundred yards upriver, arc high over the bridge and punch out their first ebony bombs. Turning, the seat of his pants flapping, he ran for the bunker by the trees, screaming at the top of his lungs.

Behind, the first bombs hit the bridge. A hot, orange flower blossomed, opened rapidly, ripened, blackened into an ugly ball of thick smoke. The explosion crashed across the encampment with a real physical presence, hammering at Kelly's back.

"No!" he shouted. He stumbled, almost fell. If he fell, he was finished.

More bombs plowed into the steel floor of the bridge, shredded the plating squares, and hurled thousands of sharp, deadly slivers into the smoke-darkened sky. These jagged fragments fell back to earth with a wind-cutting hum that was audible even above the shriek of the Stukas and the shattering explosions of more bombs.

He reached the steps in the earth and went down to the bunker door, grabbed the handle in both hands, and wrenched at it. The door did not open. He tried again, with no more success than before, then fell against it and pounded with one fist. "Hey, in there! Hey!"

The Stukas, circling back from the bridge, came in low over the bunker, engines screaming. They established a sympathetic vibration in his bones. His teeth chattered like castanets. Shuddering violently, he felt himself throwing off his strength, letting the weakness well up. Then the Stukas were gone, leaving behind them a smell of scorched metal and overheated machine oil.

Major Kelly realized, as the Stukas shot out across the trees to make their second approach on the bridge, that no one inside the bunker was going to open up and let him in, even though he was their commanding officer and had always been nice to them. He knew just what they were thinking. They were thinking that if they opened the door, one of the Stukas would put a two-hundred-pound bomb right through it, killing them all. Perhaps that was a paranoid fear, but Major Kelly could understand it; he was at least as paranoid as any of the men hiding down in the bunker.

The Stukas, which had grown almost inaudible at

the nadir of their swing-around, now closed in again, their engines winding up from a low whistle through a shrill keening into an enraged scream that made Major Kelly's hair stand right on end.

Kelly ran up the bunker steps to the surface and, screaming again, plunged past the back of the machinery building, past the latrine, and along the riverbank toward the hospital bunker. His legs pumped so hard and so high that he seemed in grave danger of hitting himself in the chest with his own knees.

The Stukas thundered in, lower than before, shattering the air and making the earth under him reverberate.

Kelly knew he was running toward the bridge, and he hated to do that, but the hospital bunker was a hundred and fifty yards closer to the span than the latrines had been, offering the only other underground shelter in the camp. He reached the hospital steps just as the first Stuka let go with its second load of bombs.

The entire length of the bridge jumped up from its moorings, twisted sickeningly against the backdrop of smoke-sheathed trees on the far side of the gorge. The structure tossed away I-beams like a frantic lover throwing off clothes. Long steel planks zoomed above the blanket of smoke, then shot down again, smashing branches to the ground, splitting the dry, baked earth.

Kelly looked away, ran down the hospital steps, and tried the door just as the second Stuka let go with its payload. The bridge gave some more, but the hospital door wouldn't give at all.

Kelly ran back up to the surface, screaming.

The last plane swooped over the gorge. Flames gushed up in its wake, and smoldering pieces of metal rained down around the major, bouncing on his shoes, and leaving scars where they hit.

The Stukas, peeling off at the apex of their bombing climb, turned over on their backs and flew upside down toward the trees, to lead into a third approach.

"Arrogant sons of bitches!" Kelly shouted.

Then he realized he shouldn't antagonize the Stuka pilots, and he shut up. Was it possible that any of them had heard him above the roar of their own planes and above the noise of bridge sections settling violently into the gorge? Unlikely. In fact, impossible. However, you didn't stay alive in this war by taking chances. It was always possible that one or more of the pilots could read lips and that, flying upside down with a perfect view of him, they had discovered the nature of the epithet which he had so thoughtlessly flung at them.

Suddenly, with the planes gone over the trees, he was alone, standing in a low pall of black smoke that rose like flood waters out of the gorge and spread rapidly across the entire camp. Choking, wiping at teary eyes, he began to run again—then stopped cold as he saw that there was nowhere to run to. Caught with his pants down in the latrine, he hadn't gotten to either of the bunkers in time to be let in with the other men. Unaccustomed to battle, the technicians and laborers in Kelly's unit of Army engineers had developed only one useful talent for battle conditions: running. Any man in the unit could make it from one end of the camp to the other and into the bunkers so fast he'd have won a medal at any Olympic track event. Unless, of course, he was confronted with some obstacle—like pants around his ankles, an exposed nail that ripped out the seat of his pants, or the latrine door. Which was what had happened to Kelly to slow him down. And now he was here alone, waiting for the Stukas, doomed.

The smoke rose around him in black columns, rolled menacingly over the C-shaped clearing in which the camp stood, obscuring the HQ building and the machinery shed and the latrines, closing out life and bringing in death. He knew it. *I feel it coming,* he thought. He was doomed. He sneezed as the smoke tickled his nostrils, and he wished to hell the Stukas would come back and get it over with. Why were they making him wait so long for it? All they had to do was drop a couple of bombs anywhere nearby, and it would be over. The sooner they did it the better, because he didn't like standing there in that smoke, sneezing and coughing and his mouth full of an oily taste. He was miserable. He wasn't a fighter. He was an engineer. He had hung on as long as he could reasonably hope to; the war had finally defeated him, had foiled his every stratagem, destroyed his every scheme for survival, and he was ready to face up to the awful truth. So where were the Stukas?

As the smoke gradually cleared, leaving only the gorge clouded in ugly vapor, Major Kelly understood that the Stukas weren't coming back. They had done all they needed to do in their first two passes. He wasn't doomed after all, or even injured. He could have remained in the latrine, watching the spider, and saved himself all this effort. But that wasn't the way to hang on, to stay alive. That was taking chances, and only madmen took chances. To stay alive, you moved constantly this way and that, searching for an edge. And now that the Stukas were gone, so was Major Kelly's pessimism. He *would* come out of this in one piece, one *live* piece, and then he would find General Blade—the man who had dropped their unit two hundred and fifty miles behind German lines—and he would kill the son of a bitch.

I had six goals in that opening chapter, and there were many techniques by which I attempted to attain those goals:

1. *I wanted to grip the reader immediately.* I believe the very first sentence fulfills that intention. It contains sudden, violent action: the attack of the dive bombers. It also creates a humorous and intriguing image in the reader's mind: poor Major Kelly in the latrine, embarrassingly unprepared when the attack begins.

After the initial sentence, I make use of another technique that I highly recommend: *the tease.* Once the bombers have been introduced and Kelly has been established in his dumb but terrifying position, I do not mention the Stukas again for eight rather long sentences. I hold the reader at arm's length, so to speak, while I give him a bit of scene setting and a touch of character development; then I return to the bomber attack. If a reader is allowed to anticipate a scene of violence or other action, that anticipation makes the action sequence considerably more exciting than it otherwise would have been.

Warning! The amount of anticipation you force upon your readers must be carefully considered and not excessively long. I would have been unwise to open with the sentence about the latrine and the Stukas . . . then wander off for two or three pages of stage dressing before returning to the bomber attack. Had I done that, I either would have lost my readers or I would have motivated them to organize a lynching.

2. *I wanted to introduce the lead character.* And he's right there in the very first sentence of the book.

3. *I wanted to plunge the lead character into terrible trouble.* Again, that is accomplished in the first sentence. If you think that being caught in a flimsy latrine during a bombing isn't terrible trouble, then you must have led an absolutely *harrowing* life.

Please note that Kelly's terrible trouble almost immediately gets even more terrible. He leaves the latrine, and bombs begin to fall. He can't get into the first bunker. More bombs fall; the level of violence rapidly increases. He can't get into the second bunker. More bombs. Shrapnel. Bone-jarring explosions, smoke, fire. Finally, Kelly is reduced to standing in the open, frozen in mortal terror, while the Stukas do their dirty work all around him. Once you have opened with your hero in terrible trouble, you must expand upon that trouble, squeeze every drop of dramatic potential out of it.

4. *I wanted to make the reader laugh or at least smile in order to set the tone for funnier scenes to come.* Throughout Major Kelly's frantic search for shelter, I worked hard to balance his genuine terror with a hysterical fatalism that would, by contrast, seem amusing. Whether I achieved this balance, and whether or not it was amusing, depends on each reader's sense of humor.

5. *I wanted to let the reader know that this was going to be a fast-paced story with lots of suspense, not merely a comic novel.* I attempted to do this, in part, by keeping Kelly on the move. I could have written a first scene in which he just sits there in the latrine, paralyzed by fear, raging at himself for his inability to move, and perhaps I could have made that scene just as amusing as the one I *did* write; however, I could not have made it as suspenseful, as colorful, or as filled with action as it is now.

Suspense is also sharpened by Major Kelly's constant fear, by his unwavering certainty that he is not going to survive. Once you have introduced a *likeable* lead character, keeping your readers worried about the character's fate is one of the best ways to keep them reading. Writers sometimes make the mistake of creating a hero (or heroine) who is utterly unafraid of danger, who is too self-reliant, too competent for his survival ever to be in doubt. Even if you plunge that kind of super-hero into terrible trouble, you cannot generate much tension. If your hero doesn't fear anything, your readers will be unable to fear *for* him, and your story will be without a trace of suspense. Of course, in the opening pages of *Hanging On,* Major Kelly's fear is dwelt upon to excess, wildly exaggerated for comic effect. A lead character's doubts and fears will seldom be stated so blatantly in a non-comic novel; nevertheless, the principle herein described holds true for nearly all popular fiction, comic or not.

Various stylistic techniques also contribute to the suspense in that first chapter of *Hanging On.* For one thing, I used strong, action-filled verbs wherever possible. When Major Kelly decides to desert the latrine in an effort to reach the safety of the bunker, he doesn't simply "leave" the latrine or "go out" of it. I wrote: "He slammed through the latrine door. . . ." *Slammed.* That colorful verb helps the reader hear the door banging open, the hinges loudly rattling, and it more accurately, more vividly describes Major Kelly's haste and excitement than would a verb like "stepped" or "pushed." In the very next sentence, I wrote:

"He was just in time to see the Stukas, four hundred yards upriver, arc high over the bridge and punch out their first ebony bombs." If I had composed that sentence using "fly" instead of "arc" and "drop" instead of "punch out," the suspensefulness of the scene as a whole might have been reduced by only the tiniest fraction—but it *would* have been reduced. Within the next dozen lines these action verbs appear: ran, hit, crashed, plowed, shredded, hurled. When you are writing a suspense and/or action sequence, colorful and urgent verbs make the action more intense and the tension more immediate; they make the terrible trouble seem more terrible—which is why I am discussing them at this point—for they assist the reader when he attempts to visualize your scenes and empathize with your story people. As you might suspect, action verbs can easily be overused. You shouldn't employ them in every sentence, or even in most, for that would give your book a shrill, one-note quality. A writer must learn to let his prose rise and fall like a rhythmic yet steadily building tide; the best prose has a complex rhythm, not only in regard to its pace, but in regard to its emotional intensity as well.

6. *I wanted to create a strong sense of reality, at least to the extent possible given the built-in comic exaggeration of this particular novel.* You might wonder what realism has to do with devising terrible trouble for your hero. It has everything to do with it. Even the most charming and sympathetic hero ever created by a novelist, combined with the most brilliantly constructed and surprising plot ever dreamed up, compounded by the most devilishly clever and truly terrible trouble ever visited upon a lead character—even *that* epic story would be flat and lifeless if it did not unfold in a setting that was believable. The reader wants to be convinced that the tale he's reading is really happening, or that it has really happened in the past, or that it could really happen in the future, and he cannot be convinced of any such thing if the author does not bother to conjure up a good illusion of reality.

Realism in fiction is attained primarily by two means: stylistic technique and the use of well-observed, accurate details. Most stylistic techniques must be learned through thousands of hours of writing and rewriting fiction; they cannot be taught, for each author's style is different, formed by his unique psyche, colored by his own view of the world. (See Chapter 11 for a few other thoughts on "style" as it applies to a novelist's work.)

As for well-observed, accurate details, they come from two sources. First there is the mundane detail that a writer draws from his own ordinary experiences. For example, look at the first paragraph of *Hanging On,* in which Kelly notices a spider spinning its web in one corner of the latrine stall. Anyone who has ever had to use an outhouse knows that spiders adore those places. This is not a big, important detail, nothing earthshaking; however, when the spider is added to the dozens of other unremarkable details that are used to establish a sense of place in that scene, a pretty good illusion of reality begins to take shape. The second source of accurate details is research. Nothing adds verisimilitude to a story more quickly and surely than obscure details that the author has gone to some trouble to unearth. Once, when writing a novel set largely in Kyoto, Japan, I researched thousands of arcane facts about Japanese customs, politics, lifestyles, architecture, theater, art, music, philosophy, and cuisine. Because my two lead characters had a scene in a taxi, I even went so far as to dig up the name of the largest taxi company in Kyoto *and* the color of its cabs. I could have put my characters into a taxi without mentioning that it was red and black, but how much more authentic the scene is when it's enriched with unobtrusively inserted facts of that nature! Another example: In the second paragraph of *Hanging On,* I mentioned that, in World War Two, Stuka dive bombers were usually accompanied by a Messerschmitt escort. That is a detail that makes no major, direct contribution to the plot of my novel, but it does contribute to the maintenance of the illusion of reality, without which the plot would collapse. The influence of realistic detail on the success or failure of a piece of fiction is indirect but vital.

Those were my six goals when I sat down to write the opening chapter of *Hanging On.* Except for number 4,

which deals with the comic aspects peculiar to that particular novel, those are the same goals (though not necessarily the only goals) with which I begin the first scene of
every novel I write. I highly recommend them as guidelines
for new authors who are having difficulty writing gripping
first chapters.

Let's look at a second excerpt, this one from *The Vision*,
first published by G.P. Putnam's Sons in 1977. Strangely
enough, I was interested in *The Vision* primarily because it
offered me a chance to engage in a stylistic experiment.
One day, looking over a shelf of books in search of something to read, I was suddenly struck with the realization
that most horror novels are written in a dense or even
baroque style. Oh, certainly, *Rosemary's Baby, The Exorcist* and a few others are not baroque, but the majority are.
Even Stephen King's books—especially *'Salem's Lot, The
Shining, and The Stand*—have a sort of *modern* baroque
quality. I began to wonder what a horror novel would read
like if it were written in brisk, stripped-down prose. That
made me think of James M. Cain and Dashiell Hammett,
and Hammett's name really started my idea pump working
at top speed. Could a horror novel be written in a style
approximating Hammett's? Could it be told in lean, almost
cold prose and still be scary? Could the hard-boiled, tough
tone of 1930s detective fiction be adapted to the horror
genre with any degree of success? I quickly sat down at my
typewriter to give it a try, and *The Vision* turned out to be
one of the most exhilarating writing experiences I had had
up till that time. The book was chosen as a full selection of
the Doubleday Book Club, through which it sold 350,000
copies. The paperback rights were sold at auction for a
substantial, six-figure advance. British rights brought a
high price, too, and translation rights were quickly sold in
other countries. This is how *The Vision* begins:

> "Gloves of blood."
> The woman raised her hands and stared at them,
> stared *through* them.
> Her voice was soft but tense. "Blood on his hands."
> Her own hands were clean and pale.

Her husband leaned forward from the back seat of the patrol car. "Mary?"

She didn't respond.

"Mary, can you hear me?"

"Yes."

"Whose blood do you see?"

"I'm not sure."

"The victim's blood?"

"No. In fact . . . it's his own."

"The killer's?"

"Yes."

"He has his own blood on his hands?"

"That's right," she said.

"He's hurt himself?"

"But not badly."

"How?"

"I don't know."

"Try to get inside of him."

"I am already."

"Get deeper."

"I'm not a mind reader."

"I know that, darling. But you're the next best thing."

The perspiration on Mary Bergen's face was like the ceramic glaze on the plaster countenance of an altar saint. Her smooth skin gleamed in the green light from the instrument panel. Her dark eyes also shone, but they were unfocused, blank.

Suddenly she leaned forward and shuddered.

In the driver's seat Chief of Police Harley Barnes shifted uneasily. He flexed his big hands on the steering wheel.

"He's sucking the wound," she said. "Sucking his own blood."

After thirty years of police work, Barnes didn't expect to be surprised or frightened. Now, in a single evening, he had been surprised more than once and had felt his heartbeat accelerate with fear.

The tree-shrouded streets were as familiar to him as the contours of his own face. However, tonight, cloaked in a rainstorm, they seemed menacing. The tires hissed on the slick pavement. The windshield wipers thumped, an eerie metronome.

The woman beside Barnes was distraught, but her appearance was less disturbing than the changes she had wrought inside the patrol car. The humid air became clearer when she entered her trance. He was certain he was not imagining that. The ordinary sounds of the storm and the car were overlaid with the soft humming of ghost frequencies. He sensed an indescribable power radiating from her. He was a practical man, not at all superstitious. But he could not deny what he felt so strongly.

She bent as far toward the dashboard as her seat belt would allow. She hugged herself and groaned as if she were having labor pains.

Max Bergen reached out from the rear seat, touched her.

She murmured and relaxed slightly.

His hand looked enormous on her slender shoulder. He was tall, angular, hard-muscled, hard-faced, forty years old, ten years older than his wife. His eyes were his most arresting feature; they were gray, cold, humorless.

Chief Barnes had never seen him smile. Clearly, Bergen harbored powerful and complex feelings for Mary, but he gave no indication that he felt anything but contempt for the rest of the world.

The woman said, "Turn at the next corner."

Barnes braked gently. "Left or right?"

"Right," she said.

Well-kept, thirty-year-old stucco houses and bungalows, most of them California-Spanish in style, lay on both sides of the street. Yellow lights glowed vaguely behind drapes that had been drawn against the chill of the damp December night. The road was much darker than the one they had left. Sodium vapor lamps stood only at the corners, and purple-black, rain-pooled shadows filled the long blocks between them.

After he made the turn, Barnes drove no faster than ten miles an hour. From the woman's attitude, he gathered that the chase would end nearby.

Mary sat up straight. Her voice was louder and clearer than it had been since she began to use her strange talent, her clairvoyance. "I get an impression . . . of a . . . a fence. Yes . . . I see it now . . . he's cut his hand . . . on a fence."

Max stroked her hair. "And it's not a serious wound?"

"No . . . just a cut . . . his thumb . . . deep . . . but not disabling." She raised one thin hand, forgot what she meant to do with it, let it flutter back into her lap.

"But if he's bleeding from a deep cut, won't he give up tonight?" Max asked.

"No," she said.

"You're sure?"

"He'll go on."

"The bastard's killed five women so far," Barnes said. "Some of them fought like hell, scratched him and cut him and even tore out his hair. He doesn't give up easily."

Ignoring the policeman, Max soothed his wife, caressed her face with one hand and prompted her with another question. "What kind of fence do you see?"

"Chain-link," she said. "Sharp and unfinished at the top."

"Is it high?"

"Five feet."

"What does it surround?"

"A yard."

"Storage yard?"

"No. Behind a house."

"Can you see the house?"

"Yes."

"What's it like?"

"It's a two story."

"Stucco?"

"Yes."

"What about the roof?"

"Spanish tile."

"Any unique features?"

"I can't quite see . . ."

"A veranda?"

"No."

"A courtyard maybe?"

"No. But I see . . . a winding tile walkway."

"Front or back?"

"Out front of the house."

"Any trees?"

"Matched magnolias . . . on either side of the walk."

"Anything else?"

"A few small palms . . . farther back."

Harley Barnes squinted through the rain-dappled windshield. He was searching for a pair of magnolias.

Initially he had been skeptical. In fact, he'd been certain the Bergens were frauds. He played his role in the charade because the *mayor* was a believer. The mayor brought them to town and insisted the police cooperate with them.

Barnes had read about psychic detectives, of course, and most especially about that famous Dutch clairvoyant, Peter Hurkos. But using ESP to track down a psychopathic killer, to catch him in the act? He didn't put much faith in that.

Or do I? he wondered. This woman was so lovely, charming, earnest, so convincing that perhaps she'd made a believer of him. If she hasn't, he thought, why am I looking for magnolia trees?

She made a sound like an animal caught in a saw-toothed trap for a long time. Not a screech of agony, but a nearly inaudible mewl.

When an animal made that noise, it meant, "This still hurts, but I'm resigned to it now."

Many years ago, as a boy in Minnesota, Barnes had hunted and trapped. It was that same pitiful, stifled moan of the wounded prey that caused him to give up his sport.

Until tonight, he had never heard precisely the

same sound issue from a human being. Apparently, as she used her talent to zero in on the killer, she suffered from contact with his deranged mind.

Barnes shivered.

"Mary," her husband said. "What's the matter?"

"I see him . . . at the back door of the house. His hand on the door . . . and blood . . . his blood on a white door frame. He's talking to himself."

"What's he saying?"

"I don't . . ."

"Mary?"

"He's saying filthy things about the woman."

"The woman in the house—the one he's after tonight?"

"Yes."

"He knows her?"

"No. She's a stranger . . . random target. But he's been . . . watching her . . . watching her for several days . . . knows her habits and routines."

With those last few words she slumped against the door. She took several deep breaths. She was forced to relax periodically to regroup her energies if she were to maintain the psychic thread. For some clairvoyants, Barnes knew, the visions came without strain, virtually without effort; but apparently not for this one.

Phantom voices whispered and crackled, came and went in staccato bursts on the police radio.

The wind carried fine sheets of rain across the roadway.

The wettest rainy season in years, Barnes thought. Twenty years ago it would have seemed normal. But California had steadily become a drought state. This much rain was unnatural now. Like everything else that's happening tonight, he thought.

Waiting for Mary to speak, he slowed to less than five miles an hour.

Matched magnolia trees flanking a winding tile walk . . .

He found it taxing to see what lay in the headlights

directly in front of him, and extremely difficult to discern the landscaping on either side. They might already have passed the magnolias.

Brief as it was, Mary Bergen's hesitation elicited Dan Goldman's first words in more than hour. "We haven't much time left, Mrs. Bergen."

Goldman was a reliable young officer, the chief's most trusted subordinate. He was sitting beside Max Bergen, behind Barnes, his eyes fixed on the woman.

Goldman believed in psychic powers. He was impressionable. And as Barnes could see in the rearview mirror, the events of the evening had left a haunted look on his broad, plain face.

"We don't have much time," Goldman said again. "If this madman's already at the woman's back door—"

Abruptly, Mary turned to him. Her voice was freighted with concern. "Don't get out of this car tonight—not until the man is caught."

"What do you mean?" Goldman asked.

"If you try to help capture him, you'll be hurt."

"He'll kill me?"

She shuddered convulsively. New beads of sweat popped out at her hairline.

Barnes felt perspiration trickle down his face, too.

She said to Goldman, "He'll stab you . . . with the same knife he's used on all the women . . . hurt you badly . . . but not kill you." Closing her eyes, speaking between clenched teeth, she said, *"Stay in the car!"*

"Harley?" Goldman asked worriedly.

"It'll be all right," Barnes assured him.

"You'd better listen to her," Max told Goldman. "Don't leave the car."

"If I need you," Barnes told Goldman, "you'll come with me. No one will be hurt." He was concerned that the woman was undermining his authority. He glanced at her. "We need a number for the house you've described, a street address."

"Don't press," her husband said sharply. With everyone but Mary he had a voice like two rough steel bars scraped against each other. "It won't do any good whatsoever to press her. It'll only interfere."

"It's okay, Max," she said.

"But I've told them before," he said.

She faced front once more. "I see . . . the rear door of the house. It's open."

"Where's the man, the killer?" Max asked.

"He's standing in a dark room . . . small . . . the laundry room . . . that's what it is . . . the laundry room behind the kitchen."

"What's he doing?"

"He's opening another door . . . to the kitchen . . . no one in there . . . a dim light on over the gas range . . . a few dirty dishes on the table . . . he's standing . . . just standing there and listening . . . left hand in a fist to stop the thumb from bleeding . . . listening . . . Benny Goodman music on a stereo in the living room . . ." Touching Barnes' arm, a new and urgent tone in her voice, she said, "Just two blocks from here. On the right. The second house . . . no, the third from the corner."

"You're positive?"

"For God's sake, *hurry!*"

Am I about to make a fool of myself? Barnes wondered. If I take her seriously and she's wrong, I'll be the punch line of bad jokes for the rest of my career.

Nevertheless, he switched on the siren and tramped the accelerator to the floor. The tires spun on the pavement. With a squeal of rubber, the car surged forward.

Breathlessly she said, "I still see . . . he's crossing the kitchen . . . moving slowly . . ."

If she's faking all this, Barnes thought, she's a hell of a good actress.

The Ford raced along the poorly lit street. Rain snapped against the windshield. They swept through a four-way stop, then toward another.

"Listening . . . listening between steps . . . cautious . . . nervous . . . taking the knife out of his overcoat pocket . . . smiling at the sharp edge on the blade . . . such a big knife . . ."

In the block she had specified they fishtailed to a stop at the curb in front of the third house on the right: a pair of matched magnolias, a winding walk, a two-story stucco with lights on downstairs.

"Goddamn," Goldman said, more reverently than not. "It fits her description perfectly."

The Vision begins with an odd variation of the narrative hook. The first sentence contains neither overt violence nor action of any kind. In an effort to seize the reader's attention, the opening line relies on two things: 1) an unusual, arresting, perhaps even eerie image; 2) the implied violence inherent in that image.

Remembering what I said about wanting to write a horror novel in stripped-down prose, you might be wondering why I didn't express that opening thought in a less exotic fashion by writing "bloody hands" instead of "gloves of blood." Well, all I can tell you is that, in my estimation, those two words would have been more prosaic and considerably less intriguing than the three-word image I used. I could list a number of reasons why "gloves of blood" is technically and artistically superior to "bloody hands," but I would be lying to you if I said that I was consciously aware of all those reasons when I began writing The Vision. The origins of fiction are, in part, mysterious. When I composed that opening sentence, I did not analyze it. I did not arrive at those three words through the application of a set of rules; rather, they floated up from my subconscious, and I knew instinctively that they were right, and I typed them out. Once again, we are dealing with matters of style, which cannot be taught.

I was, however, conscious of the need to introduce the male and female lead characters as quickly as possible. The heroine speaks in the first sentence and appears in the second. The male lead comes on stage in the sixth sentence.

In Hanging On, the lead character is in mortal danger by the end of the first sentence, but in The Vision, Mary

Bergen's terrible trouble is not so terrible as Major Kelly's. Her life isn't under the shadow of a bomb. Nevertheless, she is in *some* trouble, which has the potential to become very terrible indeed, and there are two aspects to it: 1) She is wracked by physically debilitating, emotionally shattering clairvoyant visions that are quite literally painful for her to endure. 2) She is hurrying toward the scene of a crime that is still in progress, and the possibility exists that Mary will be stepping right into the middle of a deadly situation. In fact, if I have done my job well, the eeriness and the chilly mood of that opening sequence should convince the reader that Mary *will* encounter the knife-wielding psychopath sooner or later. Her terrible trouble, then, is more terrible than it initially appears.

In the excerpt from *Hanging On,* I used "the tease" to grip the reader; in *The Vision* I made use of another trick, which I'll call "the ticking clock." If you start a novel by giving your characters an urgent task to perform, and if you establish the fact that something awful will happen if they fail to complete the task within a short period of time, you have created an almost irresistible curiosity in your readers. In *The Vision,* Mary Bergen must lead the police to the psychopath before he kills again; if she fails to perform this task within a few minutes, a woman will die horribly, and that death will, of course, weigh heavily on Mary's conscience.

Again, I was acutely aware of the need to conjure up a good illusion of reality, and most of my efforts in this regard were directed toward making Mary's psychic powers seem believable. That was the element of the scene most readers would resist, and their resistance had to be broken down quickly if the book were to succeed. We have all seen a rainy night; we can all imagine what the inside of a police patrol car is like, even if we have never been in such a vehicle. With that in mind, I spent very few words describing those things with which the reader was familiar; when I *did* make an observation about the rain or the streets along which the patrol car passed, I made my words serve a double purpose as both scene-setting and mood-setting. Most of the details in that first scene have to do with Mary Bergen's psychic process; how it affects her emotionally, how it affects her physically, what fears and other reactions it elicits from those around her. I made it tough on her because I felt that her clairvoyance would seem more real if it did not come easily to her. I didn't want her to be a television-type psychic; if she had been a female Kreskin, for instance, tossing predictions and psychic impressions off the top of her head with ease, she would have appeared to be a trickster, and readers would not have empathized with her. The pain Mary endures during her psychic visions, the physical and emotional contortions she undergoes, contribute (I hope) to the creation of an illusion of reality.

If I had it to do over again, I would probably make a few changes in that chapter. For one thing, it is almost too brisk and treads dangerously close to the line where lean, spare prose becomes thin and unconvincing.

Furthermore, when I look at that scene today, I wonder if I chose the correct point of view from which to tell it. Sheriff Barnes was a convenient device because from his viewpoint I could give physical descriptions of both Max and Mary Bergen, whereas if I opened from Max's viewpoint, I couldn't give the reader a full description of *him*, only of Mary from his point of view. Max would have had to wait until Chapter 2 to become fully visible. At the time I didn't think it was advisable to wait to bring Max all the way into the light, for the descriptions of everything else were pared so close to the bone that it seemed vital for the male and female leads to be seen physically and in relationship to one another by some outsider (Barnes) who could make judgments about them. I also avoided entering Max's mind because, later in the book, he becomes a suspect in another series of killings; I felt that I could not enter his mind and still maintain him as a viable suspect. Of course, now I realize that using Max's point of view in some scenes would have been just the kind of challenge that, if successfully met, could have lifted *The Vision* onto a much higher plane in terms of craftsmanship and artistic quality.

(For a long discussion of point of view in fiction, see Chapter 11.)

The third opening scene I will analyze is from *Prison of*

Ice by "David Axton," a short-lived alter ego of mine. In 1974, while I was struggling to shed my image as a science fiction writer and trying to establish a name as a mainstream novelist, I had the urge to write the kind of book that Alistair MacLean used to write before he changed (or lost) his direction after *Puppet on a Chain*. I had read and immensely enjoyed MacLean's early books—*South by Java Head, H.M.S. Ulysses, Where Eagles Dare, Fear Is the Key, The Guns of Navarone*, among others—and I thought it would be fun to write one of those no-holds-barred, blitz-paced adventure stories. Such a book would not comfortably fit in with the things I was then doing under my own name, so I gave *Prison of Ice* to "David Axton." J.P. Lippincott published the hardcover edition in 1976, and Fawcett brought out its paperback the following year. *Prison of Ice* has done well in England and other overseas markets, but not well enough to justify a continuation of the Axton career. This is how *Prison of Ice* begins:

11:57

The heated bit of the power drill chewed deep into the ice. Slush churned out of the hole, sluiced across the crusted snow and refroze in seconds. The bit was out of sight now, and the steel shank had also disappeared into the four-inch-diameter bore.

Harry Carpenter, watching the drill bite deeper and deeper into the ice, had a premonition of disaster. Although, as a scientist, he respected the tools of logic, method and reason, Carpenter had learned never to discount a hunch. Especially not out here on the icefield, where anything could happen—and usually did. He could not understand the source of his uneasiness—unless it was the possibility that the explosive charge might detonate prematurely, right now, in their faces. There was little chance of that. Nevertheless . . .

Peter Johnson, the American electronics engineer who doubled as demolitions expert, switched off the drill and stepped back from it. In his bulky white thermal suit and fur-lined hood, he resembled a polar bear—except for his dark brown face.

Claude Jobert shut off the portable generator which supplied power to the drill.

As the afternoon began, the three men were preparing to lower the last of the one-hundred-pound explosive charges into the ice. This was the sixtieth bomb they had handled since yesterday morning, and they were uneasily aware that they were standing on enough high-yield plastic explosives to destroy them in an apocalyptic instant.

If they died here, Harry thought, well . . . the ice cap *was* a model graveyard, utterly lifeless. Ghostly bluish-white plains led off in every direction, somber and moody during this season of nearly constant darkness, brief twilight and perpetual overcast. Visibility was fair because this was the time of day when a vague crescent of sunlight painted the horizon. But there was not much to see. The only points of elevation were the jagged pressure ridges and hundreds of house-sized slabs of ice that had popped from the field and stood on end like gigantic tombstones.

Pete Johnson joined Carpenter and Jobert in front of a pair of specially rebuilt snowmobiles. "The shaft's twenty-eight yards deep. One more extension for the bit and the job's done."

"Thank God!" Jobert shivered as if his thermal suit provided no protection whatsoever. In spite of the transparent film of lanolin petroleum jelly that protected the exposed portions of his face from frostbite, he was pale and drawn. "We'll make it back to base camp tonight. Think of that! I haven't been warm since we left."

Ordinarily, Jobert did not complain. He was a jovial and energetic little man. At a glance he seemed fragile. That wasn't the case. At five-seven and a hundred and thirty pounds, he was lean, wiry, hard. He had a mane of white hair, a leathery face and bright blue eyes as clear as those of a child. Carpenter had never seen hatred or anger in those eyes—nor, until yesterday, had he seen self-pity in them.

Since they had left the comfort of Edgeway Station, Jobert had been neither jovial nor energetic. At fifty-nine he was the oldest member of the expedition, eighteen years older than Carpenter. That was nearly the outer limit for a scientist working in this brutal climate.

Although he was a fine Arctic geologist, this would be his last trip onto the icefield. From now on, his work would be done in laboratories and behind typewriters, far from the rigors of the ice.

Maybe, Harry thought, he's not bothered by the cold so much as by the knowledge that this work has grown too demanding for him. How will I feel when I've got to face the same truth?

Pete Johnson said, "It's snowing."

Even as the black man spoke, Harry saw the dime-sized flakes.

Jobert frowned. "We weren't due for snow until this evening."

The trip out from Edgeway Station—four air miles to the northeast, seven miles by snowmobile past ridges and deep chasms—had not been difficult. However, a bad storm could make the return journey impossible. Visibility would decrease to zero. They could easily get lost because of compass distortion. And if their snowmobiles ran out of fuel, they would freeze to death, for even their thermal suits would be insufficient protection against prolonged exposure to the murderous cold that came with a blizzard.

Studying the sky, Carpenter said, "This might be a local squall."

"You said the same thing last week," Johnson reminded him. "As a geophysicist, you deserved the Nobel. As a meteorologist—"

"I'm a bust. So we'd better finish this job quickly."

"Like yesterday."

Johnson freed the drill from the shank of the buried bit and lifted it out of its supportive frame, handling it as if it weighed a tenth of its actual eighty-five pounds.

A decade ago he had been a football star at Penn State, turning down offers from six NFL teams. He hadn't wanted to play out the role the public had created for every six-foot-four-inch, two-hundred-and-thirty-pound black football hero. Instead he won scholarships, took two more degrees, and wound up in a well-paid position with an IBM think tank.

Now he was vital to Carpenter's expedition. He serviced the electronic data-gathering equipment at Edgeway; and having designed the explosive devices, he was the only man who could deal with them if something went wrong. Furthermore, his tremendous strength was an asset out here on the inhospitable top of the world.

As Johnson lifted the drill out of the way, Carpenter and Jobert took a three-foot bit extension from one of the cargo trailers that stood behind the snowmobiles. They screwed it onto the threaded shank, which was already buried in the ice.

Jobert started the generator again.

Johnson slammed the drill in place and finished boring the twenty-nine-yard shaft which would hold the tubular pack of explosives.

While the machine roared, Harry looked at the ugly sky.

Within the past fifteen minutes the weather had deteriorated noticeably. Most of the light had gone from behind the clouds. The snow stung his greased face; the wind was moving at twenty miles per hour or thereabouts, just beginning to howl.

He still sensed an oncoming disaster. It was formless, vague, but nonetheless real.

Jobert leaned toward him and shouted above the noise from the wind and the drill. "Don't worry, Harry! We'll be back at Edgeway this evening!"

Carpenter nodded. He continued to study the sky.

To satisfy your curiosity and to set that scene in context, let me explain what *Prison of Ice* is about. A team of scientists is working at the edge of the polar ice field, setting up an experiment that will show whether or not man-made icebergs can be blasted loose from the polar cap and moved southward to provide fresh water in drought-stricken areas of the world. After they plant the chain of explosive charges but before they can pull back to Edge-way Station—their permanent camp, more than seven miles away—an undersea quake breaks loose that section of ice on which they have been working. They find themselves adrift on an island of ice that is peppered with unre-trievable bombs. When the bombs explode in just twelve hours, the ice island will shatter. They must get off the berg before it disintegrates under them. Their situation is com-plicated by two developments: 1)As their ship of ice drifts out into the cold sea, the area is hit by a fierce storm which makes it quite impossible for rescue ships and planes to reach them; 2) For reasons that initially baffle the scien-tists, one of them (there are seven altogether) turns out to be a homicidal maniac, hellbent on a strange mission of his own, his inner control finally blown away by the stress of their predicament.

Of course, very little of that information is in the first chapter, as you have seen.

And as you may have guessed, I chose the opening scene of *Prison of Ice* as my third example because it breaks the rules a bit. Actually, it doesn't break them so much as just crack them a little. I *do* introduce the lead character in the second paragraph, and I *do* make a concerted effort to create a good illusion of reality that will help the reader feel the arctic weather. You may think, however, that I have forgotten two important things: terrible trouble and action.

It is true that none of the three men's lives hangs in the balance in that first short scene. The nature of the story was such that many characters had to be introduced and a lot of background had to be established before the crisis could be brought onstage. Faced with that situation, un-able to plunge straightaway into terrible trouble, I was forced to settle for a stylistic trick: *foreshadowing.* In order to keep the reader's attention, I needed to let him know in advance that a serious crisis was fast approaching. I ac-complished that by giving my lead character, Harry Carpenter, a premonition of disaster in the second paragraph, and I kept Harry uneasy and wary during the entire scene. Furthermore, I reinforced Harry's premonition by creating an ominous atmosphere through somber descriptions of the landscape and through the use of grim and eerie metaphorical images, such as the one which, at some length, compared the icefield to a graveyard. What I did was akin to reaching out, shaking the reader, and saying, "Hey, this is a potentially dangerous situation, and although everything is relatively calm now, all hell is going to break loose before long, so stick around."

Of course, if this had been a different story, a tale set in Boston—or Peoria or Seattle or Miami—and if Harry had been shaken by a premonition of disaster while taking a relaxing stroll on a glorious spring afternoon, that would have qualified as an unforgivably disruptive intrusion by the author, for in that case the premonition would have come out of nowhere. In *Prison of Ice,* however, Harry Carpenter is standing on top of a bunch of bombs, on the edge of the polar ice cap, with a blizzard building around him, and he is seven miles from the safety of his base camp; there are very good reasons why he might have a premonition of disaster. Only a fool or a blockhead would be worry-free at a moment like that! The explosive charges and the oncoming storm are the seeds of violent action; I used foreshadowing only to draw the reader's attention to the seeds I had already planted. Foreshadowing of that nature is not blatant author intrusion; it grows logically out of the situation and the characters.

Warning! Events in a story should never be foreshadowed by having the author speak directly to the reader. For example, *never* write a sentence like this one: "If only Becky could have known that Ralph would betray her on Wednesday, she would not have told him her priceless secret at dinner on Tuesday evening." And here's a sentence that's even worse than that: "As she danced and laughed and drank champagne on New Year's Eve, little did Polly know that her life would be in ruins by the end of January." During the early stages of the novel's growth as an art form, authors thought it permissible to directly address their readers in the middle of a story, either to emphasize a thematic point or to crudely foreshadow upcoming plot developments. The modern reader is sophisticated and simply will not tolerate intrusions of that sort because they shatter the fragile illusion of reality that makes a story enjoyable. The instant the author speaks directly to his audience, the reader is reminded that what he has before him is only a *story*, a mere fabrication, and with that realization the magic abruptly goes out of the reading experience. If you *must* foreshadow plot developments—and it is a technique that should be used only as a last resort—be certain that you speak through your characters, in their voices; do not reveal your own godlike hand at work.

In addition to foreshadowing, and in addition to creating an ominous mood, I used another minor but effective gimmick to intrigue the reader and to suggest to him that terrible trouble would quickly descend upon the characters in *Prison of Ice*. Instead of numbering the chapters—1, 2, 3, et cetera—I headed each with the time of day at which it opened, beginning at 11:57 a.m. and working toward midnight, thereby contributing a sense of urgency even to the unspectacular events that transpire in the first chapter. The reader is aware that some sort of countdown is underway, and in fiction a countdown virtually always leads toward some terrible, violent event which the characters must strive desperately to prevent. Thus, the reader of *Prison of Ice* is subtly told—and becomes subconsciously aware—that thrills and chills lie ahead, in spite of the deceptively low-key first scene. Again, as in *The Vision*, I used the "ticking clock" technique, except that in *Prison* I was more literal about it, in hope of compensating for the fact that the first chapter did not plunge the lead characters into terrible trouble.

I admit it: In the opening scene of *Prison of Ice*, I bent the rules. When you've read all of *How to Write Bestselling Fiction*, you can go to any bookstore and purchase a dozen novels which also, in some minor or major way, violate the guidelines I suggest for plotting, characterization, background, and so forth. Writers break rules and still get published; it happens every day. For the most part, however, the rule breakers are authors who have published numerous books; they have learned the rules, have proved they can write repeatedly and successfully within the standard guidelines. At a certain point in his career, having gained sufficient control of his prose, every established writer begins to experiment with new techniques, looking for fresh and interesting ways to tell a story. Gradually, the writer discovers that, to a certain extent, most rules can be bent, and a few broken, without the novel suffering; sometimes, bending a rule or two even makes a book better than it might otherwise have been. But just as the finest abstract painters must first learn how to draw in superbly realistic detail, so the new writer—who has not yet proved himself, who is not yet confident with the basic forms of fiction— must avoid experimentation until he is more accomplished. Your road to success as an author of popular fiction will be considerably shorter if you walk the known trail in your early days and leave the exploration of new territory for later.

Complications

Once you have plunged your lead character into terrible trouble, the bulk of the story line is then concerned with the complications that arise as he tries desperately to solve his problem. Here are five things you should carefully consider when planning the complications in your plots.

1. *Every complication must make the hero's situation darker.* Complications should never be used just to pad the length of your manuscript. Nor should complications be used if they only slow the hero down in his drive toward the solution of his problem; for if they do not actually make his task more difficult, if they only slow him down, they are not complications at all but merely *delays.* Each complication absolutely must make the lead character's terrible trouble look even more terrible, and with each new development the reader should be increasingly worried about the hero's chances of saving himself.

To make this point clear, here are examples of the right and the wrong ways to structure a story complication.

The wrong way. Mysterious, unknown villains have set up your hero, Tom, to take the rap for the murder of a powerful United States Senator. The frame-up is so cunningly perfect that Tom knows he will surely be convicted; he panics and flees before he is arrested. On the run, Tom realizes that he has an alibi for the time of the murder. While the senator was being killed, Tom was in bed with Jessica, a famous Washington columnist. If Jessica will testify for him, he will not be jailed and charged with murder. He goes to Jessica's place in the suburbs and learns from her housekeeper that she is attending a luncheon at a hotel in the city. Cautiously ducking any policemen he sees, Tom goes to the hotel, but he discovers that Jessica left the luncheon forty minutes ago, after receiving an urgent message from her office. He hurries to Jessica's office, only to be told that she has gone to the airport to catch a plane to San Francisco, where her mother is desperately ill. Tom rushes off to the airport, hoping to explain his plight to Jessica before she leaves town, but he is just in time to see the jet take off with her aboard.

That series of events does nothing whatsoever to make Tom's situation darker. Those are not complications; they are *delays*. We know that he will make contact with Jessica sooner or later, either by phone or in person when she returns from San Francisco. The repeatedly missed connections do not increase the reader's concern for the hero; they only frustrate him.

The right way. Framed for the senator's murder, Tom panics and flees before he is arrested. He goes to Jessica's place in the suburbs to ask her to testify in his behalf—and he discovers that Jessica is dead. She's naked, in bed, with a knife in the middle of her bosom. Suddenly Tom hears sirens. Someone has tipped the police that Jessica is dead. Probably the same unknown villains who killed the senator. Tom escapes from the house before the cops can get their hands on him, but they *do* see him, so now he is wanted for *two* murders.

In the second case, Tom's situation is darker because the only person who could clear him of the senator's murder has herself been killed. What can Tom do now? Suddenly the solution to his problem is no longer as easy as it once seemed. If the author now confronts Tom with a series of additional complications that arise logically out of what has previously transpired, and if each of these complications is more serious than the one before it, until at last Tom appears to be backed into a corner with no possible route of escape, and if the author then reveals a logical solution based upon all that Tom has learned from his ordeal—well, then the author has an honest-to-goodness plot.

2. *Every complication must be a logical outgrowth of the events that have gone before it.* For instance, suppose that Tom—yes, I'm talking about the same luckless fellow as above—spends two hundreds pages avoiding the police and conducting his own investigation into Jessica's and the senator's deaths. Let's further suppose that Tom is hurrying down a street, heading for a rendezvous with a potential witness to one of the murders, when two uniformed policemen turn the corner at the end of the block and start walking casually in his direction. Rather than risk being recognized—after all, his photograph is on a most-wanted list—Tom quickly steps into a bank until the policemen pass. He isn't in the bank more than thirty seconds before two of the customers pull guns and announce that a stickup is underway. Meanwhile, as the two foot patrolmen stroll past the bank, they realize something is amiss; a shootout begins; the holdup men barricade themselves inside the bank, holding Tom and a few other customers as hostages. Now Tom is in danger of being killed in the crossfire, and even if the thieves are persuaded to surrender peacefully, the police will recognize and arrest Tom in the aftermath. Not only that, but Tom will miss his rendezvous with the witness who might have been able to testify in his behalf in the matter of Jessica's death. Well, well, well. . . . All of those developments certainly make poor Tom's situation blacker than ever—but they don't arise logically out of what has gone before. The bank robbery has nothing whatsoever to do with the central story line of the novel—which is the murder of the senator and the framing of Tom—and the reader will only be irritated by this diversion. Remember, readers always just want to *get on with it!* If the author doesn't want his dust jacket photograph to be used as a dartboard in game rooms all across the country, he must be sure that each complication is a *direct result* of the hero's valiant attempts to solve his problem.

3. *The author must never use coincidence to complicate a story.* If Tom is in a car, racing toward another rendez-vous fifty miles outside of Washington, and if his entire future depends on his getting to the rendezvous point not one minute later than noon, and if his progress is abruptly halted by a sluggishly moving, two-hundred-car freight train, readers will condemn you for your lazy plotting and your arrogance. Never forget that every plot complication has to evolve from the characters' actions and must also have a logical connection with what has gone before.

4. *Complications must never arise because of a character's stupidity.* Your novel's hero is permitted to have character flaws, of course. In fact, he *must* have a couple of faults if he is to be a well-rounded, believable human being. He may, for instance, have a blind spot when it comes to beautiful women, a blind spot that leads him to misjudge the intentions of the gorgeous blond who turns out to be the ruthless killer. He may be shortsighted. He may be impetuous. He may make all sorts of mistakes based on his unique and clearly defined psychology. But he may *not* get into a jam simply because he's too dumb to see trouble coming. If Tom barges into a room, unarmed, unprepared, knowing that the killer is in there waiting for him, he deserves whatever he gets, and the reader will cease to care about him.

Ken Follett, author of the delightful *Eye of the Needle,* the bestselling World War Two thriller, stumbled into this pitfall with his most recent novel, *The Key to Rebecca.* On more than one occasion, the hero of *Key*—a British intelli-gence officer serving in North Africa during World War Two—misses the chance to apprehend the villain, and each time the chance is missed for the same dumb reason: *The hero forgets to carry his gun!* On other occasions, he walks into ambushes that any moron would have spotted from a hundred yards. The villain, who is supposed to be a bril-liant German spy, also makes incredibly dumb mistakes, and, as with the hero, none of these mistakes is a logical result of the character's faults; they are simply grotesque, numbingly stupid errors that are unimaginatively used to artificially complicate the plot. When the *New York Times Book Review* took a look at *The Key to Rebecca,* it headlined its reviewer's piece with these words: THE THREE STOOGES IN CAIRO. I don't always concur with the judgments expressed by the critics who write for the *Times,* but in this case the reviewer's assessment was in perfect harmony with my own.

Mr. Follett can get away with lazy plotting because he stands upon the huge and well-deserved success of *Eye of the Needle.* His publisher is eager to print whatever he writes, for his books have made a lot of money in the past. I sincerely believe that if a new writer, a complete unknown, had submitted *The Key to Rebecca,* either the book would have been rejected, or it would have been bought for a low advance to fill a slot on the bottom half of some publisher's list. Without Mr. Follett's name on it, *The Key to Rebecca* would surely not have received major advertising and publicity.

I can hear some of you saying, "Hey, it's not fair that a bad book by a Big Name Writer can get bestseller treatment, while far better books by lesser-knowns and unknowns have trouble even getting an editor's attention." It *is* unfair, but it's a fact of life with which every writer must learn to live. Take solace, if you can, in the fact that justice will eventually be served. If Mr. Follett writes too many books with slapdash plotting, he will use up all the goodwill that *Eye of the Needle* earned him with book buyers. After too many efforts as weak as *The Key to Rebecca,* his career will gradually but surely sink into oblivion. It has happened to others. The reading public is always willing to forgive a favorite author for a bad job . . . or two . . . or three. But readers' patience is not bottomless, and when an author totally and repeatedly disappoints his fans, he alienates them; once alienated, they can seldom be won back. That is why I advise you always to strive for quality and for the finest craftsmanship, even if that *is* the hardest road to walk.

5. *The final complication must be the worst.* Just when the reader is sure that the hero's terrible trouble cannot possibly get more terrible, the author must drop a block-buster, a devastating (but always logical) final complication that will have the reader biting his nails to the quick. Furthermore, this complication should be something the reader could have foreseen if he had been as clever as the author. It should evoke this exclamation from him: "My God, *of course!* Why didn't I see that coming?!"

Eliciting that reaction from a reader is difficult, and explaining how to do it is virtually impossible. The best way to learn how to handle the final complication is to read the three novels I'm about to recommend, each of which deals with the problem in exemplary fashion. Read each book twice. The first time, read it solely for pleasure. The second time, once you know where the book is headed, study the ever-building nature of the plot line and note how the author has prepared the reader for a truly terrible, inevitable, yet surprising final complication worse than any that has gone before.

First, read *Force 10 from Navarone* by Alistair MacLean. This sequel to the author's famous *The Guns of Navarone* was a bestseller in its own right and is, in some ways, even more suspenseful than the book that spawned it. *Force 10 from Navarone* is set in World War Two. The story concerns an Allied commando team that must sneak deep into German-held territory and blow up a vital dam in order to decimate German forces, throw a monkey wrench in the Nazi war machine, and save thousands of Allied soldiers' lives. They encounter all the complications one might expect in a story of this sort—geographical obstacles, German patrols, a murderous Nazi-sympathizer within their own ranks, failures of personal courage—but when at last they reach the dam and plant the explosives, the reader thinks the worst is surely over. "All right," the reader says to himself, "now they just slip away, get to high ground, and watch the dam go up like it's the Fourth of July." And that's where MacLean hits you with a nail-biting FINAL COMPLICATION. Because the commandos are running behind schedule, because the demolitions scheme hasn't worked quite as planned, because the Germans have figured out something is up and are searching for the invaders, and for a variety of other logical reasons, our heroes are unable to get far away from the dam before it blows. Just when the reader thinks they've suffered the worst possible slings and arrows of outrageous fortune (to borrow a phrase), they are plunged into even more terrible trouble than before: They are going to be blown to bits along with the dam—or be drowned when it collapses! "Okay," the reader says, "maybe these guys can handle Nazi machine gunners and killer guard dogs and shiv-wielding traitors who slit throats in the night, but *nobody* can stand up to a bursting dam and survive. These people are doomed." That's exactly what MacLean *wants* the reader to say. I won't spoil your fun by telling you exactly where all the characters are as the final seconds tick away; this series of scenes builds one of the half dozen most perfectly crafted final complications I've ever encountered. When you read the book, pay special attention to the logical but breathtakingly terrifying position in which the author places Andrea, the big Greek commando, for in that scene more than any other, the audacity of MacLean's final complication should be an inspiration to any student hoping to learn about plot structure.

Second, read *The Exorcist* by William Peter Blatty. In this famous novel—which has sold more than twelve million copies in the U.S. and as many as twenty-five million worldwide—the hero is Father Damien Karras, a likeable, quite sensitive priest who is undergoing a crisis of faith. When he is brought into the Regan MacNeil case, he would like very much to believe that the little girl is really possessed, for that belief would justify his years in the priesthood and restore his faith. (If Satan exists, Karras reasons, then God must exist too.) The supernatural being in possession of Regan gives Karras numerous proofs that it is, indeed, a genuine demonic spirit. But because Karras is not sure in his faith, because he is a Jesuit and a psychologist—which makes him almost an overeducated man—he is bright enough to come up with rational, logical explanations for the weird and miraculous acts the demon performs. Early in the novel, it is abundantly clear that the devil doesn't want Regan at all; the child is merely an instrument for Karras's destruction, a means of luring Karras into an ultimate test of his faith. Satan expects Karras to fail that test and, therefore, lose his soul. Blatty does a fine job of building fear in his readers; we are afraid for poor Regan, the pawn, and we are increasingly afraid for Karras, who seems to be steadily losing the battle to retain his faith and his immortal soul. Eventually, after all sorts of complications, Regan's condition deteriorates so horribly that Karras agrees to seek the Church's approval for an exorcism. He still is not able to *believe*, but he thinks that Regan might be psychologically ill and that the exorcism will be a symbol to which she can clutch and upon which she can rebuild her sanity; the power of suggestion, Karras notes, has frequently worked wonders with emotionally disturbed people. Because Karras's faith is not strong, he does not dare to perform an exorcism himself, for the ritual is rather like a wrestling match between the priest and the demon; the priest's only armor is his faith, and without it he stands no chance of either physical or spiritual survival. Father Lankester Merrin, a Jesuit archaeologist who has performed exorcisms in the past, is brought in to deal with the demon in Regan. Preparations for the exorcism and the initial stages of it are built with superb skill and enormous tension, and when the reader is totally wrung out by what these characters have seen and endured, Blatty throws in the FINAL COMPLICATION, the whopper: Father Merrin, who is strong in his faith but physically weak, dies in the middle of the strenuous exorcism, *leaving Karras to complete the job alone.* "Oh, no," the reader says. "No, no. This isn't fair. Karras doesn't have a chance. Not Karras, the doubter. Not Karras, the psychologist with his too rigidly rational view of the world. He's going to lose his life; he's going to lose his soul; and God only knows what's going to happen to poor Regan." After introducing this final, chilling complication, Blatty takes only six pages to wind up the last chapter before the epilogue. The solution to the final complication doesn't take as long to unfold as it does in *Force 10 from Navarone*, but Blatty packs a huge wallop in those six pages.

Then, read *Rosemary's Baby* by Ira Levin. The reader thinks the worst is past when Rosemary finally delivers her unholy child and is told that it is dead. Even if we don't believe it's dead, we figure that at least Rosemary doesn't have to carry the frightful thing within her any longer, and we assume the baby has been spirited away by the cultists who have been using Rosemary. We expect the book to end with the disquieting fact that the anti-Christ has successfully arrived on earth, but we don't think that Rosemary, about whom we've come to care a great deal, will be plunged into any more immediate danger. Then the FINAL COMPLICATION arises: She discovers the baby is alive, and she sets out to find it. When we start to wonder exactly what kind of *thing* she will find, and when we begin to worry about what it will do to her, the final chapter becomes the most hair-raising sequence in the book. (What happens when Rosemary finds her child is more surprising and frightening than anything the reader can imagine—a quiet terror that ends the novel on a powerful note and proves Levin's mastery.)

   As far as plot solutions are concerned, I have only a few simple do's and don't's. You should not, however, be misled by the simplicity of this list. The solution of the plot, the means by which the hero triumphs over his terrible trouble, is in some ways as important as the opening scene of the novel, for it is this last sequence of events that readers remember most vividly in the days, weeks, and months after they have finished your book. If the solution is weak, dull, and contrived, the reader will look upon the book as a failure no matter how wonderful the first four-fifths of it were. On the other hand, if the solution is clever, filled with thrilling action, and thoroughly satisfying in character and thematic terms, the reader will be primed to buy your next novel, and you will be on your way to building a large faithful following.
   With that in mind, consider these suggestions:
   DON'T let your hero lose his battle unless that is the *only* logical solution to the plot. As I said earlier, readers nearly always prefer a happy ending. Although some of the good

guys die in most of Alistair MacLean's best novels (see the reading list in Chapter 15), *none* of his novels ends with the hero dead and the hero's objectives unfulfilled. Likewise, though there are heaps of tragedy in Stephen King's *The Shining*, little Danny and his mother survive and set out upon a better life than they've known before. In *The Exorcist*, William Peter Blatty bends the rule a bit; the hero dies, but he doesn't lose his soul, and he doesn't fail to save Regan, the child who so desperately needs his help.

An unhappy ending in a popular novel is an obstacle to its sale—unless the writer is extremely skillful or already a Big Name or both. This is one rule a new writer should treat with the utmost respect, even though many well-established authors occasionally find that it is satisfyingly breakable. For instance, James Clavell kills both his hero and heroine in *Tai-Pan*, which leaves the reader devastated. But Clavell is so darned good that the tragedy of those two deaths is a catharsis for readers, an emotionally draining event that stuns yet satisfies all of our dramatic expectations. After all, sometimes readers *like* to have a good cry. Some of the most popular novels of all time—*Gone with the Wind, The Thorn Birds, Forever Amber*—are full of scenes intended to squeeze out buckets of tears. However, a new writer should not try to end a book in tragedy unless he *knows* he is as skillful as Clavell. Initially, stick with happy endings, and you'll start selling sooner. Later, when you're established, you can let your hero fall into a sausage machine at the end, and if you have developed the craftsmanship and art to write such a scene well, you can get away with it.

DO make sure that your solution is clever enough to justify all of the horrendous complications that you have piled up through the course of the story. If, at the end of a long hard struggle, your hero solves his problems in a way that he could have solved them far sooner, *or* if he solves his problems with a stroke of genius that the reader foresaw a hundred pages earlier, you are in very deep trouble.

DON'T start writing a novel until you know how to solve the hero's problems. You don't want to get to the end of a long manuscript only to discover that you have no idea at all how to get your hero out of the mess into which you have put him. More than a few new writers have painted themselves into *that* corner and have never gotten out of it.

DO speed up the pace of the book toward the end. The final chapters should not be weighted down with long descriptions of sunsets or places or characters. By the time you reach the final complication and are ready to reveal the solution, you should have nothing left to write except *action*. Your goal is to make the reader race breathlessly through the last fifty pages, so that he feels wrung out when he finally puts the book down.

DON'T let your story drag on for dozens of pages after the solution has been revealed and successfully applied to the lead character's problem. All you need after the last big action scene—in which the terrible trouble is vanquished and the villain laid low at the last possible instant—is a short coda, just a page or two, to tie up any loose ends and to give the reader a chance to coast down from the peak of excitement to which you drove him.

This mistake somewhat marred *The Stand,* a novel by Stephen King, an author whom I very much admire and who seldom makes serious or even half-way serious errors of any kind. In *The Stand,* Mr. King leads the reader through several hundred thousand fascinating words with the promise of a spectacular showdown between the archetypal forces of good and evil. When the showdown comes, its effect is watered down by the fact that another fifty or sixty thousand words of anticlimax follow. *The Stand* is nevertheless a marvelous book, toweringly ambitious, constantly entertaining, frequently enthralling, always imaginative. Mr. King is so good at what he does that he can conclude a book with fifty thousand words of anticlimax and get away with it. Most writers can't. The new writer shouldn't even consider it.

Plotting for the mainstream audience

I have already advised you not to limit yourself by seeking or accepting such labels as SCIENCE FICTION WRITER, MYSTERY WRITER, WESTERN WRITER, and so forth. Think of yourself as a WRITER, period. To achieve the widest possible dissemination of your ideas and to earn the greatest financial rewards, your book must rise above the limitations of any genre; it must have those qualities and themes which touch the hearts and minds of a large number of people. It must be complex in its intentions and ambitious in its treatment of plot, characterization, background, and theme. Today's editors are constantly on the lookout for promotable books of this nature, and they are never able to find enough of them to meet publishers' needs.

As far as plot is concerned, there is basically one difference between genre—or category—fiction and mainstream novels. In the mainstream story, the plot acts as a skeleton upon which the writer adds layers of action, characterization, theme, symbolism, background, and mood, until a living thing has been constructed. In category fiction, the plot is usually the skeleton *and* the tendons *and* the vital organs *and* the muscle; other elements of the novelist's art—characterization, theme, background—are seldom if ever given such full expression as they are in the best mainstream work. In both genre and mainstream fiction, of course, a *strong* plot—one that is based on an ever-worsening series of complications—is essential; but to achieve success in the mainstream, the writer must structure his plot so that it provides breathing spaces, opportunities for the novelist to apply himself diligently to *all* aspects of his story.

Consider the mystery novel. In the classic mystery—the "whodunit"—the plot not only functions in the manner of a mainstream plot by contributing form and narrative drive to the story; it *also* must provide an intellectual game, a puzzle. The mystery writer is burdened with the extra duty of planting clues in a subtle yet wholly fair fashion, thereby giving the reader a good chance to guess the killer's identity while simultaneously misdirecting his suspicions toward the wrong suspect. With the need to expertly juggle all of those plot components, is it any wonder that few mystery writers manage (or bother) to give us stories with strong, vital thematic structure? Is it any wonder that very few mysteries contain well-rounded, truly *human*, multi-faceted characters?

Now before you mystery fans rush to your typewriters to compose poison pen letters denouncing my view of your favorite genre, let me assure you that I *like* mysteries. I have read hundreds upon hundreds of them and have passed countless pleasant hours trying to figure out who done it. All I am saying is that mysteries are, by their very nature, simpler than successful mainstream fiction. And it is simplicity that limits their appeal; it is precisely because of this lack of deeply probing characterization and complex thematic structure that most mystery novels receive average paperback printings of no more than fifty to one hundred thousand copies. The majority of book buyers want more for their money than a genre novel of any kind ordinarily delivers.

Some mystery writers *have* managed to pull themselves away from plotting and puzzle-building long enough to develop well-rounded, convincing characters, and as a result they have enjoyed modest bestsellers and even, in a handful of cases, major bestsellers that went all the way to the top of the list. For years, in each of his many finely crafted mysteries, Dick Francis has written about people who—if not for all of a book, then at least for most of it—seem *real,* as commanding of attention as a fist in the face. Mr. Francis's *Whip Hand* had a brief tenure on the lower third of the American bestseller lists, and his new novel, *Reflex,* promises to do even better. P. D. James strives for mainstream-quality characterization, and her work has met with substantial success beyond the confines of the mystery genre. Lawrence Sanders has never been strictly a mystery writer, but he has borrowed from the genre, applying its best narrative techniques and gimmicks to large-scale mainstream novels, and he has enjoyed tremendous sales. Rex Stout created a multi-faceted, thoroughly believable character when he came up with Nero Wolfe, treading close to the line that separates characterization from caricature, but never crossing over it as did Agatha Christie with her Marple and Poirot.

However, as splendid as some of those famous mystery characters are, can we honestly say that even one of them measures up to the great characters from modern mainstream fiction? Consider these names for a moment:

Scarlett O'Hara, Rhett Butler, Michael Corleone, Mister Roberts, Captain Queeg, Dr. Sam Abelman in Gerald Green's *The Last Angry Man*, Jeeter Lester from *Tobacco Road*, Marjorie Morningstar, Youngblood Hawke, Magnolia Ravenal from *Show Boat* or any dozen other characters from Edna Ferber's novels. I could go on and on, but I think you must see my point. What character in any mystery novel has ever been so thoroughly realized as those mainstream characters I have just listed? Ross Macdonald's Lew Archer? No. Ross Macdonald sells well outside of the mystery ghetto not because his characters are exquisitely detailed and brought vibrantly to life—which they are not—but because his books have one of those other things that most mysteries lack—serious thematic purpose. Besides, Ross Macdonald has a rich prose style, a lyrical way with language, a talent which appeals to the mainstream audience but which most mystery writers, who are so focused on their Byzantine plots, never bother to develop. Does Sam Spade measure up to Sam Abelman or to Youngblood Hawke? I think not. *The Maltese Falcon* is a wonderful book for many reasons, but when the reader turns the last page he knows less about Sam Spade's soul than he could learn of Captain Queeg's in just one chapter of *The Caine Mutiny*. For my money, only one modern mystery writer has created a truly immortal character: Raymond Chandler did it with Philip Marlowe. Of course, Marlowe was brought fully to life through the course of several novels, not just in one book. Nevertheless, when you read the body of Chandler's work, you feel that, in Philip Marlowe, you have met a *real* person with a heart and a soul and a mind like no other.

(If I thought John D. MacDonald could be classified as a mystery writer, I would include his series character, Travis McGee, in the same league with Chandler's famous detective. As in the case of Philip Marlowe, Travis McGee achieves reality and perhaps even immortality not in any single book but through the course of many novels—nineteen to date. Quite a few people *do* consider MacDonald a mystery writer, but I think he has always been squarely in the mainstream of American fiction—a

WRITER, period—and after all, this is my book, so I can classify him any way I wish!)

Lest you get the idea I hold some sort of grudge against mystery writers, let's apply the same standards of characterization to science fiction, another genre in which authors often concentrate on plot and action at the expense of other elements of good fiction. Isaac Asimov, one of the biggest of the Big Names in the field, has always used his characters either as chess pieces to advance the plot or as mouthpieces to explain (or speculate upon) various scientific theories. Out of all Mr. Asimov's books, which I once read with great pleasure, I can remember personality details about only one character: Dr. Susan Calvin of the positronic robot stories. Although Arthur C. Clarke is a smoother, more lyrical writer than Mr. Asimov, his characters, too, often serve only as handmaidens to the plot. A. E. van Vogt's characters are usually merely devices for the articulation of sundry sociological and psychological theories, and they are blurred by the maniacal speed with which they move through their stories.

Just as the author of the whodunit is obliged to put together a plot that is also a puzzle, so the science fiction writer is required by his fans to create a well-planned plot that is thrilling and also provides a "sense of wonder." The analytical term "sense of wonder" is used frequently in critical essays about science fiction, and its meaning ought to be self-evident. Most science fiction writers generate a sense of wonder by the use of exotic backgrounds—alien worlds, far-distant futures—and/or by the elucidation of radically new and surprising concepts such as Robert Heinlein's "universe ship" in *Orphans of the Sky,* Hal Clement's heavy-gravity alien life form in *Mission of Gravity,* and Keith Laumer's clever twist on the time-travel concept in *Worlds of the Imperium.* Regardless of how this sense of wonder is finally produced, it is essentially an extra plotting chore, and too often it distracts the science fiction writer from the problems of solid characterization and integrated thematic structure.

In spite of what I have just written, I believe that science fiction has given us more memorable, well-rounded characters than has the mystery genre. To name just a few: Valentine Michael Smith in Heinlein's *Stranger in a Strange Land*, Horty Bluett in Theodore Sturgeon's touching *The Dreaming Jewels*, the title character in Edgar Pangborn's marvelous *Davy*, Father Ramon Ruiz-Sanchez in James Blish's stunning *A Case of Conscience*, Gulliver Foyle in Alfred Bester's *The Stars My Destination*, Hugh Farnham in Heinlein's postholocaust novel *Farnham's Freehold*, Conrad Nimikos in Roger Zelazny's *This Immortal* and Charles Render in the same author's *The Dream Master*, David Selig in Robert Silverberg's *Dying Inside*, Chyl Tarvok in Jack Vance's *Emphyrio*, and the unforgettable Mr. Tagomi in Philip K. Dick's classic *The Man in the High Castle*. But again, even among these outstanding examples, how many are as multi-faceted and as deeply affecting as the famous mainstream characters I listed earlier? A few, perhaps, but not many. And is any of them as surely immortal as Rhett Butler or Captain Queeg?

Some of the science fiction writers who launched their careers in the 1960s and 1970s are now consciously trying to expand their plots to accommodate mainstream-quality characterization. Gene Wolfe, Thomas Disch, Samuel R. Delany, and C. J. Cherryh all come to mind in this regard. Gregory Benford, in his fine and ambitious novel, *Timescape*, worked extremely hard to avoid the shorthand characterizations so common to the science fiction of previous generations. Although Mr. Benford's character details sometimes suffer for a lack of selectivity, and although the passages of characterization are occasionally self-conscious, he more often fulfills his ambitions than not, and that is a major achievement for any writer, inside or outside of the genres. I believe that efforts like *Timescape*, by authors of this caliber, are in part responsible for science fiction's recent upswing in popularity.

Characterization is not the only element of fiction given scant attention because of the genre writer's excessive concentration on plot; good thematic structure often is thrown out the window, too. If you ask a mystery writer to summarize the theme of his novel, he will often say something such as this: "Well, it's about murder in the garment industry." Or: "It's a detective story set in Honolulu, with lots of exotic Hawaiian stuff." Or: "It's about Caribbean voodoo cults operating smack in the middle of Manhattan." Those are not themes; they are *backgrounds*. Likewise, when you ask a science fiction author to sum up the theme of his latest novel, he will probably say, "Well, it's a time-travel story." Or: "It's about an alternate earth in which the American Revolution never took place." Or: "It's about an alien planet, a jungle world where the only intelligent life forms are plants, and the animals are all as mindless as carrots here on earth." Again, those are not really themes; they are simply plot engines and/or backgrounds.

Just as the plot brings order and coherence to the events within a novel, so the theme brings purpose and meaning to the plot. A theme is a statement or a series of related observations about one aspect or another of the human condition, interpreted from the unique viewpoint of the author. An old-fashioned English teacher might say that the theme is the *moral* of the story; however, that would be misleading, for not every moral is a theme, and not every theme is a moral. In fiction, a moral is concerned with upholding and encouraging behavior that society considers virtuous; a moral *instructs* the reader. A theme is more complex and less didactic than that; if the author wishes, the theme of a novel may be only a series of connected observations, without any intent to teach a lesson.

In my most recent novel, *Whispers,* the theme is set forth in an opening epigraph, a quote from Charles Dickens: "The forces that affect our lives, the influences that mold and shape us, are often like whispers in a distant room, teasingly indistinct, apprehended only with difficulty." Every major character and some of the minor ones in *Whispers* are walking, talking examples of Dickens's psychological observation. Scene by scene, chapter by chapter, that theme is explored, echoed, and re-echoed through the application of both obvious and subtle narrative techniques.

Even when readers are not consciously aware that a book contains a strong thematic structure, the presence of such a structure still makes the novel richer and more exciting than it would have been without that added dimension. Of course, if an author has nothing particular that he wants to say, if his only desire is to entertain, he can still create a wonderful, involving novel. I have spent countless delightful hours curled up with books which were cleverly plotted but which had about as much meaning and as much relevance to the human condition as the ad copy on the side of a cereal box. Nevertheless, if an author has something to say that is interesting and that is important to him, and if he has the urge and the ability to say it well, his novel will almost certainly have more energy and sparkle than virtually anything written by other authors whose intentions are less ambitious.

I am not suggesting that you interrupt the flow of your story to write miniature essays about the meaning of life! Development of the thematic structure must at all times be carried out unobtrusively, and it must be a true reflection of the twists and turns of your plot. In fact, your book's theme should be suggested by the plot and not the other way around. *The story comes first.* If, instead, you devise a plot solely to support a preconceived theme, then you are writing an essay disguised as fiction, or you are writing a "literary" novel. Do not preach at your readers. Even if you are writing in support of some personal conviction that is so important you want to persuade others of its value, even if your primary intent is to win converts, you must win them by entertaining them, by touching their hearts, by moving them, but never by lecturing them.

Plot.
Characterization.
Theme.
Action.
Mood.
Arresting imagery.
Stylish prose.
Background.

In the best fiction, those elements and many others are used together to create involving stories. When theme and/or characterization dominate, at the expense of plot and other elements, you have a self-conscious "literary" novel. When plotting overwhelms all else and leaves no room for well-rounded characters or thematic structure, you are very likely writing within the narrow confines of one genre or another. But when you devise a strong plot, keep it tightly controlled, mix it with multi-faceted characters, set it against a striking background, keep it charged with action, and describe that action with well-chosen and polished words—then you are writing the kind of popular mainstream fiction that can gain you a very large audience.

Think about this:

Dozens and dozens—perhaps even hundreds—of genre authors have written vampire stories. Every year, Draculaesque tales appear on bookstore shelves, and they are all pretty much the same: 60-, 70-, or 80,000-word thrillers told from the viewpoint of a single character, stuffed full of castles and Transylvanian landscapes, progressing breathlessly from a fight scene to a chase scene to a fight scene to a chase scene to *another* chase scene. . . . None of those books are runaway bestsellers. Most of them sell considerably fewer than 100,000 copies in paperback. Then along comes Stephen King with his 200,000-word, multiple-viewpoint *'Salem's Lot,* which is filled with *real* people, and he sells stacks of hardcovers, receives a small fortune as a Literary Guild main selection, lays off the film rights on a major studio, and eventually gets royalty checks on sales of 3,000,000 paperbacks.

Just *think* about it.

This chapter is the longest in *How to Write Bestselling Fiction,* partly because plotting is the most important thing for a new writer to learn, but also because plotting is the one element of fiction writing that can be pretty thoroughly explained without resorting to fuzzy-minded theorizing and blurry abstractions. Plotting is the most mechanical aspect of novel-making; therefore, it lends itself to lists of rules, do's and don't's, guidelines, pattern analyses, and other devices that make sense to both the teacher and the student.

Upcoming chapters are rather short when compared to

this one, for in a number of cases they deal with subjects that are, to one degree or another, artistically mysterious, even to the daily practitioners of the novelist's art. Convincing characterization, a fluent prose style marked by vivid imagery and by the imaginative use of language, successful integration of background material into the plot—well, no author can tell you *exactly* how he achieves good results when he strives to imbue his fiction with those qualities. Learning to do those things well is every bit as important as learning how to structure a story line, but the best teacher in this instance is experience.

And where do you get the experience that helps you to become more than just a plodding plotter? There are only two ways you can acquire it. First, read as much fiction as you can get your hands on; learn from the examples of published works. I do not mean that you should dissect a novel as you read it. You must approach each novel as any ordinary reader would approach it, seeking only to be entertained; sit down, lean back, enjoy yourself, and give the author a chance to affect you as he intended to affect you. When you have finished the book, then take time for reflection. Consider each element of the story—plot, theme, background, style, et cetera—and attempt to discover the techniques, the nuts and bolts with which the story was built. Do not be discouraged if, initially, you are unable to see into the novel with the requisite X-ray vision. Simply by making the effort to understand, you will be feeding vital information to your subconscious, programming it; and because your busy subconscious never sleeps, it will eventually make connections and associations, finally feeding back the understanding that you are seeking. Meanwhile, the second way to get experience handling characterization, background, and style is to write your own fiction whenever you are not reading somebody else's. In writing as in piano playing, practice makes perfect. Read, read, read; write, write, write: Those are probably the *best* two pieces of advice about learning to write fiction that you will ever get from anyone, anywhere.

5.

Action, action, action
or
A plot without action is
like pasta without garlic,
like Dolly Parton without
cleavage, and like a
writer without his
similes.

Plot is *what* happens.

Action is *how* it happens.

The more movement you work into your story and the more completely you avoid static scenes in which the characters do nothing but talk at one another, the more likely you are to end up with a novel that will sell. As I keep reminding you: Most readers just want to *get on with it.*

I have just three suggestions to make about writing action sequences:

1. *You can have too many action scenes.* Ideally, a novel's pace should rise and fall, rise and fall, reaching ever-higher plateaus of excitement every time it rises, while providing carefully placed lulls during which the reader can catch his breath and can have time to anticipate the next development. It is during those periods of anticipation that suspense can be built most effectively. Unless the author is very careful and very good, an unrelieved series of action scenes piled one atop the other can become boring from repetition and from lack of contrast, just as a symphony would be boring if it contained too many stirring crescendos.

Nevertheless, I advise would-be novelists to err on the side of action for their first few books, until they have a better understanding of how the lulls can be made as interesting and readable as the action sequences. (How? Well, for example, Arthur Hailey, who handles background better than just about any other popular novelist, makes his non-action scenes fascinating by incorporating arcane, odd, humorous, shocking, and highly informative details he's acquired through extensive reading and through hundreds of hours of interviews with experts. Most people are interested in knowing how things work, and Hailey is famous for telling them all about the tricks of the trade in books like *Hotel, Airport,* and *Overload.*) Over the years, *all* of the manuscripts I have seen from new, as yet unpublished writers have suffered from a lack of action.

Inexperienced authors have a tendency to let major plot events—murders, betrayals, airplane crashes—take place offstage. I think there are basically two reasons why so many commit this same error. First of all, they believe it is quite exciting to have a character make a dramatic entrance into a scene by announcing some terrible bit of news. They do it like this:

> "Judge Stephens has been murdered." Jenny said, rushing into her husband's study, a look of horror on her face.
>
> "My God," Burt said, standing up so suddenly that he knocked over his chair. "Murdered? How? When?"
>
> "An hour ago," Jenny said. She was pale, trembling. "He was gunned down on the steps of the courthouse."
>
> Burt was so shocked that he stood for several seconds in silence, numb, unable to speak or even think. At last he said, "Who was it? Who shot him?"
>
> Weak-kneed, Jenny slipped into a chair. "PLO terrorists," she said. "Two of them. They used submachine guns. It must have been awful."

That, my friends, is phony drama. Real drama *shows* the action; phony drama merely tells you about it secondhand, usually with a bit of histrionics. The murder of the judge could have been a very suspenseful and horrifying scene. When those two terrorists pulled the triggers, the reader should have been right there, should have heard the brutal clatter of the weapons, should have smelled the burnt gunpowder, the coppery scent of blood.

I believe the second reason so many new writers allow

dramatic events to transpire offstage is that they do not feel confident about their ability to bring such complex sequences to life. They are intimidated by the many elements that compose an action scene, and they think they can slip around the problem altogether by *telling* the reader about the gunplay in a comparatively easy-to-write dialogue such as the one between Jenny and Burt. This simply is not acceptable. Besides, the only way the new writer will ever learn to handle action is by trying and failing and trying again until he can do it smoothly and with confidence. But while you're doing all that practicing, keep the following two pieces of advice in mind.

2. *Make the most of every action scene.* The reader's attention is far more easily held during an action sequence than during any other kind of scene. Each time you write a potentially gripping chase—or fight or whatnot—in just one page or less, you are throwing away a golden opportunity to seize and deeply involve your audience. You *must* squeeze every drop of color and excitement and suspense out of every action scene in your novel.

By way of example, take a look at the first chapter of my most recent book, *Whispers.* Within that opening chapter, there is an extended scene between the heroine, Hilary Thomas, and a knife-wielding maniac named Bruno Frye. Frye pursues her through her house; from room to room, up a winding staircase to the second floor, down a long hallway, into another room. . . . During this hair-raising pursuit, Hilary desperately seeks a weapon with which to defend herself, is nearly seized and dragged down several times, and searches frantically for a door or some other sturdy barrier that will stand against Frye's fierce and relentless assault. I have seen new, as yet unpublished writers handle quite similar scenes in just one, two, or three pages, seldom expending more than 1,000 words to describe the entire episode. In *Whispers,* however, that scene ran twenty-five pages in manuscript and ate up more than 7,500 words! I like to think that not one of those 7,500 words was padding; I rewrote and repolished the scene more than thirty times, trying hard to make it as smooth and fast-paced and breathless as I possibly could. A number of reviewers have been kind enough to say that *Whispers* has one of the two or three most thrilling opening chapters they have ever read. If that is true, it is largely the result of the scene between Hilary and Bruno Frye, which constitutes one-third of that chapter.

There is no dark, mysterious secret to lengthening an action sequence without padding it. The key lies in a simple, seven-word rule: *Don't make it easy on your hero.* If he's running from a vampire in a deserted graveyard, he shouldn't simply be able to lock himself in a tomb and wait until daylight. That's far too easy. If he locks himself in a tomb, he should discover that he's in there with *another* vampire and that the chase is still on. If he's grappling with a maniacal ax-murderer and at last gets the ax away from his nemesis, he should then discover that the killer *also* has a knife; and when he gets the knife away from the man, when he's certain his adversary is disarmed and comparatively harmless, he *then* should discover that he is dealing with a karate expert. If the hero must climb a mountain in order to reach the heroine and save her life, the mountain should be *very* tough; it should present the climber with dangerous overhangs, with sheer faces that offer no handholds whatsoever, with crumbling rock that gives way under his supporting pitons. Those are trite examples, but I think they clearly convey what I mean. In its structure, each action scene should be a microcosmic representation of the larger structural pattern of the novel itself. In short, just as the book was built upon a classic plot pattern— primarily one of ever-worsening complications—each and every action scene should be similarly structured, though on a smaller scale. Hit your hero with startling and/or frightening complications, one after the other. *Be tough on him.* If you keep those words in mind, your action scenes will be well-rounded, exciting, and satisfyingly long.

   3. *Be aware that different prose styles can contribute in different ways to the creation—or to the destruction—of a sense of urgency in an action scene.* Regardless of the style in which the body of your novel is written, you would be well advised to modify—or perhaps I ought to say "modulate"—it now and then, specifically to punctuate action sequences. The reader might not always be consciously aware that the prose style—by which I mean the very soul and rhythm of the sentences—has changed, but he will subconsciously register that difference and will be affected by it.

I use various stylistic techniques to tighten the narrative tension in an action scene. I will share two of them with you in order to clarify the meaning of the third suggestion.

You can add excitement to an action scene by composing it in shorter paragraphs and in shorter sentences than those you use elsewhere in your novel. This change in prose rhythm will give your reader a feeling of headlong forward movement. Here is a small portion of a chase scene from *Whispers*, in which I judiciously (I hope) employed this technique. (Note: the "doors in the ground" mentioned in this excerpt are storm cellar doors.)

She pushed through the swinging door, into the kitchen, as Frye jumped down the last few steps into the hallway behind her.

She thought of searching the kitchen drawers for a knife.

Couldn't. No time.

She ran to the outside door, unlocked it, and bolted from the kitchen as Frye entered it through the swinging door.

The only weapon she had was the flashlight she had been carrying, and that was no weapon at all.

She crossed the porch, went down the steps. Rain and wind battered her.

He was not far behind. He was still chanting, *"Bitch, bitch, bitch!"*

She would never be able to run around the house and all the way to the car before he caught her. He was much too close and gaining.

The wet grass was slick.

She was afraid of falling.

Of dying.

She ran toward the only place that might offer protection: the doors in the ground.

> Lightning flickered, and thunder followed it.
> Frye wasn't screaming behind her any more. She heard a deep, animal growl of pleasure.
> Very close.
> Now *she* was screaming.

In that excerpt, I even used some sentence fragments to convey the heroine's desperation. Of course, short sentences and short paragraphs can be overused, leading to monotony every bit as sleep-inducing as that caused by 500-word sentences and ten-page-long paragraphs. The writer must have a good ear for prose, and he must apply some common sense when using this technique. I don't suppose that common sense is something you can consciously set out to teach yourself; but you *can* teach yourself to hear complicated rhythms in prose. How? Write, write, write and read, read, read!

The second technique for speeding up the pace of an action scene is just the opposite of the first, and it is used primarily to deal with the narrative problem that I call the "time paradox." Occasionally, a series of actions will take longer to describe than they would take to *happen* in real life. In a situation like that, the author risks shattering his carefully created illusion of reality, for if the reader suddenly becomes aware of the time paradox, he might, at least for a moment, lose all empathy for the story and the characters. I sometimes attempt to sweep the reader past the time paradox by jamming all of the action into one long, breathless, carefully structured sentence that surges like a series of waves. Following is an example from *The Vision,* in which the male lead is attacked and seriously wounded by the villain.

> The killer jerked the flashlight up, in the direction of Max's voice, temporarily blinding him.
> Although for an instant he could see nothing, Max raised the gun and pulled the trigger. Once. Twice. The shots crashed like cannon fire in the huge, high-ceilinged room.

Simultaneous with the explosion, perhaps even a fraction of a second prior to it, the flashlight spun up and up, out to the right.

I hit him! Max thought.

Even before he completed the thought, the knife ripped into him, rammed out of the darkness and into him, felt like the blade of a shovel, enormous, devastating, so devastating that he dropped the gun, feeling pain like nothing he'd ever known, and he realized that the killer had pitched the flashlight aside as a diversion, hadn't really been hit at all, and the knife was withdrawn from him, and then shoved hard into him again, deep into his stomach, and he thought of Mary and his love for Mary and about how he was letting her down, and he grappled with the killer's head in the dark, got handfuls of short hair, but the bandage came off his finger and the cut was wrenched open again and he felt that pain separate from all the others, and he cursed the sharp edge on the car's jack, and the flashlight hit the floor ten feet away, spun around, cast lunatic shadows, and the knife ripped loose from him again, and he reached for the hand that held it, but he missed, and the blade got him a third time, explosive pain, and he staggered back, the man all over him, the blade plunging again, high this time, into his chest, and he realized that the only way he could hope to survive now was to play dead, so he fell, fell hard, and the man stumbled over him, and he heard the man's rapid breathing, and he lay very still, and the man went for the flashlight and came back and looked down at him, stood over him, kicked him in the ribs, and he wanted to cry out but didn't, didn't move and didn't breathe, even though he was screaming inside for breath, so the man turned away and went toward the arch, and then there were footsteps on the tower stairs, and, hearing them, he felt like such a useless ass, out-smarted, and he knew he wasn't going to be able to recover his gun and climb those stairs and rescue Mary because stuff like that was for the movies, pain was pulverizing him, he was leaking all over the floor, dripping like a squeezed fruit, but he told himself he had to try to help her and that he wasn't going to die, wasn't going to die, wasn't going to die, even though that was exactly what he seemed to be doing.

It would be a mistake for any author to use this technique frequently. The breathlessly paced, exceptionally long, action-crammed sentence is a calculatedly pyrotechnical device, calling attention to itself in order to prevent the reader from noticing the more serious problem of the time paradox. When a writer employs this trick, he runs the risk of shattering the illusion of reality by dazzling his readers with his command of prose, and that is no better than letting the time paradox itself shatter the illusion. Furthermore, if the author unwittingly establishes an irritating rhythm—which is easy to do when handling such a long chain of phrases and clauses—or if he improperly punctuates one of those Brobdingnagian sentences, he will disrupt his story to a far greater extent than any built-in time paradox ever could. If you make use of this technique, use it sparingly.

Action writing in popular mainstream fiction does not differ greatly from action writing in the standard genre novel. There are, however, two things you can do to make certain that your book has a better chance of appealing to the larger, mainstream audience. First, avoid tired genre action scenes such as ordinary car chases, shootouts, and fist fights. Use your imagination; try to dream up something original and surprising. If your story *demands* a car chase, if there's simply no way around it, then in order to please the mainstream reader, you will have to write the car chase to end all car chases, something grander and wilder and more imaginative than anyone has done before. Secondly, do not forget that the mainstream reader prefers stories with more texture than most of those to be found in the genres. In its most exciting scenes, the average genre novel is nothing *but* action. In popular mainstream fiction, even in the middle of an action sequence, you must be concerned about background, about mood, about thematic intent, about keeping the characters within character.

6.

**Heroes and heroines
or
Your lead character
doesn't have to leap tall
buildings in a single
bound, and he doesn't
have to stop speeding
bullets with his bare
hands, but he darn well
better know the difference
between right and wrong,
and he better be kind to
animals, and it sure
wouldn't hurt any if he
brushed his teeth
regularly.**

In Chapter 4, which dealt primarily with plotting, I have already discussed the need for a hero and/or heroine. Although I have only a few additional comments, I am giving the subject its own chapter strictly to emphasize the tremendous importance I place upon it.

If your novel is to have any chance at all of reaching a wide audience, it *must* contain a sympathetic lead character who embodies heroic qualities, for it is this kind of person with whom readers are most easily able to identify and for whom they enjoy cheering. If there is not a character one can like and toward whom one can feel sympathetic, then readers will not care what happens next in the story. And if readers do not care what happens next, they stop reading. And if they stop reading your book before they reach the end of it, you can bet your boots and mittens that they won't come back to buy the next novel carrying your by-line. Worse yet, if *editors* fail to identify with your lead, and if *they* stop reading before they've gotten to the end of your book, you will never get it published in the first place. Now you understand why I italicized the word "must" in the opening sentence of this paragraph.

I have made a list of five traits you should consider carefully when creating your lead characters. In order to appeal to the average reader, your hero and/or heroine should have all five of these qualities.

Virtue. I am not encouraging you to write from a prim Victorian point of view. (Unless, of course, you are writing a novel set in the Victorian period.) I do not mean that your lead characters should be sexually virtuous. I do not mean that they should abstain from smoking, drinking, and cursing. They can do all of those things and still contain a large measure of virtue. I am speaking now of the heavyweight moral issues such as murder, assault, greed, thievery, the betrayal of trust, and so forth. Your male and female leads should understand the difference between right and wrong, between good and evil; they must always come down squarely on the side of good and right, even if they occasionally waver a bit during their descent. If at all possible, they should never do anything illegal, unethical, or immoral in their attempts to rid themselves of their terrible trouble. (We're talking about Big Time Immoral, now, not just jay-walking.) For instance, if your hero is being pursued by a rabid beast, he should not escape from its clutches by turning it against an innocent bystander.

Once in a while, your plot will put your lead characters in a no-win situation which requires them to do something immoral in order to survive. If the villain has the hero backed into a corner, with a hatchet at his throat, and if death for the hero is unquestionably at hand, he is within his rights to draw that dagger out of his shirtsleeve and skewer the villain at the first opportunity. *But he shouldn't feel all that good about it.* Even when he kills strictly out of self-defense, and even when the villain richly deserves death, the hero should be shaken and repulsed by the killing. It is difficult for the reader to identify with and have sympathy for a hero (or heroine) who *likes* to kill—or who revels in the commission of other immoral acts.

The new writer, wondering exactly how to handle this moral dilemma, could find no better examples than in the Travis McGee series by John D. MacDonald. McGee kills when he must—but *only* when he must—and he is never unaffected by what he has done. MacDonald makes you feel the cold, slick quiver of revulsion that McGee feels upon dealing death; he makes you taste the bile in the back of McGee's throat, and he makes you see the damage to McGee's soul, of which McGee is all too painfully aware.

I will admit that once in a while a novel achieves great success in spite of the fact that its lead characters are largely or entirely lacking in virtue. The classic example is

James M. Cain's incredibly brilliant first novel, *The Post-man Always Rings Twice*. One follows Mr. Cain's terri-fyingly amoral characters with the kind of morbid fascina-tion one might feel upon turning over a rock and finding a very strange and hideously ugly insect under it; the sight is disgusting, but the unexpected discovery of such alien and frighteningly energetic life in such an ordinary place is gripping, compelling.

The new writer, however, would be well advised to prove he can work successfully within the rules before he breaks them. Cain was a genius. At his best he was a mas-ter stylist and an incomparable storyteller the likes of which we see only once in a generation—if that often. Per-haps only one author in a thousand could write a first novel as splendid and as controlled as *The Postman Al-ways Rings Twice*. If you intend to launch your career with a book full of immoral anti-heroes, you had better be sure that you are that one in a thousand; for if you are not, you will wind up with a hopelessly unpublishable manu-script.

Competence. Readers do not want to settle down for an evening with a book about idiots, fools, and wimps—unless those idiots, fools, and wimps are hysterically funny. The average reader has an extremely difficult time identifying with and caring about lead characters who are nothing more than ineffective, whimpering victims of fate. The leads must stand up to adversity and fight back *in an intel-ligent fashion;* they must take the right steps toward find-ing a solution to their problems, and they must deal with each new complication in a clever—or at least in a commonsensical—fashion.

Courage. Readers also find it difficult to identify with cowards. They do not want to read about people who run from problems or who try to escape from the conse-quences of their own actions. When I say that lead charac-ters must be courageous, I do not mean that they must be brave to the point of foolhardiness, and I certainly am not suggesting that they ought to be thin-lipped, steely-eyed macho types. There are different kinds of courage, after all. The heroes of Alistair MacLean's *The Guns of*

Navarone display great courage during their commando raid on a heavily guarded German gun emplacement. In Erich Segal's *Love Story*, Oliver and Jenny, facing her inevitable death from cancer, are possessed of a quiet and tragic courage that is uplifting and, at the same time, inexpressibly sad. In Avery Corman's *Kramer vs Kramer*, the lead character demonstrates real courage by examining his long-held goals and modifying them, sacrificing some dreams in order to make a better life for his child. If your lead character shows courage, the reader will admire him and will feel that he is worth cheering for.

Likeability. Your hero might be virtuous, competent, and courageous, but readers will *still* not identify with him if he is a stuffed shirt or a self-congratulatory prig. He should be modest but not falsely so. He should have a sense of humor, and some of that humor should be directed against himself. He should show kindness, consideration, and concern for those around him; however, do not carry his sensitivity so far that he becomes a bleeding-heart do-gooder, for readers have as much trouble identifying with a saint as with a liar and a thief.

Imperfections. In a genre novel, the author can get away with a James Bond-like character, one who is pretty much perfect in every detail. In popular mainstream fiction, a Bond-type hero is usually unacceptable. Mainstream readers want the characters in a novel to be real, three-dimensional, the kind of people who might conceivably live next door. Now, we all know that the people next door have character flaws, and so must the heroes and heroines in your novels.

In my own *Whispers*, the female lead, Hilary Thomas, is twenty-nine years old but *still* unable to deal with the ugly memories of a childhood lived in poverty, in the shadows of abusive parents who were hot-tempered, violent alcoholics. As a child she had no one on whom she could depend, to whom she could turn for help or solace or understanding. She grew up to be fiercely independent—and as a result, she is unable to enjoy or even build close friendships, especially with men. She has become a loner, and she hates *being* a loner, but in the early chapters of the novel, she cannot open up to people. She is incapable of trusting anyone, even the male lead, who clearly loves her. Gradually, during the course of the story, as she and the hero strive to learn the identity of the psychopath who has targeted Hilary for death, Hilary learns to put her tragic past behind her; she learns to trust people; she *changes*.

That is the kind of character imperfection I am talking about. It is nothing so terrible that it turns the reader against Hilary. She is nothing so awful as a hit-and-run driver or a kitten-killer or anything of that sort. Her imperfection causes her pain but does not intrude seriously upon the lives of those around her. Indeed, the reader is affected by Hilary's loneliness, by her inability to open up, and she quickly gains his sympathy.

Consider these other fictional characters, marred by imperfections but nonetheless heroic and *likeable*: I.M. Fletcher, hero of Gregory Mcdonald's *Fletch, Confess, Fletch,* and *Fletch's Fortune,* is an opportunist, smug, and capable of cruelty, but he is likeable because he is as inexhaustibly clever as all of us wish we were, and he is funny, and he has more than a small dose of courage. Nero Wolfe, central character of many superb mysteries by the late Rex Stout, is a glutton who is grossly overweight; he is rude to those he considers fools—which includes nearly everyone; and he is a curmudgeon extraordinaire. But Wolfe remains likeable because he is the genius all of us wish we were and because he evinces childish delight in food, orchids, and books. Furthermore, he is unfailingly moral, always on the side of right, and he *cares* about such abstract things as justice. And Wolfe, though never called upon to exhibit physical bravery, is a courageous man—morally, intellectually, and emotionally.

In the matter of heroes and heroines, genre novels differ from mainstream novels in two major ways: 1) As I noted a few paragraphs ago, a genre hero (or heroine) may be an essentially flawless fantasy figure, but a mainstream lead should be *real;* he should have some faults, even if he completely overcomes those weaknesses by the end of the book and changes for the better. 2) A genre novel may have either a hero or a heroine—or both a hero *and* a heroine; but a mainstream novel should *always* have both. The readership of some genres—science fiction, Westerns, adventure-suspense—is largely male, and the lack of an intriguing heroine does not disturb many fans of those forms of fiction. However, marketing studies have shown that the average audience for popular mainstream novels is anywhere from 60 to 75 percent female. That statistic should explain why the smart author always includes a heroine in his story line. In some cases, if the book would be sharper and better for it, the author would be well advised to emphasize the heroine's role a bit *more* than the hero's. However, marketing considerations are not the only reasons why you ought to include a strong female co-lead in each of your books. The inclusion of both male and female viewpoints will give variety and balance to your story, and the challenge of writing interesting, believable characters of both sexes will hone your writing skills. Many new male writers fail to create vivid female characters, just as many new female writers fail to create vivid male characters; without the interaction of the sexes, their stories quickly grow stale. You must force yourself to write from both viewpoints in order to grow as a novelist.

7.

**Creating believable
characters
or
If your heroine is a
beautiful actress, a fine
painter, an engineer, a
cabinetmaker, a superb
cook, a daring test pilot, a
whiz at electronics, a
doctor, a lawyer, and an
Indian chief, don't you
think you ought to
humanize her at least to
the extent of giving her a
zit on the end of her
nose?**

When the time came for me to write this chapter, I was surprised to discover that I could think of very little more to say about characterization that would be genuinely helpful to the new writer. Of course, I had already written about various aspects of the subject, especially in Chapters 4 and 6. But surely (I told myself sternly) there must be a great deal more to be said, more than enough to fill a sizeable chapter. After all, I believe very strongly that the success of a novel hinges on good characterization every bit as much as it hinges on good plotting. To my way of thinking, those are the only two absolutely essential elements of fine popular fiction. I expend a considerable percentage of my writing time in the careful development of three-dimensional characters. Furthermore, I have shoeboxes full of reviews in which critics single out my characterization for special applause. Now I do not believe everything I read, but when I sat down to write this chapter and found myself with hardly a thing to say, I reread some of the reviews in those shoeboxes. I *still* couldn't think of much to say.

In desperation, I surveyed two dozen other books about the writing of fiction, something I had previously avoided doing in a determined effort to keep my advice fresher than what one usually finds in fiction-writing guides. To my utter amazement, I discovered that the authors of those other texts were *also* unable to tell their readers anything really useful about the conception and development of convincing characters. Some of them rambled on for ten or fifteen pages, saying nothing even half so intelligible or intelligent as the four a.m. mutterings of a booze-blasted dipsomaniac. Other authors made long lists of character names from famous novels, recommending that new writers study those shining examples; but they made no effort whatsoever to analyze *why* those examples were worth studying in the first place, which is rather like saying, "I don't know how in the devil to teach you to do this thing, but at least I know it when I see it done well." Nine of those twenty-four books avoided the thorny problem of characterization simply by never raising the subject.

When I asked an author friend of mine to explain his methods of characterization, he said, "I can't. I don't think about it all that much. Or maybe I should say that I think about it a lot *while I'm writing*, and I get a feel for it, but after I've finished doing it, I can't explain what I did. Check out what Woodford has to say. You probably won't agree with him, but his position's sure to be so outrageous that it'll get you thinking."

In *Trial and Error*, the hottest-selling fiction-writing guide ever put on paper (first released in 1933; well over a million hardcover copies sold in several editions; still in print from a West Coast specialty publisher), the author, Jack Woodford, devoted just one paragraph to the subject of characterization. The key sentence in that paragraph is a perfect example of Woodford's cynicism and of his tendency to oversimplify important issues: "*Characterization is an accident that flows out of action and dialogue;* and if I were you I would never pay the slightest attention to characterization or give it a thought." According to Woodford, that's all there is to it.

I cannot, in good conscience, pass that advice along to you. There *is* a grain of truth in Woodford's statement. Indeed, what he says is of more use to the would-be novelist than everything that was written about characterization in those other twenty-four textbooks *combined*. To a certain extent, characterization does evolve from action, but that is not, as Woodford pretends, a process that transpires without the author's conscious attention.

For example (and this is an example of the very kind that

Woodford himself uses), suppose that you place a character—let's call him "Zeke"—in a difficult moral dilemma, and suppose that you provide Zeke with a dozen ways out of that predicament, and further suppose that some of those solutions are moral and some are immoral and some are amoral. When Zeke chooses the solution that most appeals to him, he will tell us a lot about himself. Woodford claims that this is characterization arising out of action, without any real input from the author of the piece.

Baloney.

The situation I've just outlined is, more accurately, an example of *action consciously designed with the specific intention of contributing to the characterization of Zeke.* The author's desire to characterize clearly came *before* he dreamed up Zeke's predicament, before the action was planned. What Mr. Woodford seems to ignore is the fact that Zeke is not a *real* person acting of his own volition; he is a fictional being, and it is the writer who decides whether Zeke is moral, immoral, or amoral.

What Woodford should have said was this: "To achieve the highest possible degree of readability, the author ought to combine characterization with action whenever he can." Characterizing Zeke by confronting him with moral dilemmas in scenes of action and adventure is far preferable to characterizing him through long, dreary paragraphs of personal history and through the boring recitation of extensive laundry lists of dry personality details. *But characterization does not happen accidentally in either case!*

Okay. We have established that characterization does, indeed, require conscious and diligent effort on the part of the author. But the essential questions remain unanswered: How is a well-rounded character brought to life? What narrative techniques are involved? What are the tricks of the trade? Well, I am afraid I cannot completely illuminate the shadowy mystery of successful characterization where so many others have tried and failed. Creating a convincingly real character, choosing salient personality details for revelation to the reader, dropping those bits and pieces into the story without disturbing the narrative flow—those *are* things for which you must develop an intuitive sense. All I can offer are the following suggestions, which might help you nurture that seed of intuition.

———

Before you can word-paint imaginary characters with total confidence and authority, you must know them intimately, although by this I do not mean that your characters must be based wholly upon people in your own life. Graham Greene, the famous British novelist, claims he cannot model a complex fictional person entirely in the image of a real-life acquaintance; Mr. Greene says that he must always know more about the innermost thoughts, fears, and desires of his invented character than he can ever possibly know about the innermost thoughts, fears, and desires of any real-life model, even if that model is his nearest and dearest friend. I think Greene's point is valid. Yes, you *can* cobble together pieces of real people in a sort of Frankensteinian effort to build a cast for your story, but if you do nothing more than paste together observations from real life, your fictional people will be shallow. In order to create a truly unique and believable psychological profile *in depth*, you must enlarge upon those fragments of real people through the diligent application of your imagination. At some point in each novel, the author must come to know as much about each of his major characters as he knows about himself; in fact, he probably ought to know *more* about his leads than he knows about himself, for each of us hides certain truths about himself from himself. When you know as much about your major characters as God reportedly knows about every one of us poor mortals, then your story people will positively reek of authenticity.

In order to focus your attention and in order to make your fictional people seem solid to you while you are developing them, it is not a bad idea to draw up a list of character details on each of them, prior to beginning your novel. I must admit that neither I nor most well-established authors bother with character outlines of this nature; however, for the new writer who is having difficulty getting a firm grip on characterization, such lists might help him get organized before he even composes the first sentence of Chapter 1 and they might also serve as valuable guidelines during the actual writing of the novel.

These character detail lists—perhaps I ought to call them "dossiers" henceforth—should include, but not be limited to, information about the following:

Physical appearance: height, weight; body type; age; the shape of the mouth and nose; the shape of the face; the color and quality of the eyes; the color, texture, and length of the hair; the shade and texture of the skin; birthmarks; the size and condition of the hands; manner of dress; et cetera.

Voice and speech: the tone and pitch of the voice; whether the character is soft-spoken or loud; the accent, if any; odd rhythms of speech, if any; the nature of the character's vocabulary; whether he speaks grammatical or ungrammatical English; et cetera.

Movement and gestures: whether the character is hyperactive, slothful, or something in between; awkward or graceful; whether the character is or is not expressive with his hands and body; poor posture or good posture; agility or lack of it; et cetera.

Past life: date of birth; place of birth, whether parents were rich, poor, or middle class; whether parents were good, bad, or indifferent; father's occupation, mother's occupation; ethnic background; childhood traumas, if any; brothers or sisters, if any; whether or not the character was successful in school; the most influential person in the character's childhood and why; childhood hobbies; defeats; triumphs; job history; marital status; et cetera.

Religion: whether the character is a Catholic, Jew, Protestant, agnostic, atheist, or something else; how often the character attends services; whether the character is devoutly or casually faithful to the tenets of the religion, whatever it might be; et cetera.

Sexuality: whether the character is a virgin or well-experienced or even possibly promiscuous; whether the character likes sex or not; whether the character is a good or bad lover; guilt-ridden or guilt-free; et cetera.

Vocation: nature of the career; whether the character does his (or her) job well; whether the character likes the work; what the character's co-workers and bosses think of him (or her); et cetera.

Skills and talents: whether or not the character snow skis, pilots a plane, plays the guitar, plays the piano, climbs mountains, paints, composes poetry, builds fine cabinets, shoots a rifle well, knows karate, has a nose and palate for wines, et cetera.

I have suggested a series of considerations under each of those topic headings. If you think about them, you will come up with many other pieces of information that will help you draw a detailed picture of your character. In addition to the topics I listed above, you should also explore *these* subjects in as much depth as you can:

Fears
Dreams
Pleasures
Plans for the future
Sense of humor
Politics
Attitudes toward the opposite sex
Attitudes toward children
Attitudes toward money
Attitudes toward love
Attitudes toward death
Attitudes toward liquor and drugs
Ideals
Regrets
General likes and dislikes

One of these dossiers will contain far more data about the character than you will ever use in your book. For instance, your story line and theme might never demand that the character reveal his sexual history; however, you should know his sexual history, for it will have a direct bearing upon other aspects of his personality which perhaps do appear in the novel, such as his attitudes toward women and his views on love. Each major character is like an iceberg: the reader sees just the visible tip, but the author sees and fully understands the huge supporting structure beneath the surface.

When creating any character, major or minor, the author should avoid simple stock types *that can be fully described in a single short phrase*. The drunken Irishman, the promiscuous Frenchman, the gay hairdresser, the dumb jock, the wily oriental, the whore with a heart of gold—those characters and others like them have appeared in so many thousands of books, short stories, and movies that they have become clichés. I do not mean that you must never write about a man who is both drunken and Irish. However, when such a character is a necessary element of a particular story, he must be multi-faceted, drawn in rich detail; in as many ways as possible, he ought to be different from the Irish stereotype, so that he cannot be accurately described merely by the mention of his nationality and by reference to his taste for whiskey.

Another thing to be aware of is the need for consistency in characterization. Let's suppose that the author creates a fictional movie director named Ralph Celluloid, who is tall, handsome, witty, wealthy, intelligent, sophisticated, debonair, and highly respected by his peers. If, as the story rolls along, we also learn that Ralph is *shy and retiring*, the author better have a convincing explanation for this last trait, for it does not appear to be consistent with everything else we know about Ralph. Understand, I am not telling you that Ralph absolutely, positively *can't* be shy. I am only warning you that if he *is* shy, the author must present a logical and coherent psychological case for Ralph's shyness that somehow makes it consistent with his other qualities.

Finally, remember this word: *Change*. Characters who learn from their ordeals and from their mistakes, characters who gain insight into themselves throughout the unraveling of the plot, characters who grow and change *logically*—those are the characters who seldom fail to convince and involve the reader.

For additional information and suggestions about the problems of characterization:
> —refer to Chapter 4, in which the subject is discussed in relation to plotting;
> —refer to Chapter 6, in which there is an analysis of the desirable character traits for heroes and heroines;
> —refer to Chapter 8, which deals with character motivation.

After you have done all of that, there is nothing else to do but sit down at the typewriter, pound the keys, and pray for a lot of inspiration and intuition.

8.

**Achieving plausibility through believable character motivation
or
If your villain guns down sixty people, blows up an airport terminal, hijacks a jet and then crashes it into the White House—all because his Social Security check arrived one day late, you're going to have trouble selling your novel.**

Let's imagine there is a novelist named Orville Hack living in Potato Town, Idaho. Let's also imagine that Orville writes a thrilling tale called *Bite-Size Morsels,* a vampire epic filled with frantic chases through graveyards, creepy expeditions into dank tombs, battles between crucifix-wielding priests and blood-crazed immortal monsters, and suchlike stuff. Intoxicated with hope, Orville sends his script off to New York. One editor after another rejects *Bite-Size Morsels,* all with the same frustratingly vague comment: "Your writing isn't bad, but the story is too wild. It simply isn't plausible, Mr. Hack." Hurt and dejected, Orville shelves that book and starts writing another. A couple of weeks later, on a visit to the Potato Town Book Barn, the local vendor of literature, Orville sees a new novel by Stephen King. Mr. King's book, *'Salem's Lot,* is a vampire epic, crammed full of frantic chases through graveyards, creepy expeditions into dank tombs, battles between crucifix-wielding priests and . . . well, you get the idea.

"Why?" Orville asks the heavens. "Why can Stephen King sell his book for gobs of money, and they tell me that my book—*which has the same plot as his*—is too implausible for publication at any price? Why? Why, oh, why?"

A couple of reasons, Orville. First of all, the characters in *'Salem's Lot* are multi-faceted, thoroughly human, and consistent in every detail; that high-quality characterization contributes a lot to the novel's plausibility. Furthermore, King is excellent at setting a scene, integrating background material in a vivid but unobtrusive manner; each detail seems chosen for its singularity, poignancy, and accuracy. But most important of all, King's characters are believably motivated by love, hate, greed, jealousy, fear, and other recognizably human emotions.

Whether he realizes it or not, when an editor rejects a book because he finds it implausible, he is talking about character motivation, not about plot. Virtually *any* plot can be made totally plausible by an experienced writer who has control of a wide range of fiction-writing techniques. If you think I'm exaggerating, read (if you haven't already) the following successful books and consider their plot lines: *The Boys from Brazil* by Ira Levin, *The Sixth Commandment* by Lawrence Sanders, *The Osterman Weekend* and *The Bourne Identity* both by Robert Ludlum, *The Dead Zone* by Stephen King, *The Exorcist* by William Peter Blatty, *Damnation Alley* by Roger Zelazny, *Winter Kills* by Richard Condon. You would be hard-pressed to find a group of novels with plots any more bizarre than these, all of them risking a judgment of implausibility from the reader, yet all of them succeeding splendidly because of their authors' ability to believably motivate their casts of characters. When a novel crashes full tilt into implausibility, it is almost always because *the reader cannot believe that the characters would do, in real life, the things the author is making them do in the story.*

Let's take a look at some of the most common character motivations found in popular mainstream *and* genre fiction. Each of them has its uses, and some of them contain pitfalls for the unwary new writer.

Love. You don't have to be writing a straight love story in the Harlequin Romance vein in order to make love a strong motivation for the actions of your lead character. Such a universal and vital emotion is adaptable to any genre and to any mainstream plot line. Most thrillers have a love story tucked away in them somewhere. In the vast majority of Westerns, the heroic cowpoke may love his horse, but he usually finds a schoolmarm or a rancher's daughter who is also to his liking and for whom he will make some sacrifices and take some risks.

Never forget that, in their own lives, nearly all of your

readers want to love someone, to be loved, to fall in love; a supportive love relationship is what most people want more than anything else in the world. Even if psychological and sociological studies did not support that statement (and they do), evidence of its truth is to be found everywhere in human activity and most especially in the arts. Ninety-nine out of a hundred popular songs are about love. Donna Summer hasn't sold millions of records by singing about the beauty of nature or about the nobility of self-sacrifice. "Love, love me, do," sang the Beatles, and they didn't do so badly in the marketplace either. What succeeds on Broadway? Musicals, of course—with love stories between the songs (*Oklahoma!*, *South Pacific*, *A Chorus Line*). Comedies—with love stories between the jokes (*Arsenic and Old Lace*, *Barefoot in the Park*, *Cactus Flower*). Shakespeare didn't need Broadway's example to know that love was good box office. *Romeo and Juliet*, *The Taming of the Shrew* and other of his plays struck that chord solidly, and they have remained emotionally valid throughout the centuries. What about Hollywood? Do I really have to ask? From films of studied social relevance like *An Unmarried Woman* and *Guess Who's Coming to Dinner* to unpretentious entertainment like *Smokey and the Bandit* and *Every Which Way But Loose*, love stories are central to the plots. From old, classic films like *Adam's Rib* to the recent movie *Coal Miner's Daughter*, "love" is the password. From *Casablanca*, which many believe to be the best film of all time, to well-meaning but dreadful films like *Back Roads*, the central concern is love. If people weren't in love with love, Hallmark would go out of business, and Rod McKuen would have to give his books away, and there wouldn't be any such thing as Valentine's Day.

James Clavell, Herman Wouk, Joseph Wambaugh and most other bestselling authors are aware that book buyers are interested in reading about love and are predisposed to accept love as a plausible motivation for a hero's or a heroine's actions. If you hope to make the bestseller lists, you must make room for a love story within your book.

However, commercial considerations are not the only or even the primary reasons for including a love story within the larger body of your novel. Love is the noblest emotion; it lifts us above the muck and mire of human existence; it balances the hatred and selfishness and ignorance that is too much a part of us. In fiction, characters in love are characters who shine and are people about whom we can care.

Warning! If your lead character is willing to die for his woman (or she for her man), you better have the narrative skill to make their love appear real and deep; the power of their love for each other must touch, affect, and *convince* the reader. Only then will it seem plausible that your lead would sacrifice his own life for that of another. In the real world, of course, people do noble things all the time, frequently putting their lives on the line for complete strangers. In fiction, however, such selflessness rings false. George Orwell's classic *1984* is good for a point here. Though Winston loves Julia, he is prey to the thought police in their campaign to force him to deny and betray her. The thought police discover Winston's greatest fear: rats. When a cage is put over his head and a rat introduced into the cage—a *hungry* rat—Winston shouts, "Do it to her!" The police have broken him, and that scene is horribly, depressingly *real*. To make the reader believe that your hero would endure *any* torture or hardship for the sake of the heroine, you must persuasively show that losing her would be, for him, worse than death.

To be on the safe side, it is always wise to spike your hero's motivation with a large shot of self-interest, preferably even self-preservation. If he is fighting for his own life as well as for the life of the woman he loves, his actions are enormously more plausible than they might otherwise have been.

Curiosity. This is often used as a character motivation, for we humans are curious creatures. Without curiosity, we might still be sitting in caves, scratching our fleas and eating raw meat. Curiosity is responsible for every important discovery since humankind tamed fire; yet, as with love, curiosity is best augmented with another motivating force, such as self-preservation, love, duty, or greed. Sooner or later, after he has been beaten and threatened often enough, a realistic character, motivated only by curiosity, will call it quits. Perhaps curiosity killed the cat, but readers will not believe for a minute that any rational person would willingly die merely to satisfy his curiosity on some point or other; and. yes, your hero and heroine *must* be rational.

Self-preservation. The fear of death and the explicit threat of death lie at the thematic core of nearly every novel. Self-preservation is the most common character motivation in both popular mainstream and genre fiction. If your hero's life is at stake, virtually *anything* he does to preserve it will seem plausible to the reader, which makes this the easiest of all character motivations for the new writer to handle.

Self-preservation can be construed to mean preservation of one's self-image and self-respect. For instance, in Brian Garfield's *Death Wish,* the lead character is not driven entirely by a desire to revenge the murder of his wife. Her death at the hands of rapists leaves him feeling inadequate, helpless, and less of a man than he had always considered himself to be. He begins stalking street criminals in order to preserve his self-respect as well as to balance the scales for his wife.

Greed. This is not usually a hero's or a heroine's motivation, though it can be if—as in some popular suspense novels, most notably those by Donald Westlake and his alter ego, Richard Stark—the hero is a bandit. It *is* an excellent motivation for antagonists if it is supplemented with other motives to keep it from seeming cartoon-like. For example, if your villain is trying to destroy your hero financially in order to get control of the hero's business enterprises at a bargain price, greed might well be one of his primary motivations. But if he also hates the hero because the hero won the hand of a woman they both loved, then he is *also* motivated by jealousy, and he instantly becomes a more deeply drawn, believable, and interesting character. If you then show the reader what underlies this villain's greed—for instance, let's say that he was raised in abject poverty and his childhood was a nightmare of hunger and deprivation, which instilled in him an excessive, almost religious reverence for money—you have added yet another level of characterization and have made greed a complex and believable motivation. (Note: This "layering" of motivations is desirable not only when a character is driven by greed; regardless of his motivation—love, self-preservation, duty—he will be more *real* if he is shown to have complex needs, desires, and dreams.)

Self-discovery. The hero who sets out on a series of adventures primarily to test himself and to learn more about himself is very definitely a creature of "literary" fiction. Self-administered psychoanalysis, conscious striving for a better understanding of one's own mind, *can* be a viable motivation for a character in a popular mainstream or genre novel, but it should not be the *primary* motivation. In popular fiction, the hero should, for the most part, uncover truths about himself through his reaction to plot developments, not through any long, detailed soul-seaching.

Duty. In Shakespeare's day, duty was a valid motive for a writer's characters, but it is now somewhat dated. The masses no longer blindly give their loyalty to king and state—at least not in *this* country. For example, it is not sufficient to say that your detective or secret agent is investigating a case *only* because it is his job to do so. The reader finds little to empathize with in a character who is just doing his job. You must explain why he chose that job in the first place. Why would he *want* to take on the dirty and dangerous work of spying? Why would he *want* to be a homicide detective or a vice squad officer? What is there about him that makes him want to do these things; what need is satisfied; what psychological forces drove him into his profession? Therein lies his *real* motivation. (The aforementioned "layering" can help make duty a more believable character motivation than it otherwise might be. If your hero is a spy willing to die for his country, his selfless sense of duty might seem more real if we learn that his father was a no-good bum who deserted his family and left them to starve, thus creating in the hero a need to prove that his own sense of duty and responsibility is stronger than his father's.) Duty may still be used as a secondary factor in a character's behavior, but these days it cannot be his *only* concern.

Revenge. This was also a commonly used Shakespearean tool. Hamlet, for example, was in part motivated by a burning desire for revenge. In Shakespeare's time, it was often necessary for a family to revenge the murder of one of its own because there was little organized authority to handle such things. A mainstream novel set in more recent days, however, will take place in a social milieu in which society's revenge has pretty much replaced the family's revenge. Most people are content to allow police and judges to be the sole servants of justice, which makes revenge a somewhat dated motive for a hero or heroine. (Although, if the crime rate continues to climb rapidly in this country, we might witness a resurgence of vigilantism, which would invalidate what I've just said about revenge as a character motivation.)

At any time in history, even in current times, revenge is an excellent motivation for a villain. There's the story of the gunslinger who returns to Yuma after spending ten years in prison, intent on getting the sheriff and the judge who sent him to jail. There's the story of the gangster who vows and carries out revenge on the twelve members of the jury that convicted him. Or there's the story of the rejected lover, driven half-mad by jealousy, who seeks revenge upon the man who won the affection of the heroine. And many others.

Occasionally, a novel appears in which the author *does* successfully employ revenge as a motivation for the hero. Two that spring to mind are Brian Garfield's *Death Wish* and Justin Scott's *Shipkiller,* each of which deals with a man who is seeking vengeance for the cold-blooded murder of his wife. In books such as these, the hero is justified in taking his own revenge only if the police and the courts have utterly failed in their duties to society and to the victims of violent crime. That is exactly the case in both Mr. Garfield's book and in Scott's long adventure novel, and the reader can easily empathize with those heroes' anger, frustration, and terrible grief.

However, please note that neither of those books is truly a mainstream novel. *Death Wish* is strictly a thriller. It packs an emotional wallop, and it's a good, quick read, but it deals with characterization, background, and theme in the superficial manner of genre fiction. *Shipkiller* contains elements of the mainstream novel—most notably in its handling of background material—but again, its character-izations and its thematic structure never rise above those in a well-written genre novel. If you want to break through to the large, mainstream audience which can put your book on the bestseller lists, you should avoid using revenge as the primary motivation for your hero or heroine. Indeed, I cannot think of a single *mainstream* novel in which revenge is the protagonist's only—or even his central—reason for doing what he does.

Love, curiosity, self-preservation, greed, self-discovery, duty, revenge—those are not by any means the only character motivations the writer can call upon when trying to build a plausible story. My list was not meant to be definitive. But it does cover the most commonly used motivations in popular fiction and provides, I hope, a few useful suggestions.

Warning! No character should be motivated by something that is inconsistent with his basic personality. For example, if your hero is likeable and admirable, he can hardly be motivated by an insatiable greed for wealth and a maniacal lust for power. Likewise, your antagonist, if he is to be a fearsome character, should not be motivated by great, enduring love for the heroine.

9.

**Background
or
If your hero is eating
dinner in Moscow, you
better know that steak is
thirty bucks a pound; if he
is drinking *sake* in Tokyo,
you better know which
hand he should use to
hold the cup; and when
he is sunning on the
beach at Cape Cod,
remember that there
won't be palm trees.**

Background is locale, the geographic place in which a story is set. Background is ethnic culture. Background is social strata, the class of society to which the characters in the story belong and through which they move. Background is mechanical detail, such as whether or not a silencer can be attached to a revolver or only to a pistol. Background includes all of the many facts the author takes from the real world and inserts in his story in a quest for authenticity.

I have only eight suggestions to make about the development of background in a novel, but each of these scraps of knowledge was acquired through hard experience. I think new writers will find that they can save themselves a lot of time and effort in the long run by giving serious thought to these few but important pieces of advice.

1. *You can't get away with faking background details.* No matter how esoteric the subject about which you make a false statement—be it the classic patterns in Philippine basket weaving, the care and feeding of a platypus, the floor plan of the courthouse in downtown Tangier, or the inner workings of a Kalishnikov rifle—a small but significant percentage of your readership will be aware of your goof. If you fabricate a lot of "facts" on a wide variety of subjects, confident that no single reader could ever be knowledgeable enough to catch all your errors, you are only fooling yourself, for every reader will notice at least some mistakes, perhaps more of them than you might imagine. Every time a reader knows that you are faking a bit of background, your credibility slips a notch; when it slips two or three or four notches, you will lose that reader.

I am not saying that you must set your stories only in places of which you have extensive experience; neither am I telling you that you have to be an expert in every subject touched upon by your story. Extensive *secondhand* knowledge is usually good enough. With hard work and ingenuity, you can learn about even the most mundane details of life in any hamlet on earth, regardless of how distant and exotic it may be.

As I have mentioned, I once wrote a pseudonymous novel set largely in Kyoto, Japan. Never having been to Japan, I was forced to rely on secondhand sources for information about daily life in a Japanese city. I needed to know about Japanese food, table manners, music, art, nightlife, customs, social conventions, medical practices, architecture, and a hundred other things. I obtained nearly all of my background material from nonfiction books about Japan: histories, sociological treatises, eight or ten travel guides, at least a dozen voluminous full-color photographic studies of the country and its people, a book on Japan's railroads, a mapbook of the country with emphasis on the street layouts of the major cities, memoirs by famous Japanese, and other volumes.

I read one of the histories from cover to cover, for it dealt with the city, Kyoto, in which most of my story was set. I skimmed the other histories, reading only those sections bearing on the historical events that directly or indirectly shaped Kyoto. (Of course, if I had been writing historical fiction instead of a contemporary novel, I would have read *every* history book cover to cover. In historical fiction, history is a large part of the plot, and historical events appear in the manuscript. In my contemporary novel, the history of Japan was never revealed to the reader; I wanted to know about that history only so that I could have a better feel for modern Japan, an educated perspective from which to describe what Japan is like today.) I read the sociological treatises and the memoirs of famous Japanese from cover to cover because they revealed how the Japanese think, how their beliefs and attitudes and basic assumptions differ from ours. Often, the genre novelist makes the mistake of writing about people of other nations as if they were Americans with funny accents and a few charming, amusing customs; the mainstream novelist cannot get by with this superficial view of a foreign culture and expect to be widely read. The travel guides—Fodor's, Frommer's, Fielding's, and others—provided names and descriptions of restaurants in which my characters could eat, information about hotels and taxi fares and theaters and museums and entertainment districts where action scenes could be set to provide the greatest amount of local color and the most imaginative use of the Kyoto background. I never read any of the travel guides from first page to last, but I constantly referred to all of them for a host of small details. The full-color photographic studies of Japan allowed me to see—and therefore convincingly describe—the streets and buildings in which my scenes took place. The book on Japan's railroads was essential because I had a two-page scene on a train, and I wanted the reader to feel it was a *Japanese* train. The mapbook of city streets prevented me from unwittingly sending my characters on roundabout routes between two points, and their familiarity with Kyoto's layout added verisimilitude to every street scene in the novel. Without stacks of research books, I would have been utterly lost.

Furthermore at two or three spots in the novel, it was necessary, for the sake of authenticity, to have a character speak just a few lines of Japanese; to be able to write those lines of dialogue, I had to purchase and study a Japanese-English dictionary, a basic language primer, and a Japanese grammar book.

When my novel was finally published, I received a call from a friend of mine who lived for almost two years in Kyoto. He said, "My God, you never told me that *you* lived in Kyoto, too!" I told him I had never even visited Japan, except in spirit; at first he was reluctant to believe me. "But you *know* Kyoto," he said. "You've got it down just perfect in every detail." My friend's approbation not only tickles my ego, it also supports my contention that secondhand experience—if it is extensive enough, and if it is cleverly employed—can make an author appear to be a highly educated expert in *any* field or subject.

Warning! Very few reference books are perfect. It is always wise to cross-check every piece of background information, using two and preferably three sources.

Interviews with experts are also useful. Arthur Hailey employs this technique and makes voluminous notes about these conversations. One expert is, of course, never enough, for the information he gives you might be inaccurate or biased. You must cross-check one expert against another just as you would check one book against another.

I should also note that firsthand knowledge of a geographical background is always desirable. There is no better way to learn the sounds, the smells, the look, and the texture of a place—*if you are an observant and perceptive traveler* with sufficient inquisitiveness to see more of a place than the average tourist sees. Even if you are that special combination of detective and tourist, you should cross-check your observations against those of others and against the facts to be found in the kind of books I've mentioned, for it is always possible—especially in a very different culture from your own—that you will misunderstand or misinterpret the fine details of what you see.

Warning! There is a novelist—I will not mention his name—who has gone on record as advising writers to fake an obscure bit of background if it can't be uncovered in a few minutes with a reference book or two. I am a great fan of this writer's work; he has a brisk, clean, easygoing style that involves the reader, and he can tell a rousing story as well as anyone, usually with a large dollop of delightfully sly humor. If you enjoy his books as much as I do, and if you should come across his essay about writing background, don't let your fondness for his fiction lead you to accept his pronouncement about faking background details. As much as I like his novels, I have found in every one of them details that I knew to be wrong, and each time I stumbled into one of those errors, I was virtually catapulted out of the illusion of reality which the author had been striving to maintain. Keep this in mind: Although this writer's books are loads of fun, he has never had a novel that came close to being a major bestseller. Could it be because too many of his readers are jolted by fabricated "facts" and do not come back for his next book?

2. *All background material must be broken into small chunks and larded through the action.* An author can do nothing more boring than stop his story dead in its tracks to write a chapter on the history of Paris or a three-page essay on the methods by which a computer's security code can be bypassed or cracked. Background material, just like characterization, must always be unobtrusive. If you must feed the reader three pages of data about cracking a computer's security, do it in a suspenseful scene in which a character is actually sitting at a CRT terminal, breaking the code before our very eyes, while security guards are searching the building for him. Do *not* feed the reader all the facts first and *then* have the character make use of them. That is not only a boring technique; it is also redundant. Again, we return to that old saw that you are probably tired of hearing by now: Never forget that the reader just wants to *get on with it!*

3. *An exotic geographical-cultural background has advantages over a mundane setting.* For one thing, most readers find a story set in Hong Kong innately more intriguing than a story set in Cleveland. (Unless, of course, the reader lives in Hong Kong, in which case he might find Cleveland wildly exotic. However, if you wrote novels solely to appeal to residents of Hong Kong, you would be aiming at a hopelessly small market!) We have all felt the lure of far-off places; we imagine them filled with mystery and romance and surprise. That attitude is a deeply ingrained part of human nature, which holds that the grass is always greener (or at least more interesting) on the other side of the fence.

Furthermore, it is easier to write colorfully about an exotic background than it is to write colorfully about a mundane setting. If two authors of equal talent are working on two similar thrillers, one set in Pittsburgh and one in Paris, the fellow doing the French story is almost certain to come up with a more colorful, livelier tale than the one written by his colleague. Paris is ancient; Pittsburgh is not. On the streets of Paris, one can hear a dozen languages being spoken within a few blocks; Pittsburgh is *not* an international city. Paris is a boiling pot of international intrigue, a political crossroads for diplomats from all over the world, a jumping-off point for mercenaries on their way to Africa and Asia, a haven for defectors and deported political figures of all nationalities. Pittsburgh is none of those things. It should be obvious to any writer that Paris, not Pittsburgh, will give him the brightest colors and the widest range of shades with which to paint a dazzling background.

I do not mean to say that you should never set a story in an ordinary place. Some novels will demand Cleveland or Pittsburgh or Potato Town, Idaho, as a backdrop because those locales will be exactly right for certain stories. Obviously, if you were writing a multi-generational saga about a family that made a fortune in the steel industry, Pittsburgh would be one of the major stages for that drama. William Goldman's *Magic* is set largely in a bland, somewhat shabby, thinly portrayed Catskills resort area. That place—which was once the launching pad for scores of entertainers who eventually became famous—is the perfect background for the story of Corky Withers, a ventriloquist who is certifiably insane and who is acting out his violent impulses through his dummy, Fats, which he treats as a real person. The Catskills have sunk into the shabby state of depression that plagued Atlantic City prior to the advent of legalized gambling, and they function admirably as a symbol of broken dreams, lost chances, and unfulfilled promise; they offer a superb setting against which Corky, a performer who might have been hugely successful but for his psychological problems, sinks ever deeper into trouble, ruin, and madness.

Of course, if the writer works hard enough at digging up unusual background details, virtually any place can be made interesting if not fascinating. Every town and city is unique. If you are sufficiently perceptive to discover what makes it a special place, and if your talent is large enough to convey that specialness to the reader, even Cleveland can seem, at least to some degree, exotic. To accomplish such an amazing feat, one must be committed to extensive, exhaustive research. Research, research, research: That is the only piece of "how-to" advice that can help you to make the background strong when you are setting a mainstream novel in a mundane locale.

As an aside, it is worth noting that horror stories often *require* a very ordinary setting in order to achieve plausibility. The plot engines of horror novels—werewolves, vampires, ghosts, monsters—are usually so exotic to begin with that drawing an exotic geographical-cultural background would be like adding a layer of caviar to a chocolate-iced birthday cake. Stephen King's *'Salem's Lot* is set in a small, unremarkable Maine community. Jack Finney's classic *The Body Snatchers* takes place in Santa Mira, a sleepy California town that makes Peoria look like Xanadu and Sodom and Shangri-La, all rolled into one. Ira Levin's magnificent *Rosemary's Baby* does take place in New York, which usually qualifies as a colorful background, but Levin purposefully downplays that vibrant, bustling city. He does not go out of his way to tell you strange and intriguing things about New York; he paints a picture of Manhattan that is no deeper than one in a quickly written and hastily filmed television show. He wants the reader to see New York as a typical American city, a symbol of modern society and sophistication, but otherwise as nowhere really special. By setting his story in an ordinary place and by writing about ordinary people who hold ordinary jobs, the horror writer grounds the reader in gritty reality before shocking him with the appearance of blood-sucking demons or walking corpses or other fantastic developments. Once grounded, the reader is usually willing to accept the supernatural elements without a quibble.

4. *Do not hesitate to use a particular geographical-cultural background merely because it has been used often by other writers.* I have heard writers—both published and unpublished—say they wouldn't use a certain background because other writers had "exhausted" it. That's ridiculous. Hundreds of novelists have written well about Hong Kong, but that didn't stop James Clavell from tackling it in his massive *Noble House.* The shelves in bookstores groan under the weight of novels about Hollywood, but there are many writers and critics (and I am one of them) who feel that only Nathanael West's The Day of the Locust actually captures a truth about the movie business and the semi-mythical place we call "Hollywood." And West delineates only one facet of the truth. There are dozens of other aspects of the Hollywood story waiting for writers with talent and perception and vision. Before Gerald Green picked up his pen to write about both the medical profession and Brooklyn in The Last Angry Man, countless other novelists had written about both subjects, but Green's book was nevertheless a tremendous bestseller. No background can be exhausted by one book or a dozen books or a hundred; we live in a complex world, where virtually every subject is as multilayered as an onion. Besides, every writer's point of view is unique because every human being is unique; therefore, no two writers will ever see the same subject in exactly the same way, a fact that guarantees freshness no matter how often a background has been used.

When I sat down to begin Whispers, a large novel set in California (where I live), I wanted my background to be so rich and thoroughly developed that it would virtually become as important as any character in the story. I wanted California to be a living, breathing entity in my tale. I wasn't daunted by the fact that Joan Didion and John Dunne and others have written brilliantly about California. I wasn't intimidated by the fact that Raymond Chandler had created an exquisitely poetic, visual, true, and meaningful portrait of California. Nor did it ever occur to me that I could (or would have to) write better about California than those people had done. I simply knew that my vision of California would be not better but different because I am a much different person from Chandler, Didion, and Dunne.

Likewise, you are a very different person from all others, a writer unlike any other, and when you set out to write your California novel, it will be nothing like mine. I have said this before, in various ways, and I will be saying it again before I reach the end of this book, but it bears repeating: When you come right down to it, all the stories have been told countless times before, and all the settings have been used again and again, and the primary thing any writer has to sell is his special voice, his unique point of view, his *individuality* as it is reflected by and refracted in his fiction.

5. *If you write a novel in which you thoroughly explore the background of an occupation, a business, or an industry, you do not necessarily need a richly drawn geographical-cultural background as well.* In this regard, consider Arthur Hailey's *Hotel.* That novel is busy with a multitude of plots and subplots, involving a large cast of colorful characters, all set against the background of a major hotel in New Orleans. From Mr. Hailey, we (the readers) learn how a professional hotel-room thief goes about obtaining keys and successfully pulling off his burglaries. We learn how a hotel detective stalks such a thief. We learn how a hotel kitchen operates, and we discover that a surprising number of minor crises can arise there. We learn how a large building is heated and cooled, how a well-trained staff deals with belligerent guests, how a hotel doctor deals with medical emergencies peculiar to hotel guests. In several scenes dealing with the maintenance and repair of the elevators, we learn how those machines work—and all of this information is made interesting and even urgent because Hailey uses subtle foreshadowing techniques to let us know that something horrible is going to happen to people in one of those elevators before the book ends. We learn hundreds of other interesting tidbits about hotel management in the course of the novel, but we learn very little about New Orleans, only the bare essentials and a bit of color having to do with the nature of graveyards in bayou country. New Orleans is, of course, a potentially exotic geographical-cultural background; it is the city of Creole culture, the city that gave birth to jazz, the city of the Mardi Gras. However, if Hailey had made use of this rich stew of material, the dish he finally served up to his readers would have been—just like that caviar-coated birthday cake—too much of too many good things. Besides, *Hotel* is already a large novel; with a full measure of geographical background added, it would be long enough to discourage some readers.

In nearly all of his novels, Hailey forsakes thorough exploration of geographical-cultural backgrounds in favor of occupational-cultural backgrounds or the in-depth examination of an industry. *Airport* is set in Chicago, but it would be essentially the same book if it were set in New York City or Boston or Philadelphia. *Overload*, a surprisingly engaging and involving tour of a major public utility, would be every bit as readable and dramatic if it took place in Massachusetts instead of California. In a novel of this sort, the geographical-cultural background ceases to be important because the industry or occupation with which the book is concerned *becomes the entire world for the duration of the novel*. The hotel in *Hotel* becomes the universe; the microcosm becomes the macrocosm and embodies all of human experience within its narrow perimeters. The reader doesn't give a hoot what happens beyond the doors of the hotel, for it is in that building that all the plot lines tie together, and it is in that building that all the characters move toward their own personal crises, and it is in that building that the thematic purpose is arrived at and revealed.

6. *You must be careful not to stuff so much background material into your novel that you inadvertently transform it into a travelogue.* If you've done even a moderate amount of research, you will discover that you have far more background detail than you can comfortably include in your novel. You must choose for inclusion only the most interesting details and primarily those which are pertinent to your plot and theme. No one can tell you how to identify those bits and pieces worth inclusion, for the answer to that question varies radically from novel to novel and from subject to subject. However, here are a couple of suggestions to guide you in making your choices.

First, never stop the story cold for long passages of background material. If you find you've gotten away from describing the action for more than a page at a time, you have slipped into travelogue writing. Integrate your background facts with the action. In Michael Crichton's delightful *The Great Train Robbery*, a staggering amount of detail about Victorian England is painlessly brought to the reader in short paragraphs interwoven with the planning and execution of a daring robbery. I strongly recommend that you read his novel as a prime example of how to keep your background material from lumping together in long, dreary passages. In my pseudonymous novel with a Japanese setting, I knew I had to say a great deal about Japanese food and table customs, for much of the Japanese character and philosophy is expressed through that society's attitudes toward food. If you understand the methods and reasons behind the rituals of a Japanese kitchen and a Japanese table, you are on your way to understanding all of the most fundamental things about the Japanese world view; their culinary customs and habits form a microcosm reflecting every aspect of the entire Japanese experience, and this is true of no other culture on earth, not even that of the French. In order to tell the reader all about Japanese food and table customs without boring him, I broke up this data into dozens and dozens of pieces and spread them throughout several meals in several different chapters, and in each of those scenes, the meal was incidental to the conversation between the characters who were at the table. The dramatic conversations which had to be written in order to impart plot and character information to the reader could have taken place anywhere, but since I needed to squeeze in information about Japanese cuisine, I simply set some of the dialogues in restaurants. Because the characters were discussing actions they were going to take to deal with their terrible trouble, and because those conversations all contained character conflict, they were inherently gripping; the details of the cuisine and table rituals could be added in small doses, between tense exchanges of dialogue, adding color without slowing anything down. James Clavell did the same sort of thing (though much better than I did it) in *Shogun*. That novel contains a long tea ceremony rich with background detail, and yet it reads smoothly and quickly because the two characters at the tea ceremony have a great deal of bad blood between them, and their conversation contains an underlying hostility that grips the reader. Clavell has a gift for infusing every scene with unobtrusive background detail, and I urge you to read his work, especially *Tai Pan*, to see how this is done by a master.

Second, if you make certain that at least 90 percent of your background details have a direct connection to your plot and/or thematic structure, you will encounter no difficulty deciding which tidbits to include and which to leave out. For instance, if your story is about a clever financier with a plan to defraud a multinational bank, and if the chief locale of your story is Switzerland, then it would be pertinent to include every scrap of data you could find about the mysterious Swiss banking system, but it would not seem wise to include reams of material about the making of Swiss chocolate.

7. *A thoughtful choice of background can contribute to the suspense in a novel.* For example, if you set a story in San Francisco, and if you know that your hero and villain will have a face-to-face showdown at the end of the novel, you should carefully consider a list of famous San Francisco landmarks with an eye toward letting the background sharpen the drama of that showdown. Sure, you could have them fight it out in an ordinary room. But wouldn't it be more exciting if they did combat down at Fisherman's Wharf, along the docks and gangways, perhaps even jumping from one fishing boat to another? If your story is set in New York, why not have the showdown—or another action scene earlier in the novel—take place on a moving, nearly empty subway train, rather than on an ordinary street? If the scene is Washington, D.C., and the plot calls for a shootout in a parking lot, why not shift that violent encounter (if at all possible) to the Lincoln Memorial, where the hero and villain can blast away at each other while dodging among the giant pillars supporting the roof of that structure? Remember how Alfred Hitchock structured the big showdown in *North by Northwest*: It takes place high on the carved stone face of Thomas Jefferson at the Mount Rushmore National Monument! King Kong wasn't gunned down in an alley; he was mugged while clinging to the top of the Empire State Building. Evan Hunter sets the chilling, suspenseful, penultimate scene of *Come Winter* high on a mountainside; so

does "Trevanian" in his bestselling *Eiger Sanction*. The showdown in my own novel *Night Chills*—which took place in a small town in Maine—could have transpired on Main Street or in a meadow or virtually anywhere, but I chose to set it in a lumber mill, amidst large, noisy, and dangerous machines, where the background contributed to the tension. If you write a thriller set in Venice and fail to use its canals for at least one suspenseful sequence, you might as well transplant the plot to Peoria.

8. *A rich background, peppered with interesting and arcane facts, is more important in popular mainstream fiction than it is in most genre novels.* Science fiction is the only genre that frequently delivers extensively detailed backgrounds. Westerns? No. As a group, Western writers do not tend to execute thoroughly realized backgrounds; most of them traffic in the myth of the Old West, not in the reality of history. The exception, of course, is Louis L'Amour, whose grasp of background material, coupled with his narrative skill, has made him the most popular Western novelist of all time. If you compare the most successful mainstream novels—works like M. M. Kaye's *The Far Pavilions,* Collins and LaPierre's *The Fifth Horseman,* James Clavell's *Shogun,* Arthur Hailey's *Airport,* Mario Puzo's *The Godfather*—with even the best of genre fiction, you will see that the backgrounds in those mainstream novels are more convincingly drawn than any in category fiction, including the superbly portrayed locales in L'Amour's novels. If you want to break through to the large, mainstream audience, you must give background development more than cursory attention, and you must consider the first seven suggestions in this list of eight. For other suggestions about background as it applies to plot, see Chapter 4.

10.

**Grammar and Syntax
or
If you think grammar is
just a small child's
mispronunciation of
"grandmother," and if you
think syntax is a tax that
the church levies on sin,
maybe you should
consider becoming a
nuclear physicist or a
neurosurgeon or just
about anything at all
except a novelist.**

Not long ago I received a manuscript from a friend of a friend, an unpublished writer who was sure he was going to smash his way to the top of the bestseller lists with his maiden novel. I'll call him Bubba, though that was not his name. Bubba said that writing a novel was the easiest thing he had ever done. "I just sat down and typed," he said. "The story just flowed off the top of my head. I can't understand why *everyone* doesn't write novels." Bubba wanted me to help him find an agent and a publisher.

In the first chapter of that novel, Bubba commits virtually every grammatical error known to English-speaking people. In the opening sentence he writes: "If Yancy was king of England, he would still be insecure." Because the introductory adverb clause of that sentence contains a statement that is contrary to fact, correct usage demands the subjunctive "were" in place of "was." In prose dense enough to shield a reader from nuclear radiation, Bubba needs only one page to give us "if it was him" for "if it was he"; "one of them are" for "one of them is"; "shouting at each other" for "shouting at one another" (more than two people being involved in the argument); "He couldn't help but feel" for "He couldn't help feeling"; and so on.

I forced myself to read twenty dreadful pages of Bubba's epic, trying to give it a chance to win my attention, but I found each page sloppier than the one preceding it. I returned the script to the author with a note expressing—in kindlier terms than Bubba deserved—my opinion that the book was not in a publishable state and could not be elevated to that status. I gently suggested that Bubba purchase a good grammar book as well as Jacques Barzun's *Simple & Direct,* an excellent guide to the art of writing what you mean.

When reading the work of a new writer, especially one as yet unpublished, I keep in mind that he is inexperienced, and I am able, therefore, to forgive him for crude narrative technique. I am able to forgive him for deficiencies in characterization. I am able to forgive him for shaky plotting and for an overblown style that screams, "Look, Ma, I can *write!*" I am able to forgive him for all of those blunders as well as for many other ineptitudes because I know that virtually all of us begin our careers as awkward goslings; a new writer deserves the benefit of the doubt from readers and critics, a chance to learn from his mistakes and foolishnesses. If he has a modicum of talent and a vast reservoir of determination and a desire to be a *good* novelist, even the ugliest of ducklings is likely to grow up to be a swan.

There are, however, two mistakes for which I will forgive no writer, regardless of whether he is new or long-established at his trade. First, faking background details is inexcusable. Second, complete ignorance of English grammar is unforgivable. When he writes a novel, an author is imposing upon other people by hoping, suggesting, and even sometimes explicitly requesting that they read his book, and when he makes that imposition without first at least learning the basic rules of grammar, he is being arrogant and stupid. Gathering background material and writing grammatical prose are not creative tasks; they are strictly mechanical processes. The new writer does not need to have extensive experience in his craft in order to do conscientious research or to write prose that meets minimum standards of correct English usage. He doesn't even need any formal education before he can do these things well, for both of these skills can be self-taught. Failure in either task has only one explanation: laziness.

I do *not* mean that every piece of fiction must be free of even the most minor grammatical errors before it can be published. The English language is a difficult beast to master; few writers ever gain complete, unfaltering control of it. Human beings are fallible, after all. I am sure that my writing in this textbook will provide you with a few unintended examples of my own fallibility. I work hard to make my prose clear and grammatical, but I do not don a hair shirt or flagellate myself when I make a mistake. Day by day, week by week, novel by novel, I attempt to learn more about language and its proper usage.

The process of becoming more literate reminds me of that chair-and-wall example which is used by many mathematics teachers to illustrate theories of finite and infinite distances. I am certain you must remember it from your school days: If a chair is ten feet from a wall, and if you move the chair x number of times, always putting it closer to the wall, always moving it exactly half the distance that still separates it from the wall, how many moves will it take until the chair is actually touching the wall? The answer is that, in theory, the chair will *never* touch the wall, not even after a million moves, for there will always be half of *something* separating the two objects. That is how I feel about the prospect of one day attaining a perfect state of grace in matters of grammar; there will always be *something* separating me from that wall. Anyway, perfect grammar is not the primary thing I'm striving to achieve with my fiction, and I do not recommend that you set it as your own highest goal, for if you focus too intently on grammar, you risk paying too little attention to some of the many other essential elements of fine fiction. The important thing is for the writer to be aware of and to have respect for the rules of grammar, so that his meaning is communicated to the reader without being seriously distorted.

Warning! The new writer should not expect his copyeditors to strip away his shabby ignorance and clothe him in the image of an erudite linguist. I have heard several would-be novelists say something of this sort: "Well, as long as I can tell a good story, I don't have to be a grammarian. The publisher will hire someone to fix up my English." One gapes in amazement at any person capable of making a statement like that, especially when, in the very next breath, he has the gall to refer to himself as a writer. Besides, although publishers *do* employ copyeditors partly to keep authors from making jackasses of themselves, a distressingly large number of copyeditors know less about English grammar than they know about the mating habits of penguins.

On the average only four out of ten copyeditors appear to be fully qualified for the work they are hired to perform. That statistic is based on my own experience with forty copyeditors over the past twelve years. More often than I care to think about, I have been forced to re-edit a copyedited manuscript or set of galleys in order to restore correct grammar after my prose was "fixed" by a copyeditor with a weak grasp of English usage. This chore is tedious and thankless; worse, it is sometimes wasted effort, for the publisher occasionally decides to go with the copyeditor's changes in spite of the fact that the author has demonstrated the superiority of his own knowledge of grammar and syntax. I suppose that, having paid for the copyeditor's advice, the publishing house feels it must take that advice, right or wrong, in order to get its money's worth. I am well aware that's not a *rational* explanation for knowingly setting incorrect English in type, but it is the only explanation that has ever occurred to me. Whatever the reasoning behind these bizarre decisions, several publishers have issued "fixed" versions of my books that have caused me embarrassment. The changes have ranged from such minor but irritating things as the substitution of the substandard "anymore" for "any more" all the way to more serious tinkering with verb tenses and pronoun-antecedent agreement. When an author is embarrassed by his own mistakes, at least he learns from that embarrassment; however, there is no equal compensation when he must take the rap for somebody else's ignorance.

Upon selling his novel, the new writer should insist that he be sent the copyedited manuscript before it is delivered to the typesetter. This will make it possible for him to correct any serious mangling of his prose before those grotesqueries are committed to print, after which it is infinitely more difficult to get them changed. Don't be surprised if your editor tells you that the copyedited manuscript cannot be supplied to you. This disquieting announcement is usually followed by calm assurance that you can make any changes you want in the galleys, restoring your original prose if the copyeditor (or anyone else) has indeed messed with it. There are three problems with this approach: 1) Comparing typeset text on galley pages to the original typescript, in a diligent search for changes, is a tedious, mind-numbing task, requiring days of concentrated labor, whereas the changes can be spotted and carefully considered and decided upon, all within an hour or two, if one is dealing with the copyedited manuscript. 2) Publishers do not always make the changes that a writer requests on the galley pages; sometimes they simply ignore his requests in order to save the expense of resetting type. 3) If large blocks of the galleys must be reset to restore the author's original prose, and if the publisher actually allows this to be done, the typesetter will usually make several mistakes in the course of his work, and these errors may not be noticed until finished books are in the stores. To spare yourself those agonies, you should always pressure your editor to supply you with the copyedited manuscript. If you cannot win this concession on your first or second book, don't surrender; keep applying pressure. Eventually, you will win the right to protect your prose and your reputation.

Why on earth (I hear you asking) do publishers resist sending copyedited manuscripts to writers? Aren't they concerned about good grammar and syntax? Aren't they concerned about preserving the author's style and vision? Well, publishers usually say that sending out the copyedited manuscript would delay the production schedule and force a postponement of the publication date. In nearly all cases, this is untrue. With virtually every project, there is a six- to ten-month gap between the author's delivery of the final, revised script and the actual printing and distribution of the finished book. In that six- to ten-month period, there is certainly a week or two that can be spared for the author's examination of the copyedited manuscript. (Jove Books once managed to get copyedited script, galleys, and page-proofs into my hands for my approval, even though they were on an insanely tight schedule that allowed only seven weeks from the delivery of the revised script to the printing and binding of finished copies. They were running a promotion for the novel which required 2,500 advance copies five months ahead of the actual publication date, yet they had the intelligence and the grace to properly involve the author every step of the way. If they could do that on such a frantic schedule, *any* publisher with six to ten months can surely do as well.) I believe there are basically three reasons why some publishers are so stubborn in this matter: 1) They don't care enough about maintaining standards and providing a quality product, and they are contemptuous of people who do care; cynicism is a widespread and pernicious disease; 2) They like to play power politics with authors; 3) Once a script is in their hands, some publishers actually begin to think of it as their creation, as if the author is nothing more than a messenger boy who brings novels to their offices now and then.

I have given all this space to the subject of copyediting because most of the good writers of my acquaintance suffered the shock, hurt, and humiliation of seeing their prose appear in a sullied version upon the publication of their first novels. Every writer I know has at some point in his career lost days and frequently weeks of work time dealing with anger, frustration, and despair that is engendered by having one's name appear on a book filled with clumsy syntax and illiterate grammar *that is not one's own handiwork*. This is a danger of which every writer should be aware, but few are ever warned.

Fight for your grammar if you know it to be correct. Fight for your syntax. Fight for your *style*. Fight in a gentlemanly (or ladylike) fashion. Be calm about it. Be reasonable. Be erudite. But for God's sake, *fight!*

I am happy to report that, for the past couple of years, my manuscripts have been assigned to thoughtful, well-educated copyeditors. However, no matter how long this good fortune continues, even if I am blessed with brilliant copyeditors for the next thirty years, I will never forget the pain that others caused me. It is for this reason that I warn the new writer to be well-grounded in the rules of grammar and syntax. You must not expect others to clean up your sloppy act; you must work hard to keep it clean yourself. *No one cares half so much about your work and your future as you do.* If you don't care enough to write well, you are destined to fail, and you deserve to fail.

All right. I admit: There is a chance you can get an ungrammatical novel published. It happens all the time. But if you go into the marketplace with four hundred pages of illiterate maunderings, you are starting with one strike against you. Ungrammatical writing makes your fiction more difficult to read; if it becomes *too* difficult to read, no editor will buy it.

I own seven grammar books, and I keep them all near my desk. I have never found a single text that answers every question about English usage. I recommend that you stock your shelves with a variety of reference works on grammar.

I own half a dozen dictionaries, but there are only two that I can countenance. The first is the *Oxford English Dictionary*, which is the finest dictionary ever compiled. It is the final authority on our language, and its support of your word choices is the best ammunition you can fire at a recalcitrant copyeditor. I own the compact, two-volume *Oxford*, which is printed in such small type that it comes with a magnifying glass. We are currently remodeling our house; and when we are at last finished with that messy project, I will have sufficient space in my office for the standard twelve-volume edition of the *Oxford*, which contains neither more nor less than the two-volume edition, but which can be consulted sans magnifier. As a handier backup to the *Oxford*, I recommend the *American Heritage Dictionary*. It is not as permissive as other American dictionaries, and though it is not as large as some other volumes on the market, it is far more reliable than its competitors. (As I write this, the *Oxford American Dictionary* has been released; it's from the same people who brought you the aforementioned *Oxford English Dictionary*, which means it is of very high quality indeed. However, I feel that it makes too many concessions to unjustifiable American usages and is somewhat less reliable an authority than the *Oxford English Dictionary*. Even if you are a patriotic, red-white-and-blue-blooded American writer, I would still recommend you consider the *O.E.D.* as the final arbiter of word choices.)

I have already mentioned *Simple & Direct: A Rhetoric for Writers* by Jacques Barzun. This wonderful book is not only a fine guide to effective writing, it is also *humorous*.

Finally, I urge you to purchase a copy of *Paradigms Lost: Reflections on Literacy and Its Decline* by John Simon. Reading and re-reading this witty, trenchant, uncompromising writer will keep you humble. He keeps *me* humble, anyway.

11.

**Style
or
You can paint like
Rembrandt or Grandma
Moses and be
acclaimed in either
case; but if you paint by
the numbers like my
Aunt Matilda, no
museum is going to
hang your pictures of
flowers and sailing
ships.**

Writing about style is rather like writing about love; in both cases, words cannot convey a complete understanding, for "style" and "love" are best defined by the feelings they inspire. One of my dictionaries tells me that style is "(in a literary composition) the mode and form of expression, as distinguished from the content." Does that clear everything up for you? No, I didn't think it would. I don't think *I* can make it clear, either. The best I can do is offer some thoughts on the subject and give you some rather mechanical suggestions about writing techniques that can help you attain a smooth style. As for creating an *individualistic* style that is uniquely yours, that is something you must do on your own; your style will gradually rise out of your own soul; no one can teach it to you.

Dialogue

Many new writers think—erroneously—that fiction should be a mirror of reality. Actually, it should act as a sifter to *refine* reality until only the essence is before the reader. This is nowhere more evident than in fictional dialogue. In real life, conversation is often roundabout, filled with general commentary and polite rituals. In fiction, the characters must always get right to the point when they talk. For example, if one of your characters has been threatened by a psychotic killer and is sure his house is being watched at night, he would not approach a neighbor for confirmation of his fears in this natural but extended manner:

Jack Moffet hesitated, then knocked on the Halseys' front door.

In a moment, Bill Halsey answered the knock. "Why, Jack! How are you, you old sonofagun?"

"Fine, fine," Moffet said, though he wasn't fine at all.

"Come on in."

Jack followed Halsey into the quiet of the front hallway and then to the living room where Lena Halsey was sitting in an easy chair reading the evening paper.

"Look who's here, Lena," Bill said.

"Jack! We haven't seen you in a couple of weeks."

"Yes, I have been busy."

"Sit down," Bill said.

Jack took a seat.

"Can I get you coffee or anything?" Lena asked.

"No thanks," Jack said.

"It's past coffee time," Bill said. "I'm going to make myself something, so you might as well join me."

"Scotch, then," Jack said. "On the rocks."

When they had their drinks, Bill said, "Now, what brings you over here after two weeks of being a hermit?"

"I have a problem," Jack said. "Maybe you can help me with it."

And so on. Though a real life conversation would run something like that, it is not adequate for fiction. You must trim and get to the point:

Jack Moffet hesitated, then knocked on the Halseys' front door.

In a moment, Bill Halsey answered the knock. "Jack! How are you? We haven't seen you in weeks."

"Actually," Moffet said, "I'm not too good, Bill."

"Oh?" Halsey said, ushering him into the living room. "What's the problem?"

Jack nodded to Lena, Bill's wife, and said, "I may sound like a paranoid, but I honestly believe someone is trying to kill me. I think they've been watching my house at night, waiting to build up their nerve."

That's more to the point. However, you can go overboard when compressing dialogue. Avoid something as hasty as this:

> Jack Moffet hesitated, then knocked on the Halseys' front door. In a moment, Bill Halsey answered the knock. Before he could say anything, Moffet said, breathlessly, "Someone is trying to kill me, Bill. I need your help!"

Dialogue is essential to the rhythm of a story, and few novels are bought that contain less than 20 or 30 percent dialogue. A book filled with heavy, narrative paragraphs is not as psychologically appealing to the browsing book buyer as one in which the narrative is broken regularly by sprightly stretches of short, conversational exchanges between characters.

However, a thirty-page section of dialogue can become as boring as thirty pages of long, leaden narrative paragraphs. Sometimes, in mystery and suspense novels when the hero finally explains how a situation is to be resolved or when he identifies the killer for the enlightenment of the other characters, the writer must present a great deal of information as dramatically as possible. In order not to bore the reader with page-long soliloquies by the hero, you can interrupt the hero by having other characters challenge his facts, his conclusions, or pose other questions for him to answer. And, if the reader has already been shown the killer's identity and how the hero arrived at his conclusions, you will not want to repeat everything verbatim to enlighten the other characters. In a situation like this, you can employ indirect dialogue to sum up what has already been shown. For example:

> Joe Black waited until they were all seated in the drawing room, then, succinctly, told them how Mrs. Housel had been murdered, who the killer was, and why the crime had been committed.

Direct dialogue is preferable in every case except these:

1) when one character must tell another of an event the reader has already seen, as in the example above; 2) when one character must explain to another character something which the reader does not have to hear in detail ("Joe Black told Lord Randolph how to load and use the pistol if he should need it"); and 3) when a long section of direct dialogue could be made more rhythmic and interesting by the use of a few lines of indirect dialogue, as in this example:

> He got to his feet a moment before Tilly entered the room, and he smiled at her, weakly. He was surprised he could smile at all.
> "Are you all right?" she asked.
> "Yes, Tilly."
> "What was that noise?"
> "A shot." He had decided to hide nothing from her.
> She was shocked. "A shot?"
> "Yes." He pointed to the broken glass and said, "It came through the window."
> "Are you hurt?"
> "No, no," he said. "I dropped out of sight when I saw him standing there, just before he pulled the trigger."
> "For heaven's sake, before *who* pulled the trigger?" she asked, her elfin face drawn up in a knot of tight lines.
> "It was Richard," he said.
> "Why would he want to kill you?"
> As quickly as he could, he told her why, told her everything he had learned last night.
> She sat down in the nearest chair. "It's hard to believe!"
> "I found it hard to believe too, at first."
> "If he means to kill you, he means to kill me as well."
> He agreed.

The lines "As quickly as he could . . ." and "He agreed" are examples of indirect dialogue mixed with direct to give a more varied tone.

Another thing: Don't identify the speaker after every line of dialogue unless that is absolutely necessary for the sake of clarity. Consider this exchange between two characters:

"Did he hurt you?" Jack asked worriedly.
"No," Sandy said. She was shaking.
"But his knife—"
"I managed to knock it out of his hand."
"My God."
"I'm just bruised."
"Did you see what he looked like?"
"He was big. Dark hair."
"What color were his eyes?"
"Gray. They were spooky, too."
"Did he have any scars?"
"Yeah. Now that you mention it . . . at the right corner of his mouth. It was a little half-moon mark."
"Great!" Jack said. "This is the first time we've been able to get a description of the creep. The other women he's attacked never got a look at his face."

Notice that most of those exchanges are not identified with the names of the speakers. When only two characters are involved in a conversation you should not need to attach a dialogue tag—he said, she said, or something similar—to every line of the conversation in order to make it clear who is saying what to whom. If you *do* need to identify every line in such a scene, then something is woefully wrong with your dialogue; it should be rewritten and re-rewritten until it can stand by itself.

When you've got three or more people speaking within one scene, you will have to use substantially more dialogue tags than in a one-on-one exchange. However, regardless of the number of characters involved in a conversation, do not expend a lot of thought and energy searching for synonyms to replace the word "said." Never, never, *never*, write something like this:

"Did he hurt you?" Jack asked worriedly.
"No," Sandy gasped. She was shaking.

"But his knife—"

"I managed to knock it out of his hand," she quaked.

"My God!" he exclaimed.

"I'm just bruised," she assured him.

"Did you see what he looked like?"

"He was big. Dark hair."

"What color were his eyes?" Jack queried.

"Gray," she declared. "They were spooky, too."

"Did he have any scars?" Jack probed.

"Yeah. Now that you mention it . . . at the right corner of his mouth. It was a little half-moon mark."

"Great!" Jack erupted jubilantly.

Gasped, quaked, exclaimed, queried, declared, probed, erupted—those and even more offensive substitutes for the word "said" are found frequently in the manuscripts of new writers. Such clumsy substitutes merely interrupt the smooth flow of the prose and add nothing but an unwelcome note of melodrama. Ninety percent of the time, if dialogue tags are needed at all, "said" and "asked" are sufficient. The other 10 percent of the time, when a somewhat stronger word seems called for, the writer can usually get by with a forceful but not exotic verb: shouted, called, replied, insisted. The use of dialogue tags like "quaked," "exclaimed," and "erupted" is a sure sign that the writer is either an amateur or an unfortunate sod who has absolutely no ear for the rhythms of language.

I believe there are four reasons why new writers often resort to exotic dialogue tags: 1) They simply don't know any better; they have not developed a sufficiently sensitive ear to be able to hear how such substitutes for "said" jolt and even derail the reader. 2) They think that repeatedly using "said" is dull and that employing colorful substitutes shows how clever they are. In reality, it shows only that they know how to use a thesaurus. Listen, you do not *want* too much variety in your dialogue tags, for that only calls attention to them; and when you call attention to the tags, that is like grabbing the reader, shaking him, and saying, "This isn't a *real* conversation between *real* people. It's only dialogue in a novel; it's all made up." Exotic dialogue tags shatter the illusion of reality into which the reader has allowed you to draw him. 3) Many new writers seem to think that a melodramatic tag can make the dialogue more exciting. This does not work. If it isn't clear from context that the characters are involved in an exciting scene, then the entire scene desperately needs to be reworked. It can't be improved merely by tacking on colorful dialogue tags. 4) New writers often are afraid their readers will not perceive the tone of voice in which a line of dialogue is spoken and will therefore fail to grasp the speaker's emotional/mental condition. However, if an exchange of dialogue is meant to be tense, freighted with fear and rage and other strong emotions, those feelings must be inherent in the dialogue itself, in the speakers' choices of words, in the way they phrase their thoughts. We must hear the rage and the fear without the assistance of gaudy dialogue tags. If we can't hear it, then the dialogue is poorly written and needs to be polished until it has the desired effect.

Warning! You can find published novels in which authors use one flashy dialogue tag after another. Don't send me a list of those authors, please. I didn't tell you that the frequent use of such tags would prevent you from being published. I only said that they indicate the author is an amateur or that he lacks the sensitivity to appreciate the musical qualities of language. Books full of inept dialogue tags get published all the time. Of course they do. Not all published writers are *good* writers.

Clichés

You cannot produce stylish prose if it is weighed down with leaden clichés. If your hero is "as proud as a peacock" and "hungry enough to eat a horse" and "as wise as an owl," and if your story opens on a "dark and stormy night," you are in trouble. Clichés are used by writers who are too lazy or too short of talent to think of fresh, interesting ways to say things. Clichés are a sort of shorthand which allows writers to keep writing without pausing to think.

Warning! Even if you are conscious of the need to avoid clichés, they are such pernicious things that you will probably use one now and then without realizing it. When doing your final draft and again when reading galleys, make cliché-hunting one of your primary tasks.

Simplicity

Less is more. Five adjectives in one sentence are better than six; four adjectives are better than five; three are better than four; two are better than three. . . . By using fewer words to obtain the effects you desire, you will force yourself to use more accurate and more powerful words than you otherwise might have done.

Communication is the primary function of the novelist, and the kind of prose that most successfully communicates ideas is that which is simple and direct. You can't entertain the reader if you can't communicate the story line to him with ease. You can't inspire the reader if you can't communicate your thematic intentions in easily grasped terms. You can't affect your reader emotionally if your prose is so dense that he becomes bogged down in it. Anything that interferes with communication—excessive adjectives and adverbs, overly complicated phrasing, too elaborate metaphors and similes included *solely* because the writer is showing off—should be discarded.

(Of course good prose contains vivid metaphors, similes, and other striking images. A novel would be flat and dull without them. But if you find yourself using such devices in every third sentence, or if your similes become so involved that you need a full page to present—or explain—one of them, you have ceased to communicate with your readership.)

I am reminded of the anecdote that journalism teachers traditionally recount for their students. It concerns a city editor who sent an inexperienced cub reporter to cover the Johnstown flood. After waiting hours and hours for the young reporter's coverage to start coming in over the wire, the editor was close to apoplexy. What was taking the cub so long? Finally, the teletype began to clatter, and the kid's story, ten thousand words long, began to print out. It contained dismayingly few facts and was composed in a melodramatic style hardly suited to newspaper reportage. The first sentence over the wire was: "God sits tonight in judgment at Johnstown." The city editor was furious but not without a sense of humor. He immediately sent his own wire to the cub reporter: "Forget flood. Interview God."

Now, I am certainly not suggesting that your fiction should be as spare and colorless as journalism or even as straightforward as nonfiction. As an art form, fiction is superior to all varieties of nonfiction because the novelist can go inside characters' minds, which journalists can never do. Novelists can be everywhere at once in a story, viewing every event firsthand, a power given to no reporter. A novelist can stack the cards, slant the events, twist and shape the entire story so that every word of it carries the message he wishes to spread. No good reporter ever slants his story to support his own preconceived opinion. (I'm ruling out those "journalists" who indulge in so-called "advocacy journalism," for they are not reporters at all, even if they do work for some of this country's leading newspapers; they are propagandists.) When I stress the need for simplicity in your fiction, I am talking about pruning the gaudy metaphors; I am not suggesting doing away with them altogether. I'm telling you to carefully select the best adjectives to convey your meaning; I am not advocating the elimination of adjectives altogether. Hemingway's *The Old Man and the Sea* is a simple tale, simply told, yet it is a thousand times more powerful than any journalistic account of a similar incident could ever be.

Transitions

Well-crafted transitions contribute to a smooth, readable style. Reams have been written about the transition, most of it to the confusion of new writers. Transitions can be easily handled; any mistakes you may be making with them can be easily corrected.

The transition is the change from one scene to another in a dramatic narrative; it usually involves moving your characters from one place to another or from one time to another. By stepping in at the end of the following scene, we can see a *poorly done* transition:

"Are you going to just sit there like a stone?" Lou asked her, looming over her where she sat in the big easy chair.

She didn't answer him. She looked straight ahead, her eyes on the wall behind him, her lip trembling but her determination otherwise unbetrayed.

"I don't have to take this, and I'm not going to," he said, turning away from her. "I can always find some- one else—someone who *will* talk to me."

Still, she sat, silent.

"Damn you," he snapped, crossing the small room, slamming the big oaken door behind him.

He went down the steps and out into the clear spring morning, walked two blocks down Elm Ave- nue to the bus stop, where he caught the 9:45 for town. He rode there without incident, brooding over the scene with Rita, got off at Market Street, and went to his favorite bar on the square.

Max, the bartender, wasn't as moody as Rita had been. He was willing to talk. In fact, he had some interesting news. "Selma's been in here the last cou- ple of days, Lou. She's been asking around about you."

The longest paragraph in the example is essentially all transition, getting Lou from one place to another. It stalls the story because it adds nothing.

It should have been handled this way:

Still, she sat, silent.

"Damn you," he snapped, crossing the small room, slamming the big oaken door behind him.

Thirty minutes later, he was in his favorite bar on the square downtown. Max, the bartender, wasn't as moody as Rita had been. He was willing to talk. . . .

As soon as one scene is over, you should lead your reader into the next, with no excess prose between them. The details of how the character got from here to there do absolutely nothing for the story except retard it.

Another popular way of changing scenes is by using the space break, a blank space on the page between the blocks of print to indicate where one scene ends and another begins. A film director might call this a "quick-cut." To make the best use of this technique, the writer may want to end the first scene with a lead-in for the opening of the second. For example:

> Still, she sat, silent.
> "Damn you," he snapped, crossing the small room to the big, oaken door. "I'm going down to the bar. If you won't speak to me, at least Max will!" He left, slamming the door behind.

> Max put the beer down before him and, in that matchmaking tone of voice some bartenders culture, he said, "I've got some news for you. Selma has been in the last couple of days. . . ."

Another transition of the same sort might run like this:

> The voice on the phone said, "Have the ransom money at the museum by midnight tonight. Otherwise, your wife is dead."
> Mike swallowed hard, wiped at his mouth, and said, "I'll be there—midnight on the dot."

> The museum was dark and deserted when he rounded the corner and walked toward the stone lions that flanked the steps.

As you can see, writing good scene transitions is really a simple matter; as I said, when discussing style, simplicity is the password.

Viewpoint

"You open the door and walk into the room, and you see the corpse at once. You are shocked, and you wonder if you should run. You can't be sure if the murderer has left, yet you have a duty to find out what has happened." That is an example of the second person viewpoint, and it is too affected to be suitable in any but the most special cases. Both the mainstream and genre writer have four effective viewpoints from which to tell a story: the omniscient and modified omniscient, which are both forms of third person narration; the third person limited; and the first person.

Omniscient and modified omniscient viewpoints

An omniscient viewpoint is one from which the author may look in on any of his characters. He may write from the hero's point of view in one scene, from the heroine's p.o.v. in the next scene, from the villain's p.o.v. in a third scene, then return to the hero's viewpoint in a fourth scene. He may vary his viewpoint in whatever order or fashion his plot requires, although *he may not switch points of view within a single scene.* Free to view the unfolding events from many vantage points, the writer can develop several plot threads, building suspense by letting the reader see how all the pieces will come together while the characters are kept ignorant of the true situation. When the reader knows something the characters don't, you have created "dramatic irony," and it can be quite effective. Furthermore, by spending some time in third person with every character in the book, the writer is better able to create believable people all down the line than if he used only the eyes and mind of the hero to present the rest of the story people.

In previous centuries, the pure omniscient viewpoint was most popular with writers. Writing from this perspective, the author was a god who halted the action to comment on his story people, and he often addressed his comments to the reader, like this:

Robert stepped away from the overturned coach, brushed off his britches and looked up the long road toward the mansion that rested at the top of the hill. It would be a long walk in the dark, but he was determined to make it. Foolish man! You suspect nothing, anticipate only joy. But ahead, for you, lies more evil than you ever expect to encounter. Pity him, gentle reader, for the unutterable horrors he must soon face, and pray that his moral fiber and his long-held convictions will see him through these tribulations.

Ninety-nine percent of the novelists who used the pure omniscient viewpoint have passed into total obscurity; their work is now unreadable. As for those few whose talent was strong enough to permit such indulgences, their work is edited or abridged in modern editions to eliminate the worst of these stylistic ineptitudes. A modern writer must never permit himself the pure ominscient viewpoint, must never obstruct the plot with asides to the reader or with small sermons. First of all, such asides often give away events or at least reveal the outline of events to come, thereby destroying the illusion of reality for the reader. (If he *knows* the story is carefully planned out, he cannot kid himself that all of this is unfolding before his eyes.) Second, such pauses in the narrative flow tend to *tell* the reader what he should be *shown* through dramatic action.

Many new writers use the pure omniscient viewpoint without being aware of it, shaping it a bit to fit modern tastes but making the same basic mistake as all those long-forgotten novelists. They may begin a piece like this:

Leonard turned the car around and drove back toward the house, sorry that he had yelled at Ellen. He was going to have to apologize; otherwise, he would be awake all night with the knowledge of what a fool he'd been. As it turned out, he would have been far better off had he gone to a motel as planned and stayed awake until the small hours. He couldn't know that then, however.

This foreshadowing is less irritating than the long-winded omniscient commentary popular in the early days of the novel, but it is equally undesirable. If you want to create a sense of impending doom, you must do it with mood words and suspenseful events, not with coy hints to the reader.

The modified omniscient viewpoint differs from the

pure omniscient in that it never stops to sermonize or comment directly to the reader: the author must show, not tell. The only similarity between the two voices is that the author may tell the story from many different character viewpoints, which is advantageous.

Warning! At least three-quarters of all successful mainstream novels are written from the modified omniscient point of view. The mainstream audience demands a story with greater breadth and depth—in terms of characters, background, and thematic structure—than does the genre audience. Most writers find that it is easiest (though never *easy*) to create a story with breadth and depth by writing in the modified omniscient voice, for there is total freedom to enter the minds of all the characters, whereas other narrative voices limit the author to the mind of just one character, the lead. The modified omniscient point of view also offers total freedom in placing the reader at all of the major dramatic story events, rather than restricting him to those events witnessed by the lead character.

It *is* possible to write an artistically and commercially successful mainstream novel from the first person point of view, but you need great skill to pull it off. The new writer would be smart to stick with the safest viewpoint— modified omniscient—if he hopes to produce a novel with the broad scope and rich texture that appeals to the mainstream audience.

Warning! If you choose to write primarily in the modified omniscient voice, as I have recommended, you must understand that it is never permissible to switch points of view from one character to another *within a single scene*. You cannot do something like this:

> "What are you doing in my office at this hour of the night?" Tom asked. He wondered if he should have brought his gun. He felt vulnerable.
>
> "I wanted that roll of film," Henderson said angrily. He wondered if he was strong enough to beat Smith in a fight. He had a forty-pound advantage on the other man. It's worth a try, he thought. I'd like nothing better than to break his damned neck.

Tom picked up the brass paperweight from his desk. He knew that violence was coming, and the prospect of it made him sick, but he was prepared to defend himself. He's bigger than me, Tom thought, but I'll bet I'm a hell of a lot quicker.

Dropping into the minds of both characters in a single scene is jarring, and it shatters the illusion of reality. It smacks of pure omniscient point of view, and it reveals the author's hand too openly to the reader. Here's how to rewrite that example to keep it in Tom's point of view without leaving anything out:

"What are you doing in my office at this hour of the night?" Tom asked. He wondered if he should have brought his gun. He felt vulnerable.

"I want that roll of film," Henderson said angrily. His hands were curled into tight fists. In his eyes there was rage and speculation.

He's wondering if he's strong enough to take me, Tom thought nervously.

Henderson had a forty-pound advantage. He probably also had the nerve and the desire to kill.

Tom picked up the brass paperweight from his desk. He knew that violence was coming, and the thought of it made him sick, but he was prepared to defend himself.

When the author changes points of view from one scene to another, with the scenes separated by chapter numbers or at least by space breaks, the reader can easily shift gears and roll with the new point of view; the pause at the chapter number or at the space break gives the reader sufficient time to slide from one character's perspective to another's. But when the author dances through several points of view in a single scene, the result is confusion and chaos.

Third person limited viewpoint

The third person limited viewpoint differs from the omniscient viewpoints in that the writer stays with the hero, showing the reader only what transpires around the hero, describing other characters mostly through the hero's perceptions of them. The advantages here lie in the ease with which the lead can be made sympathetic. If the author does not have to jump from character to character, he has plenty of time to make the hero vivid; the reader knows at once where his sympathies should lie and can quickly identify with the hero. For example, in the average 4,000-word first chapter of an 80,000-word suspense novel, it is far easier to develop a likeable, single lead than to attempt to sympathetically describe four or five different characters. And once attention is focused primarily on the one hero, that character can be even more well rounded and strengthened in subsequent chapters. The third person viewpoint is therefore well suited to genre fiction, but it is seldom useful when writing for the mainstream audience.

First person viewpoint

When you employ the first person narrative voice, in which the hero tells his own story, you further strengthen the advantages of concentrating on a single lead character. If your lead is fresh, unstereotyped, and individual, he can sometimes be best presented by letting him color the story events with his own judgments.

One serious drawback to first person narration is the awkwardness with which the hero must speak of himself. Writing in third person, you can be objective; but if your hero is talking about himself, he cannot dwell too much on his own appearance or thoughts, lest he appear unsympathetic and egomaniacal.

Another drawback to first person narration is the difficulty of thoroughly revealing the inner workings of characters other than the hero. The writer cannot delve into the minds of any characters other than the hero; he can never tell the reader what the other characters are thinking or feeling. All characters other than the hero must be developed solely through the hero's eyes, which means that even with a perceptive and sensitive hero, the other characters will always be superficially drawn.

(Somehow, John D. MacDonald often manages to tell a

story in the first person and *still* create a large cast of vivid characters. He is one of only a handful of writers who have pulled this off. See my notes on MacDonald in Chapter 15.)

Final thoughts

Dialogue, viewpoint, transitions—those are mechanical problems, *craft* problems. If you handle them well, you will increase the clarity and readability of your prose style. But doing all of those things well is not a definition of style. Your choices of words, your choices of phrasing, your images all contribute to your style, but they are not the *only* elements that go into it. Your attitudes, your view of life, your hopes, your dreams, your fears and hatreds, your virtues, your weaknesses, your fantasies—all of those fertilize your style; it grows out of them. But still a definition eludes us. The dictionary offers us no assistance, for its definition manages to be both vague and mechanical. Any true definition of "style" in fiction must be somewhat mystical. Try this one: Style is the soul of fiction; it is the heart; it is the author's essence, the thing about his prose that makes it uniquely his and nobody else's.

The only thing you really have to sell is your style. All the stories have been told. There are no new plots. (Dickens was convinced of that a hundred years ago.) We just keep reusing old story elements in new permutations. The only thing that keeps fiction fresh and popular is the constant rising up of new voices, new authors with unique perspectives and special ways of expressing themselves.

Style is personality transferred to the printed page. That is one reason the new writer should avoid slavishly imitating his favorite authors. The more time he wastes in mimicry, the longer he will take to develop his own style—the single commodity that might just possibly make him rich and famous.

Most of a writer's style evolves without conscious intent. It is admirable to strive consciously for clarity and simplicity, and it is good to learn and observe the rules of grammar and syntax, but if you struggle too hard to "write pretty," you will wind up with a style best suited to the composition of advertising copy for travel brochures about Hawaii and Polynesia and quaint old Amsterdam.

No one but Philip K. Dick writes like Philip K. Dick. His style is very much his own.

No one writes like Raymond Chandler wrote, though countless lesser artists imitate him every year.

No one writes like Dashiell Hammett wrote.

No one but Ray Bradbury writes like Ray Bradbury.

No one but Richard Condon writes like Richard Condon—or ever will.

And no one writes like you write. Every time a new writer sits down to tell his version of an old story, it's a whole new ballgame. That's why publishers seek fresh talent; there is always new ground to be broken.

12.

Two genres:
science fiction and
mysteries
or
If you absolutely insist on
confining yourself to a
literary ghetto for the rest
or your life, here are a few
tips about how to get
along well in a couple of
those neighborhoods.

Throughout this book, I have urged you to think of yourself as a WRITER, period. I have gently—and sometimes not so gently—nudged you toward the mainstream of popular literature. But I can only suggest; ultimately, the choice is yours. I know some of you will choose to write category fiction. Although I think you are making a mistake by choosing a genre career, I wish you well.

By showing you how to write mainstream fiction, I have also shown you how to write more simple, genre novels. As I have tried to make clear, the difference is primarily in degree: Mainstream demands more than most genre work—deeper characterization, more background, better-realized thematic structure, more attention to character motivation, fresher action scenes, and a better balance among the sundry elements of fiction. Otherwise, the patterns of mainstream and category fiction are not terribly different from each other. (Of course this matter of degree, while simple, is enormously important. It explains why a mainstream novelist can sell a million, two million, even ten million copies of a book, while a genre novelist sells 50,000 or 100,000 copies.)

There are, however, two genres that present special problems to the author. Although I urge you not to work in either of these fields, I will suggest a few things that will help you make it as a science fiction or as a mystery writer, if that is really what you want.

Science fiction

SF is the one category in which you can write a straight,

very narrowly defined genre novel and *still* have a chance
at the bestseller lists. Science fiction has become quasi-
respectable in academe, and movies like *Star Wars* have
made it more popular with the general public. Frank
Herbert's books sell more than a million copies each. Anne
McCaffrey's novels do well on national lists, as do those of
Philip Jose Farmer, though he has yet to have a million-
seller. Robert Heinlein's latest book, *The Number of the
Beast,* was far below the quality of his best novels, yet it
reached the top of the trade paperback lists. All of these
writers have hit big without making any effort whatsoever
to please the mainstream audience. The chance for enormous success is here, though it remains a small chance;
most SF writers still struggle to keep bread on the table.
Nevertheless, let's take a look at those writing problems
that are unique to science fiction.

Creating believable aliens

A common mistake made by good, new science fiction
writers is that they attempt to fully realize the *human*
characters, but they construct the aliens out of cardboard,
spit, and prayer. The nonhuman members of your science
fiction cast must be as believably motivated and as individualistic as any of their human counterparts, with but
two exceptions: 1) when the alien is used as a comic foil or
focus for satire or slapstick humor; 2) when the aliens
never appear directly in the story, or appear only
fleetingly, chiefly revealed as a sinister, unseen force. (Examples of the latter are *Out of the Deeps* by John Wyndham, which recounts a horrifying battle between mankind and unseen aliens who live beneath the seas, and *The
Shores of Another Sea* by Chad Oliver, which describes a
first contact between man and unseen aliens as they try to
conquer fear of each other and learn to accept each other's
existence.) Otherwise, your extraterrestrials must be as
realistic as you can make them.

The reader can be made to *feel* the unhumanity of your
aliens in several different ways. Most obvious, and the first
technique you will use when introducing aliens, is their
appearance, which will be either subtly or radically differ-

ent from mankind's. The more detailed you make their appearance, the more solid is your first step toward making them credible beings.

In my own novel, *Beastchild,* which was voted one of the most popular science fiction novels of the decade in one poll and received a Hugo Award nomination in its year, I was especially conscious of creating a believable alien, Hulann, for he was the hero of the story and had to capture the reader's interest and sympathy from the outset. Careful, thorough delineation of his race's physical and mental standards helped to make him real, as the following passages from the book should indicate. (As I look at *Beastchild* now, it seems rather clumsily written in parts and at times even embarrassing. I was tempted to polish the following examples, but I decided that would be unfair. After all, the book's popularity and its Hugo nomination indicate that it is up to the average standards of the field, and the one requirement of any example is that it be representative of the thing it exemplifies.)

In his onyx-walled room in the occupation tower, Hulann had disassociated his overmind from his organic regulating brain. He removed it from all stimuli, including the cells of his memory banks, where it could not even dream. He slept the perfect death-like sleep that only his kind, in all the myriad worlds of the galaxy, seemed to be able to achieve.

The naoli? The lizard men? They're the ones who die every night, aren't they?

To Hulann in his sleeping state, there was no sound whatsoever. No light. No images of color, no heat or cold. If there was a taste upon his long, thin tongue, his overmind could not know. Indeed all the stimuli were so censored that there was not even darkness. Darkness, after all, represented only nothingness.

He could return to wakefulness in any one of three ways, though there was a decided order of preference among these methods. First, and most unpleasant, was his body's built-in danger alarm. If his regulating brain, the heavily convoluted organic portion of his mind, should discover something seriously amiss with his temporal shell, it would be able to contact and wake his overmind through a fail-safe system of seldom-used third-order nerve clusters. Such a contact would shock its own grey cortex, opening the nether-world pocket in which the ethereal overmind sleeps.

(Pause here for an anecdote or two. In a thousand places across the stars, stories are told which concern the naoli and the seriousness with which alcoholic beverages affect their "danger alarm" waking system. These stories are told in barrooms in port cities, down in the basements of questionable buildings that lease their rooms to even more questionable businessmen, or in sweet-drug centers on better looking but no more honest streets. It seems that while sweet-drugs bring only euphoria to the naoli, alcohol transforms them into bobbling, bouncing, scaly-tailed clowns who—after half an hour of making total fools of themselves—collapse into their death-sleep. They stretch out stiff as ice right on the floor. In some less reputable establishments (which is to say most of these places) the other patrons make great sport out of carrying the unconscious lizard men to odd places like garbage bins and ladies' washrooms and leaving them there to wake. This damages nothing but the naoli's ego. A far more nasty pastime among these same drunken buffoons is to see how far they must go to trigger the naoli's "danger alarm" system. But the alarm is stupefied by alcohol and does not work well. The stories you hear later are about naoli lying there with their webs sizzling, not even twitching in response. Or of a naoli with fifty pins stuck in its legs, sleeping peacefully while its heavy blood seeped out through its tough gray skin. Naoli do not often drink liquor. When they do, it is usually alone. They are not a stupid race.)

Much less unpleasant but still not desirable, a naoli could come awake if the Phasersystem had something to tell him. That could, of course, be anything from urgent news to another spate of propaganda from the central committee. More often than not, it was the latter.

Finally, and best of all, the overmind could awake of its own accord. Before retiring into the netherworld, the overmind could plant a suggestion with a time-trigger. Then, ten or eight, or fifteen or twenty hours later, it would click into consciousness with the clarity of a tridimensional screen being turned on.

Here, the reader is confronted with an alien quality so fundamental that it becomes impossible for him to think of the hero, Hulann, as a fancily dressed human. If naoli and man are so different in the way they sleep and wake, how much more must they differ on complex questions? Also, with the key words and phrases like "lizard men," "scaly-tailed," "webs," and "tough gray skin," the unhuman appearance of the aliens is kept in the front of the reader's mind.

Other physiological references abound:

He snorted, opening his second set of nostrils now that he would need a full air supply for movement. When his lungs swelled and adjusted to the new air flow, he got out of bed.

And:

Hulann moved closer, raising the double lids completely free of his huge, oval eyes.

And this:

Hulann winced. His double stomach burned on both levels with acidic agitation.

Aside from their physical peculiarities, alien creatures will have habits and gestures unlike those of humans. Instead of alcohol, for example, the naoli use sweet-drugs, a substance with no effect on human beings. As for their gestures:

> He tucked his tail between his legs, wrapping it around his left thigh in the age-old reaction to danger, to the unknown, to that which made the scales of the scalp tighten and ache.

A human being's reaction to fear might be a hunching of the shoulders, a stiffening of the back, balling of the fists. But the naoli are not human beings. Another gesture:

> [Hulann] passed the others without comment, noticing the odd looks he drew from them. Realizing that his lips were pulled in over his teeth, giving him a look of shame, he quickly rearranged his facial composure. . . .

When we say a man looks shamefaced, we certainly don't mean that he has his lips drawn in over his teeth! Having convincingly established the differences in appearance between the aliens and mankind, you must make continual application of these differences, elaborating on them throughout the story. This can be done in any of three ways: (1) through the alien's relationships with his own kind, (2) through his contacts with men, and (3) through his reactions to events in the story.

Let's look, for example, at alien-to-alien interaction in *Beastchild;* this particular scene concerns naoli sexuality:

> She licked her lips with her tongue, then stuck more of it out and flicked at her chin. She was pretty. He did not understand how he had almost walked by without stopping.

Certainly, a man would not be attracted to a woman whose tongue was so long she could lick her chin with it and did so, apparently, with some regularity. But naoli values of beauty will be different from those of a man.

And, having established a naoli's sexuality, one must also expect it to be satisfied in a manner unlike human satisfaction:

> He watched her a moment longer, reluctant to leave. More than any other female he had seen in the last two hundred years, she made him want to make a verbal commitment. It would be a delight to go away with her, into the warren of his own house back on the home world, and fuse for sixteen days, living off the fat of their bodies and the ceremonial waters they would take with them.
>
> He could envision her in ecstasy.
>
> And when she came out of the warren, she would have the gaunt, fleshless look of a desirable woman who has mated for the standard fusing period.
>
> She would be gorgeous in the aura of her femininity.

In a few simple paragraphs that don't interrupt the narrative flow, the reader gets a glimpse of another basic difference between men and naoli, as profound a difference as the way they sleep and wake.

Through contact with men, the alien's unhuman qualities will also be driven home, as in the following exchange between Hulann and a human child, Leo, whom he has befriended against all the laws of his race, which has been at war with ours for many years:

> "Doesn't that hurt?" Leo asked.
>
> "What?"
>
> "Your lips. When you pull them in over your teeth like that."
>
> Hulann quickly showed his teeth, put a hand to his lips and felt them. "No," he said. "We have few nerves in our outer layers of flesh."
>
> "You look funny," Leo said. He drew his own lips in over his teeth and made talking motions, then burst out laughing.
>
> Hulann found himself laughing also, watching the

boy mimic him. Did he really look like that? It was a mysterious expression on a naoli; or at least he had been raised to respect it as such. In this mock version, it truly was humorous.

"What are you *doing?*" the boy squealed, laughing even harder.

"What?" Hulann asked, looking about him. His body was still. His hands and feet did not move.

"That noise," Leo said.

"Noise?"

"That wheezing sound."

Hulann was perplexed. "Mirth," he said. "Laughter like yours."

"It sounds like a drain that's clogged," Leo said. "Do I sound that bad to you?"

Hulann began laughing again. "To me . . . you sound like some birds that we have on my world. They are great, hairy things with three legs and tiny little bills."

In other words, the writer must realize that the aliens will find human beings as strange as men find them.

Finally, the writer must apply these alien peculiarities to plot developments. In the following example from *Beastchild,* while Hulann and Leo are fleeing pursuers by means of a cable car dangling above a snowy landscape in the midst of a storm, we see the naoli react in a very individual and different manner, based on his race's traits:

Hulann's tail snapped, then wound around his left thigh, tight.

"What's the matter?" the boy asked.

"Nothing."

"You look upset."

Hulann grimaced, his reptilian features taking on a pained look. "We're awfully high," he said in a thin voice.

"High? But it's only a hundred feet down!"

Hulann looked mournfully at the cable sliding past

above them. "A hundred feet is enough if that should break."

"You've been in shuttlecraft without even a cable."

"The highest they go is fifteen feet."

"Your starships, then. You can't get any higher than that."

"And you can't fall, either. There's no gravity out there."

Leo was laughing now, bending over the waist-high safety bar and giggling deep down in his throat. When he looked up again, his small face was red, and his eyes were watery. "This is something else!" he said. "You're afraid of heights. Naoli aren't supposed to be afraid of anything. Do you know that? Naoli are vicious fighters, hard, ruthless opponents. Nowhere does it say they are permitted to fear anything."

"Well . . ." Hulann said weakly.

"We're almost there," Leo said. "Just steel yourself for another minute or two, and it'll all be over."

Because he has irrational fears, the alien becomes that much more of a believable character, amusing and sympathetic.

Appearance, habits, gestures, expressions, sexual and nonsexual value judgments, actions and reactions to plot incidents in accordance with his otherworldly origins all serve to make a nonhuman character real. You must further explore his eating habits, manner of dress, social customs, forms of entertainment, religion, philosophy, and a hundred and one other facets of his unusual daily life.

Then, when you have created a believable extraterrestrial race, you must make sure that the aliens in your story—if more than one appears—are as unlike each other as one human being is unlike his neighbor. Certainly, the aliens will share attitudes and reactions as a species, in the same way that human beings, regardless of race or nationality, laugh at the same things and cry on the same occasions. But of equal certainty is the fact that the personalities and opinions of the aliens will differ wildly from one individual to another—unless, of course, you have postulated a race of ants with a group mind and a single social goal.

Creating science fiction backgrounds

Because most science fiction takes place in the future, the backgrounds are largely the products of writers' imaginations. The future can be researched only to a limited extent, for when it comes to saying exactly what the years ahead hold for us, even the most well-informed scientists can offer only conjecture. The SF writer's vision of the future must be detailed and believable, or ultimately the reader will not believe *anything* about the story—not the characters, the motivations, or the plot.

The near future. Structuring a story background of the near future—twenty, thirty, or forty years from now—is in some ways more difficult than creating an entire alien planet in some impossibly distant age, for the near-future background cannot be *wholly* a product of the imagination. The writer must conduct extensive research to discover what engineers and scientists project for every aspect of future life. From that data, the author then *extrapolates* a possible world of tomorrow, one which might logically rise out of the base for the future which we are building today.

This does not mean that every science fiction novel set in A.D. 2010 must be placed against the same background. The future is amorphous; even extrapolating from today's conditions, twenty different science fiction writers will reach twenty different and entirely credible conclusions about the world of 2010.

For example, in *The Space Merchants* by Frederik Pohl and C.M. Kornbluth, the authors project a future within this century, a society in which high-pressure advertising agencies have gained terrible influence over the minds of the masses and have become, in effect, the rulers of the world. The same authors, in their *Gladiators-at-Law*, intricately develop another near future in which big business has grown so large that it has begun to collapse from within, pulling all of society into ruin with it. Each future is set in approximately the same period; each future is radically different from the other; each is believable; each could come to pass; and both of those novels are science fiction classics.

The trick lies in how well you detail your imaginary world, no matter if it lies in the near or the far future. If you paint it only in broad strokes, no one (including the editors) will accept your vision. When considering the background for any science fiction novel of the near future, be sure to give careful thought to each of the following subjects:

Moral codes of the future. Assume that morality will change, and that it will change radically. Don't assume that your own code of moral conduct will inevitably lie at the center of the societies of the future or that present-day morality will continue to be acceptable. Remember that, in the early 1950s, no one would have believed that "free love" and "group marriage" would become, if not commonplace, at least unremarkable just a couple of decades later. Likewise, no citizen of America in 1950 would have imagined that homosexuals could finally gain the right to "come out of the closet" and live without shame. Though moral codes will most likely continue to become increasingly humanistic and less predicated upon religious guilt, even that is not a certainty. The future has infinite possibilities under its cloak. The only thing of which you can be sure is that it *will* be very different from the world in which we live now. Here are a few moral questions for you to consider in the context of your imaginary near-future society: Will sexuality be more openly or less openly expressed than it is today? Will murder still be considered immoral? Will murder in the service of one's country still be considered *moral*? What about mercy killing? Will marriage survive as an institution? Will researchers' findings about the intelligence of dolphins, whales, and selected other animals induce us to pass laws making the slaughter of those species a capital crime? As you can see, the list of questions you must mull over will be very long indeed.

Domestic politics. Will there still be only two major political parties in the United States, and will they still be the Republican and the Democratic parties? Will the United

States still be a democracy? What effects will data banks on private citizens (being put together even today) have on the conduct of government and politicians? Will war be an issue? The space program? Poverty?

World politics. Will the United States still exist? Will the Soviet Union and China still exist? What new power will have arisen in world affairs—Brazil, Israel, or one of the Arab states that is already gaining tremendous influence upon world affairs? If your novel is set on an alien world, what is the nature of galactic politics and diplomacy?

Religion. Will the United States remain predominantly Christian? Set aside your own religious view and extrapolate honestly. Will religion play an even more important role in politics than it does now, accumulating even more establishment power? Or will the ongoing boom of scientific discovery eventually be the death of belief in supernatural beings? What new religions might arise? While you're thinking about these questions, you ought to read Robert Heinlein's brilliant short novel *If This Goes On . . .*, which concerns a future America that is dominated by a repressive religious organization.

Day-to-day life. This is the most important kind of background detail in any futuristic setting, for it is the sort of thing that will be constantly in the reader's eye. Perhaps morality will play an important part in your story; perhaps politics or religion or the international situation will be a major influence on the plot line; however, the details of day-to-day life in the future will be more important than the specifics of any one of those larger issues and will be visible in every scene. Will the population explosion do away with single-family homes, as it now seems likely to do, thereby forcing everyone to live in space-conserving highrises? Will people eat the same foods we eat today, or will they be forced to consume flavored algae because of worldwide food shortages? Will automobiles exist, or will they have been replaced with other transportation systems? How will citizens of the future dress? Will books exist, or will they be replaced by mechanical devices? Will children go to public schools or be taught at home by television and computers and robots? Will the pollution problem have been solved, or will people wear gas masks on the street and salve their skin to ward off deterioration and irritation caused by a caustic atmosphere? Will drugs be legalized? How will food be prepared—perhaps without human contact? Will cancer have been cured? Will all forms of madness be curable? Will mankind have spread out to colonies on the moon? On Mars? On the asteroids? Beyond?

The questions go on and on, and you must have answers to them. You must know your futuristic setting so well that, if a friend quizzed you about it, you could answer questions with the same alacrity with which you can answer questions about the real world, the world of today.

As a potential writer of science fiction, you would be well-advised to read *Dune* by Frank Herbert, a science fiction classic that is set in the far future and has sold a couple of million copies. *Dune* contains one of the most detailed futures imaginable. Likewise, Robert Heinlein's multimillion-copy classic, *Stranger in a Strange Land,* is a book that deals with a *near* future so well that few authors have ever created anything comparable to its catalogue of extrapolative minutiae.

Not *every* novel in this genre requires such a wealth of background in the finished draft, but you should have your future so well thought out that you can supply consistent background details in any scene that demands them. Some SF writers keep elaborate notebooks full of background data for the imaginary future they are constructing. Robert Heinlein has even gone so far as to plot a Chart of Future History, outlining major events over several hundred years and slotting his stories into that future history. When I wrote science fiction many years ago, I found that careful planning plus a few notes were all that I needed to handle background adequately; I never kept fat notebooks or charts. I held the entire scheme in my head in order to keep the setting more flexible than it would have been if I had outlined it on paper. Each SF author must discover, through trial and error, which method best suits his temperament.

Warning! When constructing your future world, you

must be sure that all elements mesh into a coherent whole. For example, if you extrapolate a future United States run by either a right-wing or a left-wing dictatorship, with democracy abolished, do not also portray a society in which the arts flourish unless you can explain that special situation. Those two elements—dictatorship and a flowering of artistic expression—have rarely coexisted in the history of mankind. Do not portray a future in which the Christian Church governs the world *and* in which sexual liberty is encouraged; the church would have to change drastically for such a thing to be credible.

The far future. When your story is set centuries from our time, on this or another world, you have greater freedom to create bizarre cultures, and you have correspondingly less research to do than when you are writing about a near future. No one can know what life will be like two thousand years from now. No human being alive at this moment can know how life on other worlds is structured and conducted. No amount of research into the sciences can prepare the author to make accurate predictions when such great spans of time are involved. The only rule for far-future stories is this: Your background must be consistent in its details (not so different from the rule for *near*-future settings).

For example, if you were to construct a future in which mankind has made robots as able, intelligent, and sensitive as human beings, and if you were then to have your hero and other human beings tending to mundane jobs, you would be hooted out of the genre by SF fans. In that future, the robots would probably do all of the drab work—unless you can provide a logical explanation as to why they wouldn't replace men on production lines and in hazardous occupations like fire fighting.

Another example: If you set a story on an alien world with three times Earth's gravity, and if you then let the heroes move about as easily as if they were at home, your novel will never sell. After all, Earthborn men would move slowly, painfully, and clumsily on a three-g planet, for they would weigh three times as much as they weighed on Earth, and they would feel as if they were carrying heavy burdens. Furthermore, if you put aliens that resemble men on this planet, you're again making a serious mistake. Any life form evolving on a three-g planet would be smaller than men, with only vague—and perhaps no—resemblance to intelligent life as we know it.

Researching these backgrounds is not a simple matter. Where do you find a nonfiction book about life on a planet with three times Earth's gravity? The answer, of course, is that no such book exists. You will have to begin by learning everything you can about Earth's gravity and about the subject of gravity in general; with that knowledge as a base, you can convincingly extrapolate a three-g planet. Unless you are accustomed to the often dreary prose of science books, you would do well to have a look at juvenile and even children's nonfiction books on any science that you need to research. You will find that in children's books, the fundamentals of a difficult subject are clearly and simply explained, and the fundamentals are usually all you need to know in order to begin your story. In addition, while the average library may have a poor selection of advanced science texts, it will possess thousands of children's books covering every topic from stars and space travel and gravity to the operation of a jet plane and the construction of an oil well.

These are not by any means the only things you need to know to write *great* science fiction. That subject would require an entire book of its own. But I hope you will benefit from this discussion of writing problems that are *unique* to the genre. With that same goal in mind, let's look at the special requirements of the whodunit.

The mystery novel

The classic murder mystery appears to be a moribund genre. (See my discussion of the mystery novel in Chapter 3.) Only a few fresh voices are heard in the field, and most of those writers quickly move on to more ambitious novels, achieving success in the mainstream. Nevertheless, if you insist on being a mystery writer, you should be aware of these fifteen special requirements of the form:

1. *Does your story open with a crime in the first chapter?* It should. The sooner the puzzle is presented to both the reader and the hero, the stronger your narrative hook. You may even open after a murder has been committed and the police have arrived. Or you might begin with the discovery of a body, or with a brief scene of a murder in progress. However you start, start with a bang.

In the first chapter of *The Bridge That Went Nowhere* by Robert L. Fish (one of his Captain José Da Silva mysteries), a plane lands in a clearing in a dense Brazilian jungle, carrying three men. One of the men is shot on the second page of the story; another is blown up, along with the bridge that leads into the clearing, by the fifth page, well before the end of the chapter. It would be difficult to imagine a bigger bang of a start, and the novel goes on successfully from there.

In the first chapter of Donald E. Westlake's *Murder Among Children* (published under the pseudonym Tucker Coe), the hero, Mitch Tobin (who has appeared in five Coe mysteries to date), goes into the West Village, in lower Manhattan, looking for his cousin, Robin Kennely. On the third page of the book, he finds her in a daze, holding a bloody knife; she appears to have killed someone.

Thus ends a very short first chapter. Though the killer's identity would seem certain, the second chapter brings up other possibilities, other suspects, and launches the reader on the trail of the solution.

2. *Does your hero appear in Chapter 1?* He should. In most mysteries, he will be, by title and/or circumstance, a detective: a policeman, a private detective, a private citizen caught up in a situation only he can unravel (Agatha Christie's Jane Marple mysteries are good examples of this form), a scientist sorting through clues to a disaster only he can explain, a soldier-detective, a spy-detective. His entire role in the story will be that of the sleuth seeking and evaluating clues. If the crime is committed at the outset, then you'll have a good reason to focus on him from the first page.

Some mystery writers favor the first person viewpoint for telling a story—that is, telling it through the eyes and the mind of the lead character. In fact, the mystery genre supports more first person narratives than any other. Though this makes the early introduction of the hero almost no problem at all, it should be avoided; the vast majority of published novels are told in the third person. A great many editors and, apparently, readers as well, share a prejudice against the first person. Since you must please the editors *and* the readers, you should not tackle a first person narrative until you can do it well enough to squelch any editorial dissatisfaction with the method.

In Rex Stout's enormously popular Nero Wolfe series, even though the initial crime is usually committed offstage, the heroes are onstage in the first chapter. With only a few exceptions, the Wolfe stories begin with a client who comes to Wolfe's 35th Street townhouse in an attempt to get Wolfe and his trusted associate, Archie Goodwin, to take on a case. We know our heroes straight off, and we soon learn the nature of the puzzle; from then on, it's easy reading. (Some of the Wolfe novels include *The Doorbell Rang, Plot It Yourself, Death of a Doxy, The Father Hunt, The Mother Hunt,* and *Might As Well Be Dead.*)

3. *Does your hero have a sound motive for becoming involved in the investigation of the case?* He should have some reason besides the most obvious—i.e., it's his job. For example, Stout's detective, Nero Wolfe, is quite often motivated by a desperate need for cash. Wolfe lives lavishly, with a full-time chef, a half-day orchid specialist who helps him tend his hundreds of greenhouse orchids, and other expensive accoutrements of the "good life." Naturally, there are times when he is desperate enough for ready cash that he will take on even the most unpleasant cases. When it isn't money that motivates Wolfe it may be curiosity, because that overweight private investigator is as much a puzzle fancier as any mystery reader. Or he may be motivated by self-preservation, to the extent that Wolfe must preserve his rich lifestyle by preserving his reputation as a private investigator.

Occasionally a writer creates a mystery novel protagonist with more depth to him than most. Donald E. Westlake's ex-detective, Mitch Tobin, the focus of a series of novels (*Kinds of Love Kinds of Death, Murder Among Children, Wax Apple, A Jade in Aries,* and *Don't Lie to Me*), is a man with a monkey on his back: the monkey is guilt. It's like this: Tobin was once a respected detective on the police force. However, when he arrested a burglar named Dink Campbell, he met Campbell's wife and fell for her at once. The attraction was mutual. While Campbell was serving his sentence for burglary, Tobin and Linda Campbell carried on an affair; since Tobin was married, the affair had to be during working hours. Tobin's partner covered for him when, during their tour of duty, Tobin wanted to see Linda. One day, while Tobin was in bed with the woman, the partner was killed. Tobin was disgraced, thrown off the force, and left with a load of guilt he was almost unable to bear—guilt because he had cheated on his wife, guilt because he had embarrassed his son, guilt, most of all, because he had shirked his responsibility and had not been there to back up his partner when the partner arrested a heroin pusher. In each of the novels, one of Tobin's motivations, either unspoken or quite evident, is his guilt, his need to make up for what he's done, to repay the debts, to help other people and thereby his own moral record. In some cases, he actually would prefer not to be involved at all, but does get involved out of this sense of duty to his family, his dead partner, and himself.

4. *Is your fictional crime violent enough?* You cannot expect a reader to get terribly excited about a stolen car or a mugging. You should begin with a murder, attempted murder, threatened murder, or missing person.

5. *Is the method of murder or the way the body was found unique and attention-getting?* It should be. Not every mystery must contain a clever murder method, but those that do have another plus. You should be anxious to acquire as many story values as possible, and you should try to think of something unique, something besides a simple stabbing, shooting, or strangling. An ax murder? Hit-and-run in a supermarket parking lot? A forced drowning? A murder made to look like a suicide, but so obviously bungled that the killer intended the police to know it was murder in disguise? A case of deliberate poisoning?

In the first chapter of Donald E. Westlake's *Don't Lie to Me*, the body is discovered nude, in the middle of a museum, as if it had been dropped out of the sky. Since the victim was strangled, he would have eliminated from bowels and bladder as he died, yet here he is clean as Christmas. Evidently, he was killed, then washed carefully, dried, and brought here in the dead of night, with the guard on duty. Why? How? *And by whom?* The circumstances of the body's discovery are startling enough to carry the reader through the book, wondering about the answer.

6. *Do you introduce at least one potential suspect by the end of Chapter 2?* You should, so that both the hero and the reader will have something to mull over. This doesn't necessarily mean that the suspect must be blatantly obvious (though he may be). You need only introduce an associate, friend, relative, or lover of the dead man, someone who might conceivably have a motive for killing him; this person may seem like a very unlikely prospect for the role of the killer, at first, but the important thing is that he remain at least a possibility.

7. *Do you introduce a second suspect by the end of Chapter 3?* The sooner you expand the list of possible killers, the more difficult the puzzle becomes—and the more firmly your narrative hook is implanted. For this reason, you should establish murderous motives for at least three characters. Even four or five suspects are easier to work with and better for the creation of a real puzzle.

For example, if in Chapter 1 the president of a prosperous and busy city bank is found dead in his office immediately after his lunch hour, you might have the following suspects for your detective to question. The president's own private secretary, a beautiful young woman who has been angry with the president of late because he's been vacillating about his intentions of marrying her. She was out to lunch, but can't prove where she was when the murder took place. The vice-president of the bank, who has long coveted the top job and feels the board would put him in if the president retired or left for another position in another bank. The banker's "cousin," who turns out to have been his mistress. This girl often visited him during his lunch hour, for the purpose of quick sexual relaxation, and might have been there today—and might have been mad at him because he vacillated about rejecting the notion of marrying his secretary. The banker's desk drawer contains a typed note indicating that his ex-brother-in-law borrowed $20,000 from him a year ago, agreeing to pay it back in twelve months. Perhaps the brother-in-law couldn't pay back the money and was there to plead, unsuccessfully, for an extension on the loan. Here you have four characters with murderous motives; in the course of this story, others could easily arise.

8. *Have you provided legitimate clues to the killer's identity?* You should hide at least three in the course of the story. These may be introduced so quietly that the reader never picks them up. Perhaps, for example, your story opens with a body found in a muddy flowerbed behind a mansion. When the detective covertly steals a glance at the shoes of each member of the household as he questions them, he may notice that most are wearing scuffed or dusty shoes, and that one man's shoes are freshly polished, but that no one is wearing muddy shoes. Later, it may dawn on the hero that the man with the freshly polished footwear had, just before the interrogation, scrubbed away the traces of mud; his shoe shine could have been an attempt to eliminate the evidence. This is, of course, an exaggerated example, but it should give you an idea of how the clue can be presented deceptively, the meaning quietly covered until later.

A clue may also be introduced with fanfare. A pair of work gloves, covered with garden mud, might be found in the room of the dead man's stepson, for example. This kind of thing is usually used to throw the reader off the track, to get him looking in all the wrong places. Later, it will turn out that the blatantly delivered clue was false; the muddy gloves could have been put there by the killer to throw suspicion on the stepson, or the stepson might have some perfectly legitimate explanation for them.

Likewise, the very obvious clue can be used to make the reader think: "Well, I'm supposed to suspect the stepson.

That much is obvious. Therefore, it couldn't possibly be the stepson." Then, in the end, it is the stepson, after all.

The idea is to give the reader the pertinent data but to try to fool him into employing it incorrectly. When the real killer's identity is disclosed at the end of the book, the reader should be able to go back, spot-check you, and say, "Now, why didn't I see that?"

9. *Does your narrative tension come from the reader's desire to know* who *more than from his desire to know* how *to stop him?* It should. The killer's identity, the why of the crime, is more important to the reader than any chase or race against time or anticipation of a violent event. Again, the Nero Wolfe books, or those by Agatha Christie (especially *The Mystery of the Blue Train, Murder in the Calais Coach,* and *The Murder of Roger Ackroyd)* serve as fine examples of this.

10. *Does your hero exhaust one avenue of investigation after another until it seems impossible to assign guilt for the crime?* He should reach this point no sooner than halfway through the book. He should seem stumped, or so confused by new developments that the reader almost suspects the killer will get away with his crime.

11. *Is your police and laboratory procedure genuine?* Does your detective follow established investigatory procedure, as it is known in most public and private police agencies across the country? If you're writing about an autopsy, do you know just how one is done? Do you know what the police can learn from an autopsy: old injuries, evidence of rape, traces of the killer's skin and hair, a thousand other useless and valuable bits of data? Do you know what surfaces take fingerprints well, what others take them poorly, and which ones don't take them at all? Do you know the different techniques for lifting fingerprints? Do you know how or why a shoe print or tire track can lead the authorities to the villain? All these and hundreds of other things can easily be researched in a university, city, county, or state library. If they do not have any books on criminology, they can borrow them from other libraries for as long as you will need to study them and make notes. One of the best resources on criminology is Jurgen Thorwald's *Crime and Science,* a Harvest Book published by Harcourt Brace Jovanovich in a moderately priced, oversized paperback. Thorwald's book is not only a valuable reference work, but an entertaining compilation of famous crimes that were solved through the clever application of forensic science.

12. *Does your hero's sudden realization of the killer's identity evolve from a juxtaposition of events that he has been playing with, in his mind, all along but which he has been unable to interpret thus far because of some preconception or character flaw of his own?* It should. You must never drop the solution into the hero's lap through some twist of fate or stupid mistake made by an otherwise clever villain. His own best efforts should solve the puzzle, his own wit.

13. *Does the revelation of the villain's identity come close to the end of the book?* If it comes in the first third, or in the middle, you are probably writing a suspense novel and not a mystery. Remember, the mystery reader wants to be kept guessing until the end.

14. *Is the revelation of the killer's identity delivered in an action scene, as opposed to a dry, verbalized accounting made by the hero to other people in the story?* Long summations, after the detective has called all the suspects into one room, are trite and tend to slow the plot nearly to a standstill. It is true that your reader, having come that far in the story, will read to the end no matter how you present the last few scenes. But it is better to leave a reader perfectly content with the final chapter, for it is this last sequence of events that he will most clearly remember. If he is displeased with your handling of the conclusion, he will not rush out to buy your next mystery novel. Instead of a tell-'em-about-it climax, incorporate the detective's summation into an action scene.

For example: The hero goes to the suspect's apartment, breaks in, and searches for that one last piece of evidence that will clinch the case. He finds it, but he is surprised by the villain before he can steal safely away. At the antagonist's mercy, perhaps at gunpoint, he bargains for time by trying to unsettle the killer. He laughs at him and tells him how inept he was at trying to hide his identity; in the course of delivering this ridicule, the detective explains how he came upon the clues, how he put them together, and why he decided the killer must be Mr. X. Like this:

> I rested my hand on top of the paperweight. It would make a good missile; even if I could not hit him with it, I could distract him long enough to close the short distance between us.
> "But how did you know Rita was my old girlfriend?" he asked.
> "You provided that clue yourself," I said. I gripped the paperweight, ready to throw it. "Do you remember when we were talking about—"
> "Let go of the paperweight," he said, smiling. "I'd have a bullet in your chest before you could pitch it."
> Reluctantly, I did as he said.
> "Now, go on," he said.

As you see, there is a dramatic element intertwined with the explanation. As the detective tells how he put two and two together, he also searches for a way to turn the tables on the antagonist. This is much more readable than a dry summation.

15. *In the course of your story, does your hero gain some piece of data from every interview and avenue of investigation that he conducts?* Some new mystery writers construct paper suspects who can easily be proven innocent in the detective's first confrontation with them. Then they propel their protagonist through a series of interviews and surveillances that lead absolutely nowhere—except that the hero can say, at the conclusion of each dead end, something like: "Well, Walters, we don't know anything more about Lady Randolph's death now than when we started. But at least we can be certain that Lord Biggle is not the man we want!" It is acceptable to have your protagonist follow up a *few* bum leads, for this gives the story a realistic touch; but the majority of tacks he takes must provide some information, no matter how minimal, that has a bearing on the solution of the case.

Other types of genre fiction present the author with pretty much the same kinds of narrative problems that were discussed in Chapters 4 through 11. Only science fiction and the whodunit pose unique problems for writers, and I have attempted to restrict my discussions of those two categories to the things about them that are special. I have purposely not taken an exhaustive look at SF or mysteries.

Of course, there *are* other genres besides science fiction and the whodunit—Westerns, straight historicals, the previously mentioned "bodice rippers" exemplified by the work of Rosemary Rogers and Laurie McBain, fantasy, horror, men's action novels of the sort written by Don Pendleton and much better written by Warren Murphy, sweet and chaste romances in the well-mined Harlequin-Barbara Cartland vein, and so forth. I am *not* going to discuss any of those genres, not even in the limited way that I touched upon science fiction and mysteries. I do not recommend as I did a decade ago in *Writing Popular Fiction,* that the new writer should launch his career as a genre novelist. For a number of reasons—which are spelled out in the first three chapters of this book—that old advice is no longer valid. In fact, the exact opposite is true and will continue to be true for many years to come: a new writer should make every attempt to begin his career as a mainstream novelist and avoid being labeled as *any* brand of genre wordsmith. If I expended tens of thousands of words showing you how to write in a wide variety of genres, I would appear to be endorsing the concept of a genre career for new writers, which is precisely what I am *not* doing.

I took the time to discuss the special problems of SF and mystery stories in part because those problems also apply to mainstream novels that have elements of science fiction or the whodunit in their makeup—books like *The Andro-*

meda Strain by Michael Crichton and *The Second Deadly Sin* by Lawrence Sanders. The advice and suggestions in this chapter *can* be applied to mainstream novels that take an SF or a mystery idea and—through superior characterization, richly drawn backgrounds, carefully thought-out thematic structure, and fresh action sequences—elevate it out of the genre classification.

Avoid the genre label

Think of yourself as a WRITER, period.

If you are *obsessed* with being an SF writer, then you must, of course, follow your obsession, regardless of what I say.

But why should you write books reaching tens of thousands of readers when you can perhaps write books reaching millions? If you have an idea for a good genre novel, play with it, work with it, pull and tug and reshape it, until you have broadened the concept and can write it as a larger, more ambitious mainstream book. You will not be sorry.

13.

A few more pitfalls to avoid
or
Just when you thought it was safe to go into the literary waters, here are a few more sharks no one's told you about.

The traps to which I have called your attention in the preceding twelve chapters are not by any means the only ones into which you are likely to step. If I tried to warn you about every pitfall that is out there, this book would be at least two thousand pages long. (It's a tough profession, my friends.) I have tried, however, to mention the most serious problems with which the writer must deal. Here are a few which did not fit comfortably into other chapters.

Don't get the idea that writing is easy work. It is the hardest thing I have ever done. In my younger days, I held a few jobs that involved heavy physical labor. Among other things, I worked in a grocery warehouse, stacking hundred-pound bags of sugar and cases of canned goods for eight hours at a stretch; it wasn't unusual to have lifted burdens totalling thirty or forty thousand pounds by the end of a shift. That grueling job never tired me out as completely as writing does. I also worked for a year in the Appalachian poverty program, tutoring underprivileged children, many of whom had severe behavioral problems. The day I reported for that job, I was told that some of my teenage charges were given to violence and that the man who had held the position before me had been run off the road by some of his students, had been beaten senseless, and had spent a nice long time in the hospital. Many of the kids I was trying to help were big, strong, coal-country boys who did not take kindly to discipline. Most days, when I staggered home from work, I was physically, mentally and emotionally exhausted. Nevertheless, many eight- or ten- or twelve-hour days at the typewriter have been far more demanding and exhausting than even the worst day's work in that coal-country community.

During the last two months of writing *Whispers*, when I was trying to make an important deadline, I worked seven days a week, never less than twelve hours a day; many days I worked *sixteen* hours, even taking meals at the typewriter; and during the last two weeks, I missed six nights of sleep, working right around the clock for as many as thirty-six hours in a shift. When I finished *Whispers*, I had lost ten pounds even though I had been eating normally and had had *no* exercise—and I slept twelve hours a day, every day, for a full week, recuperating.

Even when you are not trying to beat a deadline, writing is a very demanding activity, for it requires you to focus your mind more than in any other line of work. Even a brain surgeon does not spend most of his day with his attention riveted on one fine point; the operating room is the only place such total concentration is required of him. But a novelist must keep his mind tightly reined in, directed upon the gradually evolving imaginary world that he is putting together; each time he is distracted for two minutes, he needs twenty minutes to refocus.

If you want to be a writer because it seems like easy work, you are heading for two pitfalls. The shallower of the two is a pit of disappointment which will open under you when you discover that writing will not be a loafer's life. If you put too little time and effort into your writing because you think it's *easy* to just type out a gripping story, you will eventually discover that easily, lazily written stories do not sell and that your stacks of manuscripts represent nothing more than misspent time; that is the second pit, the deeper one. Time is precious.

But if you realize that writing is hard work, you will not tumble into these pits, and given time and talent and application, you *will* succeed.

■

Don't think of writing as a competitive enterprise.

Writers should be supportive of one another and should take pleasure in one another's successes. Don't waste time stewing in envy when another writer receives a larger advance than anything you have ever been paid for book rights or movie rights or whatnot; just work harder than before and put in longer hours than ever, until you finally get your own huge advance.

I have known writers who have become so jealous of a friend's success that they have broken off the friendship. This has even happened to me. A couple of writer friends of mine became deeply disturbed by the fact that my career was pulling ahead of theirs, and they went so far as to tell editors lies about me, lies which might have damaged my career if the editors hadn't checked them out. This vicious betrayal stunned and hurt me, for I had been friends with these writers when their careers had been a lot hotter than mine, and I had always been happy to hear the news of each of their successes.

Professional jealousy is silly. It's wasted effort. All of that misdirected energy should be put into writing. A novelist should be in competition only with himself, trying to make each new book better than the one before it.

———

Do not regard your writing as gospel. Be open to suggestions from your editors. When was the last time you read a good story that had been graven in stone?

———

On the other hand, do not automatically take every suggestion your editors make. You must learn to separate the proverbial wheat from the proverbial chaff, and you must have confidence in your own abilities and talent.

———

Do not worry about or be scared by that dreaded nemesis, the Writer's Block. If you worry about it or fear it too much, you will be playing right into its hands. The psychological mechanism in your own mind that generates the block will feed off your worry and fear, and the block will only get worse.

A writer's block is most often caused by one of five things: overwork, boredom, self-doubt, financial worries, or emotional problems between the writer and those close to him. If overwork is the cause, stop writing for a couple of days or weeks; when you're ready to start again, you'll know, because the typewriter will no longer appear to be a formidable opponent and will seem, instead, like a delightful toy. If boredom with the piece in progress has slowed you to a standstill, put it aside and begin something new, no matter how close to the end of the piece you may be; chances are, if it bores you, it will bore editors and readers as well. To cure a case of self-doubt, shame yourself without restraint for your lack of confidence; read a novel by a really bad writer whose work you despise, and tell yourself, "If *this* junk can get into print, publishers will fight one another for the rights to *my* book"; start something new right away, for this new thing might, by its freshness, restore your confidence. Don't worry if you go through a dozen ideas before you hit something that gets you going again. Financial worries must be solved before you can write again, even if that means you—the full-time freelancer—must take a temporary job to keep above water or that you—the part-time writer—must take a part-time job and forsake writing until your financial position is less chaotic. If emotional entanglements occupy your mind and keep you from producing, sit down with your boyfriend/girlfriend/husband/wife and talk about the things that are bothering you, work out solutions. Not only will such sessions improve your love life, they will improve your writing as well.

Many authors find that each day starts with a miniature writer's block, a one- or two-hour thing, before the mind is nimble enough to create. This is a depressing way to begin the day—sitting alone in a room, staring at a blank page, unable to string even a noun and an article together. But there's a cure for the mini-block. Each morning—or afternoon or evening—when you sit down to work, begin by retyping the last page or two that you finished the day before. Look for small ways to improve it—a different adjective here, a different adverb there, a slight rearrangement of this sentence, a better word-order for that phrase. This little trick will put you back into the mood you were in when you were working steadily and happily the previous day, and it will eliminate the mini-block for almost anyone.

It also helps to keep your work area clean and uncluttered, and your resource notes or material well arranged. I have read countless articles about how "psychologically valuable" it is for a writer to work at a cluttered desk; proponents of this theory insist that the jumbled mess of books and papers will give the author a feeling of excitement and fertility. Phooey. A writer is a professional, and he needs that sense of order that is so evident in the offices of other professional people such as doctors, lawyers, and accountants. I have never heard the cluttered-desk theory proposed by any truly *successful* author. I know you will find it easier to start writing each day if you are working in a pleasant, businesslike room.

Even the worst writer's block, even one arising from the deepest and blackest despair does not have to last longer than one or two days if the writer is determined to overcome it.

14.

**Selling what you write
or
Money is freedom; money
is time; money is fame;
money is respect; money
is a yardstick of many
things, but most of all,
money is money.**

There are writers who don't give a damn about art; at a party, three-quarters of their conversation is about money. Then there are the craftsmen, the artists, those writers who are *deeply* committed to their work; at a party, three-quarters of *their* conversation is about money, too.

In order to earn some useful currency with your fiction, you have first got to find a publisher willing to print it. New writers frequently ask me questions related to that holy quest for a good publisher; here are a few of them with the best answers I can provide:

1. *Should I begin my writing career with short stories or with novels?* A novel requires a greater commitment in terms of a writer's time, energy, and emotional resources than does any other form of writing, fiction or nonfiction; nevertheless, for several reasons, including financial return, I advise you to take the plunge into novel writing at the very start of your career. There are not one percent as many opportunities for selling short stories as there are for selling novels; the marketplace is oriented toward the longer form, for that is what readers want. Even if you sell every short story you write, the money won't be good; a hundred thousand words of short pieces will not earn you a tenth as much as a good novel of equal length. Short stories are sold for flat fees; novels earn royalties in addition to advance payments. For every short story sold to a Hollywood studio or to an independent motion picture producer, a hundred novels receive lucrative film deals. A short story has no chance whatsoever of selling to a book club; on the other hand, a novel can earn tens of thousands, even hundreds of thousands of dollars, if it is chosen as the main selection of a major club. Translation rights to short stories are occasionally sold, but not nearly as often (or for nearly as much) as the translation rights to books.

It is also difficult to build a reputation as a writer by turning out only short stories. Short fiction receives little or no attention from critics; the contents of magazines—in which short stories appear—are not regularly reviewed. Until it is collected in an anthology, a short story has a lifespan limited to the on-sale time of the publication in which it appears. It is true that Ray Bradbury has established himself as a major American writer almost entirely with his short stories. He has written two exceptionally fine novels—*Fahrenheit 451* and *Something Wicked This Way Comes*—but his fame rests primarily on the hundreds of short pieces he has published in magazines and collected into such outstanding books as *The Martian Chronicles, The Golden Apples of the Sun, R Is for Rocket, S Is for Space, The Machineries of Joy, The October Country,* and others. But Mr. Bradbury is a special case, and the new writer will find it most difficult to follow his example.

Finally, writing a lot of short stories, to the exclusion of all other forms of fiction, teaches you only short-term discipline. That can cause you a great deal of agony later, when you begin your first novel and discover that it demands considerably more than you are prepared to give. Short story writers are accustomed to completing a project in a day or two, a couple of weeks at most, and they are frequently rewarded with that exhilarating rush of high spirits that comes upon the completion of any piece of fiction; often they are not able to cope with the fact that, when writing novels, that rush comes only once every few months.

2. *What kind of advance against royalties can I expect to receive from a publisher?* If you are a new writer, you will most likely receive a small advance, a couple of thousand dollars, certainly no more than five thousand. A few times every year, a new writer comes along with a first novel that is a blockbuster—or that some publisher *thinks* is a blockbuster—and he makes hundreds of thousands, sometimes even millions of dollars from it. If you expect to erupt upon the publishing scene in Vesuvian splendor, amidst a lava flow of cash, you are setting yourself up for much frustration and disappointment. Sure, you might get lucky; you might actually be such a good storyteller that your first novel deserves major promotion and a million-dollar paperback sale. But the chance of that is so small that you can't waste time counting on it. Most writers' careers evolve slowly; their advances rise from book to book, and their audience increases year by year. That has been the pattern of my own career; the advance I received for my latest book was one hundred times greater than the advance I got for my first novel, fourteen years ago.

3. *How many books must I write before I achieve financial independence?* Many new and would-be writers start wondering about financial independence the moment they sit down at the typewriter for the first time. This is a question I'm frequently asked, and one to which there is no single answer. Some writers hit it big with their first book and have no money worries thereafter. Others write three books or six or thirty before breaking onto the bestseller lists. Some writers never achieve bestseller status; they write a lot of books and their books all stay in print, selling modestly but steadily year after year, until they *gradually* become independent. And now the bad news: Many writers, perhaps even *most* writers, never achieve even minimum financial security. I know a great many authors, especially those working in the genres, who face at least one financial crisis every year. The possibility of utter failure and the equal possibility of enormous success are what make the writing profession so exciting—if sometimes a bit nerve-wracking. The nine-to-five office worker will never starve—but he will probably also never make a fortune. The full-time writer always faces the prospect of starvation, at least in his early years (if you will allow me some hyperbole)—but he may also look forward to the chance of becoming truly wealthy to an extent that few people ever do. The nature of the publishing business is such that the writer always has hope, and hope is what makes this writing life so interesting.

4. *How easy is it to sell the film rights to a novel?* Not easy at all. For every novel that is purchased for motion picture production, hundreds go unnoticed by Hollywood. Being handled by a good agent helps your chances of getting your hands on some studio money, but what helps most of all is writing good stories. Just do your work as a novelist, and if you are any good at all, Hollywood will eventually find you.

More often than not, your books will be optioned by producers rather than bought outright. An option can amount to as little as $5,000 against a purchase price of $50,000 or $75,000 or $100,000 or more. Higher-end option deals can range from $75,000 to $100,000 against a total purchase price of $200,000 or $500,000 or more, but that is definitely getting toward the upper limits of the option game, and happens only when several producers or studios are bidding competitively for a hot property. In many cases, rather than lay **out** as much as $75,000 or $100,000 just to get a one- or two-year hold on a book, a producer will decide to go all the way, pay the larger sum, and thereby acquire film rights to the book in perpetuity. When a book is bought outright by a producer, rather than optioned, it can bring anything from $25,000 for a TV movie of a novel that is not a hot property, all the way up to $1,000,000 or more for the novel that everyone in Hollywood is desperate to film.

Even when a book is sold for a lot of money to a major film studio, that does not guarantee that a movie will be made from it. Countless problems can sideline a project before it ever gets in front of a camera. Usually, the problem is the script. It is not unusual for a book to be passed to half a dozen screenwriters, one after the other, as the studio bosses search for a script in which they are willing to invest the millions and millions of dollars that a major production requires. In the process of looking for that shootable script, a studio may spend a million dollars on screenwriters' fees and on the original purchase price of the novel itself—all of which they write off to operating losses if the film is never made. If you are fortunate enough to get a deal with a studio for one of your novels, take the money and run; do not waste time worrying about who will play the lead roles; don't get hung up on the idea of meeting and mingling with movie stars. Remember: You are a *writer*.

5. *If one of my novels sells to the movies, will I be given a chance to write the screenplay?* Once in a while, a producer will hire a novelist to adapt his own book to the screen, but it doesn't happen often. Novels and screenplays are very different forms, and few novelists seem able to handle screenplays well. When a novelist writes a script based on his own book, he usually finds it both difficult and painful to cut his story down to filmable size. It *is* hard to compress a 400-page novel into just 110 pages of action and dialogue, which is what you must do when you write a screenplay; inevitably, nuances are lost. I know of a best-selling novelist who badly wanted to write movies; when he was given the opportunity to adapt one of his own books, he turned in a 400-page screenplay. If that doesn't strike you as funny, consider this: One page of a screenplay equals roughly one minute of screen time; a 400-page script would result in a film almost seven hours long! Is it any wonder that producers are wary of letting the novelist adapt his own book?

I have written a few screenplays, and I haven't had too much trouble with the form. In fact I think that screenwriting is a great deal easier than novel writing. Several years ago, a major studio took an option on one of my "Brian Coffey" novels, *The Face of Fear,* then paid me quite a lot of money to write the screenplay. The producer, a charming woman who was easy to deal with, was surprised that I delivered the script on time and that what I delivered was quite adequate. I was, she informed me, the first novelist who had ever given her a shootable script—and she had dealt with nineteen others before me!

Does that mean I'm brilliant? No.

Does it mean the other nineteen writers were slow-witted? No.

Does it mean they failed to take their scripting jobs seriously? Quite possibly, yes. Many authors have a snobbish attitude toward screenwriting and refuse to admit that it might actually require some effort and special talent. But most likely, it means those nineteen were so fond of their own brilliant prose they couldn't bear to prune it into movie form.

If you ever get the chance to write a screenplay based on your own novel, you must regard your original story as nothing more than the launching pad for the movie. You must be willing to make *any* changes in characters, background, story line, and thematic structure that are demanded by the screenplay form. If you can bear to carve away relentlessly at your own golden prose, and if you have solid narrative skills, and if you have any visual sense at all, and if you *like* movies, then you will probably succeed as a screenwriter.

One other thing: To be *happy* writing screenplays, you must understand that a movie is a collaborative effort. Nothing you write for the medium will wind up exactly the way you originally imagined it. Your scenes and characters will be filtered through the producer, the director, the cameraman, the actors, and through countless other people as well—technicians and craftsmen in vast array—all of whom add their viewpoints and talents to the mix. In the end, no single person can legitimately claim that a movie is *his,* in spite of the fact that some directors lay just such a claim to every picture they make. For the writer, film is a far less creatively satisfying medium than print; when a book is set in type, it is frozen forever as you intended it, and you can rightfully say, "This is mine."

6. *Is there any way I can slant my novel to insure a sale of the film rights?* Because several of my books have sold to the movies, I hear this question frequently from new writers. I am sorry to report that the answer is no—there is no special slant, no magic trick that will enable you to "insure" a sale of the film rights. Producers and studio executives are as mysterious as the migratory habits of the fiddler crab, as unpredictable as Mount Saint Helens. I have written books that, when finished, seemed like naturals for Hollywood—and they never sold. I've written others that seemed, for many reasons, too difficult and expensive to film—and they sold within a few weeks of the moment when I typed "the end" on the final page.

Never write a book with one greedy eye on Hollywood. That is a fool's game. Some writers try to cram all the right movie scenes into a novel, borrowing from every hit since *Casablanca*. But that doesn't cause a producer to bounce up and down with glee in his leather-covered mogul's chair; Hollywood can film cheap imitations of its past triumphs *without* spending a lot of money to buy the rights to your book. Something new and fresh is more likely to catch a producer's attention. I've heard of writers structuring their novels with all quick-cut transitions, so that their books could be more easily adapted to screenplay form; I've heard of an author who struggles hard to write each of his novels primarily in dialogue, so that every one of his books will look and read somewhat like a screenplay. None of these tricks will guarantee you fame and fortune in Tinseltown. The best way to get a film sale is to write a fast-paced, involving, well-told novel. Good books are likely to make good movies.

If you are a serious novelist, the only thing you should care about is doing the best book you possibly can. If the story *demands* to be told largely through dialogue, then by all means tell it that way; but don't force the form upon it solely because you want the finished page to look like a movie script. A movie sale is a serendipitous bonus. When you strike it rich, enjoy every moment and every penny of it. Otherwise, don't worry about whether you should make your heroine look like Sally Field or Bo Derek or Jill Clayburgh; if a major studio *does* buy your book, they will probably change the role anyway—so that Flip Wilson can do it in drag.

7. *Why do writers use pen names?* Some writers use pen names because their real names are too harsh or too plain. No one can say for sure whether a phonetically pleasing by-line sells more books than does a name that grates on the ear, but most writers *feel* this is true. "Ross Macdonald" is a more pleasant-sounding name than Kenneth Millar, which is the author's real name. "Mark Twain" has a much nicer ring to it than Samuel Clemens. I feel that my own name has too harsh a sound for a novelist's by-line.

When I began writing, however, my need for recognition (translation: my ravenous ego) was such that I simply could not bear to write under a pseudonym.

If a mainstream author writes more than one novel a year, he will probably need to adopt a pen name for a portion of his work. Most hardcover publishers feel they cannot adequately promote more than one book a year by any writer. Furthermore, if your novels sell well, your publisher will want the exclusive right to use your name so long as you are writing for his house, and he will be eager to pay a little extra for that privilege; he doesn't want *his* new Sam Hepplefinger novel to be in competition with some other publisher's new Sam Hepplefinger novel. Thus, if your work is at all successful, you will probably be quickly locked into a contract that calls for one book a year and forbids you to use your name with any other publishing house.

If you are a popular mainstream author, paperback publishers also will express a desire to get an exclusive hold on your name. Sometimes, if you are writing bestselling paperback originals (a paperback original is a book that never had a hardcover edition), a publisher will stretch the one-a-year rule and occasionally issue two books with your by-line in a twelve-month period. This is possible because paperback publishers' schedules are, for many reasons, more flexible than those of the hardcover houses, where production and distribution progress at a comparatively slow pace. But even if you *are* a bestselling author of paperback originals, and if your publisher *does* bend the rules in order to issue two of your books in one year, you *still* will need a pen name if you write *more* than two—and some successful authors write three or even four books each year.

A genre novelist whose books do not reach the bestseller lists will probably not be asked to sign a contract in which there is an exclusivity clause. This is good news and bad news. The good news is that the genre author can satisfy his ego by publishing any number of novels under his own name each year, spreading his by-line all over bookstore shelves. The bad news is that a publisher's failure to ask for an exclusivity clause means that the publisher places little or no value on an author's name.

Finally, a writer will sometimes use a pseudonym when the book he is writing is far different from the kind of books that readers have come to associate with his name. Donald Westlake writes comic novels under his own name, but when he publishes hard-boiled thrillers, he uses the nom de plume "Richard Stark." Evan Hunter writes sensitive, superlative mainstream novels under his own name, but he calls himself "Ed McBain" when he writes mysteries. In cases such as these, the pseudonym is simply a device by which the author avoids confusing—and possibly disappointing—his readers.

8. *Is it really possible to sell a book without the help of an agent?* Yes. Publishers are always hungry for product. A few companies refuse to consider unsolicited manuscripts, but most publishing houses employ first readers who go through all unsolicited submissions, reading at least a couple of pages of each. When a first reader finds a script that shows promise, he keeps reading until he either gets bored with it or finishes it. If he actually finds a script worth reading to the end, the reader passes it up the chain of command to an editor.

My first three novels were sold without benefit of an agent. I believe I gained valuable marketing experience by handling my own books in those early days. However, I do believe it is wise to get an agent as soon as you can. (See question number 10.)

9. *If a novel is repeatedly rejected, how many publishing houses should I try before giving up?* Try all of them. Never give up on a novel in which you have faith. Some of the most successful books ever published were rejected by several houses before finding a home.

10. *How can I get an agent to handle my work?* You will not be able to get a first-rate agent or even a second-rate agent until you have sold at least one novel on your own. Most good agents will not accept a new client until they have proof that he is professional, talented, and hardworking. The best proof of those things is a finished manuscript that has hooked a publisher.

As soon as an editor tells you he wants to buy your novel, ask him to recommend you to an agent who will be willing to handle the contract. That is the best and just about the only way for a new writer to connect with a good agent.

A reputable agent will not force you to sign a contract with his agency. He will want to represent you only as long as you are happy with his representation. A good agent earns your loyalty; he does not obtain it with a binding legal document. You should be wary of any agent who tries such a thing.

In all likelihood, you will not remain forever with the first agent who represents you. The agent-author relationship is, for the average writer, almost as important as his relationship with his spouse. You should be totally comfortable with your agent both in a business and in a personal sense. Over the years, I have had three agents. The first was intolerable on every level, both business and personal. The second was an absolutely charming man; I liked him enormously as a person and always had a great deal of fun in his company. However, he and I did not see eye-to-eye about the direction my career should take, and eventually we came to a parting of the ways that was not without pain. I am now represented by a woman with whom I am very compatible on a personal level and reasonably compatible on a business level. If you find the *right* agent the first time out of the gate, you have my envy and best wishes.

Always remember this: When everything is said and done, the only thing that sells your work is the quality of the work itself. Not even the best agent in the business can sell a lousy book. An agent *can* get a higher advance and better royalty terms than an author can usually negotiate for himself. An agent *can* identify and strike out of a publishing contract nasty clauses that might slip past the author's untrained eye. An agent *can* be a go-between for disputes between an author and an editor. An agent *can* offer advice, sympathy, and encouragement; and this is one of an agent's most important functions. An agent can help an author plan for the future in terms of both finances and creative direction. (However, no writer should allow his agent to be his business manager, too, and no writer should put all of his incoming funds and financial affairs in the hands of a business manager who is associated with his agent. After all, would you allow an IRS attorney to represent you in tax court? Would you allow a surgeon to operate on your heart if you knew that half his income came from the ownership of several cemeteries?) An agent can be a shining light in the darkness, making this basically lonely occupation less lonely. There are a lot of things an agent can do, but no agent can make you rich and famous if your writing is tired and sloppy and unimaginative. Work hard. Constantly polish and improve upon your prose. If you write good books, you will be found and published and paid well. I have heard of dozens of supposedly brilliant authors who swear no one will give them a chance; but every time I've taken a look at their work, it has been unpublishable, usually because it has been self-indulgent to the point of being incoherent. Every good writer is "discovered" sooner or later. The work sells itself. Publishers need new writers; without them, publishing companies would go out of business. The work sells itself. Never neglect the work; never do a sloppy job; never take shortcuts. Give the reader his money's worth, and you will prosper.

11. *If a publisher is interested in my book and, based on that interest, I manage to obtain an agent, will I be able to rely entirely on my agent in all business matters?* No. As much as an agent may like you and admire your work, as much as he may want the very best for you, the time he can spend on you is finite. You must be aware of the needs of the marketplace, and you must be aware of what money and terms other writers at your sales level are receiving, so that you can intelligently evaluate whatever offer your agent brings to you. If it isn't a good enough offer, you must be able to explain why you feel it is inadequate, and you must have the nerve to demand a greater effort from your agent. Even if an agent loves you like a sister (or a brother), you are not number one in his book and never can be; *he* is number one in his book, just as you are number one in yours. He is always thinking about his commission; without a sale there is no commission, which means he will usually be willing to settle for a price that is "almost right" when you feel that a more aggressive bargaining stance is called for. The agent has lots of other projects to sell and lots of other commissions to earn from other clients; but you will be financially limited by whatever contract is negotiated, and you must do your best to see that the most advantageous deal is struck.

12. *Do you mean that, even after giving my approval of the verbal deal, I should force myself to read through the tedious prose of the actual contract?* Absolutely. Read every word of it. If there is anything you don't understand, ask your attorney about it. You must learn to interpret the legal and quasi-legal jargon in which publishing and film contracts are written, for not all agents look out for their clients' interests as well as they should. Besides, even the best agents occasionally overlook small details that, unnoticed and unchanged, could later give the author *big* headaches.

13. *Are there any particular clauses I should be on the lookout for when I read a publishing contract?* Yes. Here's a list of ten clauses damaging to the author's interests.

ONE: Never agree to give a publisher more than a thirty-day option on your next project. When you sign a book contract, it usually contains a clause providing for the publisher to have first look at your next outline or finished novel. There is nothing wrong with that. It is to your benefit to develop a lasting relationship with a single publishing company *if* that house intends to promote your books and keep them in print. However, the publisher should not ask for or be given an excessively long time to decide whether or not he wants your next novel. I have heard of publishers asking for sixty days, ninety days, and even as much as six months! If you should be foolish enough to agree to such an extended option period, you will be forced to sit twiddling your thumbs for months while your cash flow comes to a screeching halt. Thirty days is long enough.

One publishing company—let's call it Super-Duper Fantastico Books—introduced a new contract with an absolutely horrendous option clause. At a glance, the clause appeared to be a simple, thirty-day option. But there was another, attached paragraph which stated that the publisher didn't even have to consider a new proposal until sixty days after the author's previous book had been published; then the publisher had thirty days to decide. The intention of the clause was to give Super-Duper Fantastico a chance to see how well the first book sold before committing to a second. Considering that the elapsed time between delivery of a script and publication of a novel can be anywhere from six to eighteen months, Super-Duper Fantastico actually was asking for at least a nine-month and as much as a twenty-one-month option! When this new contract appeared, the screams of agents and authors broke windows all over America, and Super-Duper backed off. But if this clause, which shows the publisher's contempt for the author's well-being, could be proposed by one major publisher, it will eventually be proposed by others; be on guard.

TWO: Never agree to an option clause that gives your publisher your next book at the same price he paid for the previous one. If book number one garners a movie sale or a book club sale or a handsome reprint sale prior to publication, the size of your advance for the following project should increase.

THREE: Never agree to a clause that requires you to pay back any unearned portion of the original advance. An advance is just what it says it is: an advance against royalties, not a sum paid in addition to royalties. If your publisher advances you $10,000 for a novel, that book must sell enough copies to earn $10,000 in royalties before you will be paid an additional penny. If the book is successful, it may earn many times $10,000. If it is a failure, perhaps it will earn only $7,000. However, no reputable publisher should ever ask the author to repay the other $3,000, for the fact is that *both* parties have taken risks in the relationship, and the author should not be expected to cover his own losses as well as those of the publisher. Yes, it is true that the publisher risked his money, in effect placing a bet that the book would earn more than $10,000. But the author takes a risk, too, by selling the book to publisher A rather than to publisher B, for it is always possible that publisher B would have promoted the book better and would have made a far greater success of it than publisher A.

Consider this experience of mine: Several years ago, I wrote a novel titled *The Vision,* under an existing contract with a publishing company henceforth referred to as Colossal Books (not, of course, its real name). When I finished *The Vision,* I thought it broke just a bit of new ground in its field, and I knew it was a pretty good read, a page-turner. I had high hopes for it, and so did my agent. We strongly suggested that Colossal Books give *The Vision* a fairly sizeable first printing and a good advertising budget. But Colossal couldn't see things our way. "Look," said the editor at Colossal, "this is a nice little book, but it isn't special in any way, shape, or form. There's no point in putting a push behind it because nothing will happen for it. We'll be lucky to get any reprint sale at all, and there's no chance of a book club selection. We'll do *The Vision* but only as a genre mystery." We asked the editor if we could sell the book elsewhere and repay the advance that Colossal had given me, and that was acceptable to him. We moved the novel to Putnam's, where there was at least *some* enthusiasm for the book. Through Putnam's, *The Vision* was placed as a main selection of the Doubleday Book Club, from which it earned substantial royalties; it was also sold to a paperback house for a very solid six-figure advance. If we had left the book at Colossal, it probably would not have earned out the original advance, for Colossal would not have handled it properly. Colossal would have lost money—but *I would have lost money, too.* Both the publisher and the author take risks, and the author should *never* be expected to protect the publisher's at-risk funds by repaying any portion of an unearned advance.

FOUR: Never agree to an exclusivity clause unless you are being paid well for locking up your name. (For an explanation of the term "exclusivity" as it applies in a publishing contract, see question number 7, where the term is used in a discussion of pen names.)

FIVE: Never relinquish a percentage of the film rights to

the book publisher. The publisher has nothing to do with the selling of film rights or with the making of the movie, and there is no reason why he deserves to share in that revenue. He will benefit by the sales of movie tie-in editions of the book when and if the film is released, and that should satisfy him.

SIX: If your novel is first published by a hardcover house, never agree to share more than half of the income from book club or reprint sales with the publisher. The standard split of this income has been 50-50 for a long time, and that is generally considered a fair division. Many hardcover houses could not survive if they didn't share in book club and paperback money with the author. If the author is hugely profitable for the publisher—as are James Clavell, Herman Wouk, James Michener, Robert Ludlum, and others of their celebrity—the 50-50 split on paperback income is sometimes revised to the author's advantage. I know of one contract where the division of paperback income was arranged like this: 50-50 on the first $100,000; 55-45 on the second $100,000; 60-40 on the third $100,000; and 65-35 on everything thereafter, with the larger piece going to the novelist. For the new writer, and even for most moderately successful authors, the 50-50 split is fair enough—*if* the publisher does a reasonable amount of promotion and publishes the book with some enthusiasm.

If your original contract is with a paperback house, the question of how to split the reprint money will not arise. But some paperbacks are picked up for hardcover reprint by the book clubs; when this happens, a 50-50 split between author and paperback publisher is standard and fair.

SEVEN: If you are a new writer, your contracts will almost surely arrive with a clause giving the U.S. publisher anywhere from 25 to 50 percent of all foreign language rights, as well as an equally outrageous percentage of any income provided by a British publisher. Try your best to hold on to 100 percent of all foreign rights. The only time that a U.S. publisher deserves a share of foreign income is when he pays you a higher advance for permission to act as an agent for the foreign language rights to your novel.

Foreign income can amount to just $5,000 or $10,000 for a modestly successful book, but it can escalate to hundreds of thousands of dollars for a book that was a bestseller in America. Perhaps it won't hurt you to surrender 25 percent of $10,000, but imagine how you'll feel if your book *is* a hit and you have to let the publisher take 25 or 50 percent of $300,000 in foreign income! Even when your publisher boosts your advance in return for the right to handle foreign language sales, his share of those monies should amount to no more than 20 percent or, at the very most, 25 percent.

EIGHT: Never sign a contract that lacks a reversion clause. Simply put, a reversion clause returns all rights to the novel to the author at the end of a specified length of time, usually five years, sometimes as long as seven years. When a book reverts to you, the potential exists for resale, and you can make additonal money from it. If the book was published when you were an unknown beginner, and if you are a bestselling author by the time that early book reverts to you, it might actually be worth a far larger advance the second time around because your name has become an asset. A novelist is in the business of licensing books; he should *not* be in the business of selling them outright and relinquishing all rights in perpetuity.

NINE: Never agree to a clause that gives the publisher the right to alter your prose without your approval. If your name is going to be splashed on the cover of the novel, you want to be very, very sure that whole paragraphs of inept narration aren't jammed in among your own scenes and that the sense of your plot hasn't been destroyed by massive, poorly considered cutting. In matters of art and craft, the author must always be the final authority.

TEN: If your book is to be published under a pen name, never agree to a contract clause giving the publisher ownership of that pseudonym. If you do and your book is a success, you will not be able to go to another publisher with the pen name; the original publisher will feel safe in offering you any advance and royalty terms he wishes, for you will have no choice but to write for him. If you refuse, he will have the legal right to hire another writer to work under the pen name that *you* made successful in the first place.

The only exception to this rule is when the writer is hired to produce a book under an already existing house name. For example, hundreds of "Nick Carter" novels have been written by scores of authors whose real names never appear on the books, but in this case the writers don't deserve to own a piece of the house name. The Nick Carter series was created by the publisher and originally conceived as a project to be parceled out among many writers in order to keep a one-a-month release schedule.

Those ten clauses are not the only dirty tricks to be found in publishing contracts, but they are the ones most often encountered.

In Chapter 3 of this book, I said, ". . . I would be the last to claim that publishing is a safe and worry-free business. The book trade *does* have serious problems." In the interests of fair play, I promised that I would outline some of those problems in Chapter 14, and here we are. This seems the best place to take up the subject, for publishers' troubles automatically become writers' troubles in the most fundamental financial terms. To obtain the most money and the best treatment for your books, you must understand the problems that plague the industry.

Returns

Let's imagine there's a huge, nationwide chain of discount stores—like K-mart—called . . . oh, Everything Mart. Let's suppose that Everything Mart decides its customers would buy flibber-gidgets. Everything Mart obtains competitive bids from a number of flibber-gidget manufacturers, then orders one million flibber-gidgets from the supplier who can give it the best price. Let's further suppose that Everything Mart pays a wholesale price of $2 for each of those one million flibber-gidgets. Everything Mart then puts the item on its shelves with a $4 price tag, a figure that provides for overhead, advertising, and a reasonable profit. Much to its dismay, the discount store finds that its customers have all the flibber-gidgets they need; only 200,000 of the one million are sold. What does Everything Mart do with those other 800,000 flibber-gidgets? The only sensible thing it can do is put them on sale—say, at $2.75. At this new price, Everything Mart moves another 400,000 flibber-gidgets, but it is still stuck with 400,000 more in its storerooms. Now it reduces the price to $2.25. Another 300,000 are sold, leaving just 100,000 of the damned things. Everything Mart prices these at $1.95, a nickel below its wholesale cost and considerably more than a nickel below its real cost when you add in overhead. In fact, the break-even point was probably around $2.80. Everything Mart moves just 30,000 additional units at its new low price. In desperation, the price is slashed to a dollar, then to half a buck, and finally the store begins giving away flibber-gidgets as premiums with every purchase of a jibbery-doodad, until the entire order is disposed of. The Everything Mart warehousemen are relieved that they no longer have to shift around the crates of flibber-gidgets, and the assistant buyer who thought of the deal in the first place is suddenly working as a stock clerk in a dry goods store in the Australian outback.

Now let's look at a similar situation in the book business. Let's suppose that Colossal Books is publishing a paper-back original novel titled *Runaway Blockbuster* by Roderick Futility, a book that everyone believes will be a monster hit. (Futility is the star of that popular daytime soap opera, "Despair and Potroast," so how can his book possibly miss?) A fiction buyer for the Hugely Massive Book-chain orders 150,000 copies to supply Hugely Massive's 500 retail outlets—300 copies per store, a strong commitment. *Runaway Blockbuster*, a tired retread of a million other Hollywood novels—disguised in a die-cut, foil-stamped, double-embossed, three-dimensional, sequin-flocked, etched, rainbow-colored, tassel-fringed package—is released with a blaze of television ads and a cacophonous roar of radio commercials. In its first month in the Hugely Massive stores, *Runaway Blockbuster* sells just 11,126 copies—6,000 of which have been secretly purchased by Roderick Futility's agents, who are trying frantically to get the novel on Hugely Massive Bookchain's in-house bestseller list, for it is this list which most influences the composition of more important bestseller lists, like that of the *New York Times Book Review*. Theirs is a wasted effort, for word-of-mouth on the novel is so bad—worse than bad, dreadful, cataclysmic—that many bookstore browsers will not even touch the novel for fear of contracting some hideous, unnamed disease. At the end of the first month, it is clear to everyone at Hugely Massive that *Runaway Blockbuster* has been an unqualified disaster. At the end of two months, Hugely Massive has still not sold 132,000 of its initial 150,000-copy order.

Does the fiction buyer suddenly find himself working in a used paperback shop in Iceland? Not at all.

Does Hugely Massive reduce the price of the book to its wholesale cost or below, sell it at a loss, and take a financial bath on *Runaway Blockbuster*? Not on your life!

Unlike flibber-gidgets, unlike all other kinds of merchandise, books are returnable. The retailer is permitted to send them back to the manufacturer for *full* credit. In the case of a slow-selling hardcover title, the entire book is returned. With an unsalable paperback, the cover is ripped off and sent back to the publisher, while the remainder of the book is destroyed or sold for its value as paper pulp.

Because the financial responsibility for a failed book rests entirely with the publisher, several bad editorial judgments, clustered within a single year, can play havoc with a company's profit and loss statement. Returns can run as high as 50 or 60 percent on an unpopular title, and the losses on a single book can mount into the hundreds of thousands of dollars. The risks are staggering, and authors should have some understanding and sympathy for the stressful conditions under which editors and publishers must function.

However . . .

Publishers should not exaggerate the very real problem of returns in an effort to deprive writers of their fair share of book profits. But many of them do, and they have developed two extremely successful techniques for exploiting the situation, techniques that frustrate and enrage every hardworking, professional writer.

First, there is the royalty statement device known as the

"reserve against returns." This means that publishers are permitted to delay paying royalties on that percentage of sales that might possibly be returned by bookstores for credit. This is a fair clause in a publishing contract, for every book will have some copies returned by retailers; publishers should not be forced to overpay royalties and then later be forced to waste time and energy trying to recover overpayments from authors.

Unfortunately, the majority of publishing houses exploit the situation by routinely withholding 60 or 70 percent of sales as a reserve against returns on the first and often the second royalty statement following publication. In other words, they treat every book as if it were one of the worst-selling titles of the year. Even if they have published an author many times and know from experience that his returns are never greater than 20 percent, they *always* withhold 60 percent through at least one and usually two royalty periods. These delaying tactics have a devastating effect on the writer's financial well-being.

I'll give you an example that is all too typical of what most writers endure. For this purpose, let us imagine that there is a writer named Merle M. Merkle and that he has written a novel titled *Lust and Greed*.

JANUARY 2, 1981:

    Lust and Greed is published as a paperback original by Colossal Books. The first printing is one million copies.

JANUARY 19, 1981:

    Lust and Greed is selling well. Colossal Books orders a second printing of 100,000 copies to fill reorders.

JANUARY 26, 1981:

    Colossal Books orders a third printing of 100,000, for a total in-print figure of 1,200,000. Word comes that the book will be number ten on next week's *New York Times* bestseller list and number nine on the *Publishers Weekly* list.

FEBRUARY, 1981:

    During the month of February, *Lust and Greed* climbs as high as the number four position on the bestseller lists and attains an in-print total of 1,500,000 copies.

JUNE 30, 1981:

    The six-month royalty period closes. *Lust and Greed*

has not been on the bestseller lists since the end of April, but it had one hell of a run.

OCTOBER 1, 1981:

The first royalty statement on *Lust and Greed* is due. Yes, the royalty period closed on June 30, and Colossal Books' accounting department had plenty of time to correlate sales reports and issue statements to authors by August 1; however, publishing contracts traditionally give publishers ninety days after the close of a royalty period to issue statements to authors, and this is a tradition that publishers guard with savage fury. No other business operates on such a schedule; their suppliers would not tolerate it.

NOVEMBER 15, 1981:

Merle M. Merkle receives his first royalty statement from Colossal Books. You're saying, "Wait a minute, even considering the traditional snail-like schedule of the publishing business, the royalty statement was due no later than October first." Yes, but with 95 percent of all publishing houses, there are delays. Publishers' excuses are drearily familiar to any professional writer: malfunctioning computers, a terrible epidemic of flu in the accounting department, misplaced records and confused sales reports . . . ad nauseam. Anyway, when the royalty statement finally arrives on November 15—for sales through June 30—Merle Merkle receives a check. His royalty rate is a flat 10 percent of a $2.50 cover price. The publisher printed 1,500,000 and has sold at least 80 percent or 1,300,000, but he holds a large reserve against returns and pays Merkle for sales of only 400,000 copies. Since Merkle was originally advanced $25,000, his royalty check is for $75,000. The publisher is keeping a royalty pool of $225,000 as a reserve against returns. At this point, the author has irretrievably lost a great deal of money. For starters, if he had received the $75,000 on August 1, as he should have, he could have put it in Treasury certificates paying 12 percent (the current rate), and even without figuring the effect of daily compounding, it would have returned $2,637.55 interest for August, September, October, and half of November. That money is lost forever. Furthermore, during those three and a half months that the publisher was unfairly holding that $75,000, inflation was eating away at its buying power. For the past few years, as I write this, the rate of inflation has been around 14 percent. At that rate, Merle Merkle's $75,000 lost $3,062.50 in value during the extra three and a half months that the publisher held it. In addition, if the publisher had held only a *fair* reserve against returns—say, one-third the print run in the case of an unquestioned bestseller like *Lust and Greed*—then Merkle would have gotten another $150,000 on August 1. Because he *didn't* receive it then, he has already lost the investment potential plus the portion eaten up by inflation. This means there was an additional loss of at least $11,401.17. Added to the previous losses, the author is already out a total of $17,101.22, and he will continue to lose money steadily as the publisher parcels out his total royalties over a period of at least two years, probably three. In the meantime, of course, the publisher is investing that money, the *author's* money, and earning a tidy return on it. Fair? No!

Perhaps you find it difficult to sympathize with an author like Merle M. Merkle, who will, after all, earn $325,000 over two or three years from just that one book. Nevertheless, he is being hurt by this creative bookkeeping, and it isn't right. Besides, for every bestselling novelist like Merle Merkle, publishers apply the same creative accounting to scores of less successful writers whose royalty checks amount to only a few hundred or a few thousand dollars. No one escapes.

The second way that some publishers use the returns problem for their own benefit is by wildly exaggerating the seriousness of the problem in order to hold down authors' advances. Because of the creative bookkeeping outlined above, many authors have decided that they must insist upon very large advances, prior to publication, in order to avoid being victimized. During the past couple of years, frightened by the fact that they have millions upon millions of dollars tied up in non-earning advances far ahead of publication dates, some publishers have been saying that *average* returns on *all* books are running 50 percent or higher. This simply isn't true. Studies made by the federal government and other independent organizations indicate that average book returns are below 20 percent. Even as I write this, *Publishers Weekly* has printed an article outlining its findings in an in-depth survey of bookstore owners and managers all across the country, and according to this venerable and generally reliable magazine, returns are indeed averaging below 20 percent. So we have a situation in which some publishers appear to be lying about the rate of returns in order to solve another problem—high advances—which was caused at least in part by those same publishers' attempts to wring out a bit more profit by delaying authors' royalty payments. They are partly to blame for their own worst dilemmas.

Publishers face very real, very scary problems in the area of book returns. Every writer ought to make an effort to understand his publisher's anxieties in this regard. But I'm afraid that not more than a handful of writers will actually make this effort so long as publishers continue to use such unfair procedures in the calculation and payment of royalties.

I should also stress that there is absolutely nothing illegal about the way most publishers handle their royalty statements. Contracts and tradition give them the right to operate as they do. Furthermore, I'm certain many of them genuinely believe that they must make use of authors' royalties in order to keep their companies solvent. I just happen to think they're wrong—besides, isn't it bad management to reduce a company to such a state that it must operate on the float? And I am sure they would find writers more willing to bend, more sympathetic, and more cooperative if they abandoned their sometimes Draconian accounting procedures in favor of a fairer system that would protect the interests of both authors and publishers.

Overexploiting trends

In 1969, Mario Puzo's *The Godfather* exploded onto the bestseller lists and became one of the two or three most successful novels of the decade. It was a fine piece of work, a stunning tour de force, and at the very least a minor American classic.

As soon as it was obvious that Puzo's book was not

merely a bestseller but a runaway smash, a true phenomenon, editors all over New York began calling agents with the same frantic message: "If you have any clients with books about the Mafia, we want them. We want them real bad."

The better agents looked over their client lists, and if they saw no one who was working on a Mafia novel and no one who might be interested in working on one, they shrugged and turned their attention to other things. The very best agents do not encourage their clients to drop long-planned projects in order to write books that cater to current fads, for the best agents try to build lasting careers for their clients, and they know that quick and easy money for quick and easy books is usually damaging to an author—and actually less profitable in the long run. For one thing, if a writer becomes known to editors as a hack who will grind out *any* sort of book to fill a sudden scheduling need, regardless of his commitment or lack of commitment to the work at hand, that does *not* contribute favorably to his reputation as an artist and a craftsman. Editors will use him, but only to get books for the bottom or the middle of the publisher's list, never for lead titles. (As I explained earlier, I began writing when I was terribly young and hopelessly naive, and I fell into this trap in the first years of my career; later, when I became very serious about writing only polished, ambitious books, I had some trouble living down my reputation as a typewriter-for-hire. I've managed to change my image entirely, but it's taken eight years of extremely hard work, eight years of struggling to do a substantially better novel each time around, never daring to backslide for a moment.) Another reason the very best agents did not press their clients to write Mafia novels was that they know that the most successful books are nearly always those that spring from the writer himself, books that well up from his own imagination, books that he *must* write because he is obsessed with them. Books suggested by editors, books that do not have roots in the writer's own psyche, seldom do as well as the other kind.

Many second-rung agents are aware of these truths, too,

but they don't care; they are concerned only about the relatively quick commission they can earn from the easy-money book. They lack the ability or the desire (or both) to plan for the long-term success of their clients. When editors cried out urgently for imitations of *The Godfather*, many agents *did* encourage some of their clients to feed the publishers' ravenous hunger for Mafia books. A dismayingly high percentage of the resulting *Godfather* imitations were dreary, wooden, and unreadable.

In addition to commissioning new Mafia tales patterned after Puzo's book, editors combed their backlists, looking for previously published novels that had even the slightest association with the subject of organized crime. They repackaged these titles, slanting them toward the audience that loved Puzo's masterpiece. Cover blurbs were not shy about making comparisons: "BETTER THAN *THE GOD-FATHER*"; "SLASHES DEEPER THAN *THE GODFA-THER*"; "HOTTER THAN *THE GODFATHER*"; "MAKES *THE GODFATHER* LOOK LIKE A FAIRYTALE"; "MORE EXCITING THAN *THE GODFATHER*." Unfortunately, the book buyers who purchased these titles in good faith, believing the cover blurbs, were nearly always disappointed. Most of these revived, repackaged novels were simply thrillers in which Mafia types were the villains. They were not family sagas, as was Puzo's book; they were not novels with panoramic scope and thematic ambition, as was Puzo's novel. In short, although some of these repackaged books were well written and entertaining, they were not at all what they pretended to be.

Most of these imitations—both the repackaged novels and the brand new ones that were expressly written to the Puzo model—bore covers that used the lettering style and the general *look* of Neil Fujita's original cover design for *The Godfather*, which was quite distinctive, striking, and eye-pleasing. Some of the imitations so closely resembled the Fujita package that one might have thought at first glance that Puzo himself had written them. Fawcett, the paperback house that owned the reprint rights to Puzo's book, released a small flood of Mafia novels, mostly paperback originals, all with the look that Fujita had created—

and with an incredibly cheeky advertising blurb on each title that proclaimed, "FROM THE PUBLISHERS OF *THE GODFATHER*." For the first time in anyone's memory, a publisher seemed to be claiming primary credit for the quality of one of its titles, as if it and not Puzo was principally responsible for the superior readability and entertainment value of *The Godfather*; to some, Fawcett seemed to be saying, "Hey, look, we published Puzo, so we obviously have taste, and *anything* we release in the Mafia genre is bound to be 1,000 percent better than anything that anyone else publishes in the Mafia genre." Of course, that wasn't true; Fawcett published just as many rotten Puzo imitations as did everyone else. At the same time, Lancer Books (now defunct) reissued *The Fortunate Pilgrim*, Puzo's second novel, written prior to *The Godfather*, and they carefully copied the Fujita design; their cover art and sales copy led the book buyer to believe that *The Fortunate Pilgrim* was sort of a prequel or sequel to *The Godfather*, when in reality it was something of a "literary" novel that bore virtually no resemblance to Puzo's more famous book.

What was the result of this excessive exploitation?

Initially, most of the Puzo imitations enjoyed good sales. Readers, in search of a book as richly textured and as involving as *The Godfather*, took a chance that these similarly packaged novels would provide them with similarly rewarding reading experiences. Encouraged by these early successes, publishers rushed more and more and still more Mafia novels into print.

Eventually, after being repeatedly disappointed— "ripped off" would be more apt—book buyers realized that the use of Mr. Fujita's original design did not automatically guarantee a good read. They stopped buying Mafia novels.

Not surprisingly, book buyers' disenchantment with Mafia tales coincided exactly with that moment when the greatest number of those books were being released. (Most publishers seem to believe that the latest craze will continue to grow forever, even while they are issuing the cheap imitations that are absolutely certain to kill the reading public's interest in the entire form.) Suddenly, publishers were stuck with dozens of Mafia novels—totalling millions of copies—that nobody wanted. Here was a case in which returns really *were* running 60 and 70 percent on a significant number of titles. Whereas the Puzo imitators initially had contributed handsomely to the credit columns of publishers' profit and loss sheets, now they brought in only oceans of red ink.

Except for an occasional high quality novel with a Mafia background, this manufactured genre was dead. Its collapse was abrupt and devastating.

This pattern of excessive exploitation is repeated over and over again in the publishing industry. Science fiction has gone through a long series of booms and busts, a cycle primarily caused by the issuance of a large number of horrible SF books toward the peak of each upturn in the cycle. The romantic historical saga also suffered a decline in popularity due to unrestrained exploitation of the form. The Gothic romance, which was wildly popular in the 1960s and early 1970s, was virtually wiped out after the release of hundreds upon hundreds of poorly and hurriedly written Gothics designed to make quick, easy money for their publishers and authors.

(To a lesser extent, the horror novel has been plagued by excessive exploitation, which disturbs me because, both as a reader and as a writer, I have more than a casual interest in that kind of fiction. However, the horror story is in many ways a special case, with unique strengths and adaptability; it has thus far remained popular in spite of what the exploiters have done to it, and there is every indication that killing the horror story will be as difficult as killing Count Dracula.)

Since imitations of successful novels are profitable in the early stages of a wave of unrestrained exploitation, is this copycat syndrome really such a big problem?

Yes. Although the rip-off books are at first quite profitable, they later lose money by the bucketful, when readers wise up to what's happening. Unrestrained exploitation alienates book buyers, something which no one in publishing should want to do. Furthermore, serious writers often have trouble getting their work noticed in a marketplace dominated by poorly and hurriedly written imitations of blockbuster successes.

Can anything be done about this problem?

Yes again. Publishers can choose not to publish books that are strictly exploitative. If horror novels are popular, editors can encourage their best writers to do ambitious, well-crafted horror stories instead of encouraging their most mediocre authors to grind out quick, cheap imitations. Exploiting a popular trend is not necessarily a bad thing to do; it can provide book buyers with the kinds of novels they most want to read; exploitation is a sound business practice—as long as it is done with a measure of common sense, with taste, and with respect for both the written word and for the intelligence of the reading public. If publishers were to exploit each new trend carefully, if they were to eschew hack imitations, if they were to make an honest effort to publish only well-crafted and freshly conceived books in their efforts to exploit a trend, the boom and bust cycle would be broken, for book buyers would not be disappointed by reams of trash born of sheer opportunism.

Clearly, something can be done about the problem, but *will* anything ever be done?

No. Every time a new trend begins, there are a few publishers who *do* show restraint in their plans to exploit that trend. But there are always those publishers who cannot resist the quick and easy profits to be made by jumping into a new market with hastily conceived and rapidly written rip-offs. As this second group begins to rake in money, the few publishers who showed restraint start to wonder if they've been wrong to opt for quality over speed and quantity; they begin to feel as if they're missing the boat, and they, too, flood bookstores with cheap imitations. The book business is highly competitive. This competition gives the industry tremendous vitality and is, generally, more beneficial than not; but in some cases, such as the matter of excessive exploitation, the compulsion to compete has a negative effect on the publishing business.

What can the new writer do to insulate himself from the boom-and-bust cycles that so strongly affect many authors' financial well-being?

The answer to that one is simple. Don't become part of the problem. Don't write quick, cheap imitations of other novelists' work in order to take advantage of the current hot subject or genre. Don't write romantic historical sagas merely because they happen to be at a peak of popularity; write romantic historical sagas only if you take enormous pleasure in reading them and only if you are also fascinated, *as a writer*, by that form of fiction. Don't write horror novels just because *Stephen King* is making millions with them; write horror novels only if you genuinely feel that they offer the perfect vehicle for what *you* want to say. If you labor solely on novels that interest you, that excite and obsess you, then with a bit of luck and some talent and a lot of stubborn persistence, you might even produce a book that becomes a bestseller and spawns its own legion of imitators! Stay ahead of the pack, and you will not only make more money; you will also find that your work is taken more seriously by critics, editors, and readers than it otherwise might have been.

Failure to develop proven authors

Many editors and publishers (not all of them by any means, but at least half of them) seem unable to understand that a novelist can grow and change as a craftsman and as an artist. If Walter Words (or Paul Prose or Frank Fiction) begins his career writing several simple novels with only modest sales potential, many unimaginative editors and publishers believe Wally should and will write only the same kind of modest little novels for the rest of his life, as if he were a machine unable to alter his brutish function; it seldom occurs to these editors and publishers that Wally Words might *evolve* the talent to write bigger, more ambitious novels. Unimaginative editors and publishers think that every bestselling author must spring up in full bloom, smashing onto the bestseller lists his first time out. If an author's first several titles fail to achieve million-copy sales figures, many editors say, "He just doesn't have what it takes," and they dismiss him as a poor risk; they are extremely reluctant to *ever* reconsider their judgments in these matters. As a result, when Wally Words begins delivering wonderful, well-written, exciting novels with the potential to reach wide audiences, many in the publishing industry fail to see that his work has changed, and they publish his potential bestsellers without fanfare, in small printings, thereby insuring that Wally's sales will continue to be modest. Some writers are mentally and/or emotionally destroyed by this treatment. I know a few who have "burnt out"; some have left the writing game altogether. Other authors, caught in this trap, become cynical; they retreat, cease writing ambitious novels, go back to writing simple books, increase the volume of their output as they forsake quality, and settle into the role of the anything-for-a-dollar hack. A lucky few encounter an editor and a publisher who see the value of their current work and don't give a damn that their previous novels weren't bestsellers.

For years, Harry Patterson, a British author, wrote tight, fast-moving thrillers under several pen names, including "Jack Higgins." It should have been obvious to everyone that Harry Patterson had the potential to become a best-selling novelist. Many of his books—*The Keys of Hell, Night Judgment at Sinos, East of Desolation, In the Hour Before Midnight,* and a long list of other titles—were just a half-step below the kind of thrillers that warrant bestseller promotion. But it wasn't until 1975, when *The Eagle Has Landed* was published under the "Jack Higgins" by-line, that Mr. Patterson's work was given the kind of promotion that put his books squarely in the eye of the reading public. Holt, Rinehart & Winston (hardcover) and Bantam Books (paperback) took a chance on *Eagle,* and they were handsomely repaid. *The Eagle Has Landed* was a number one bestseller in hardcover and paperback, and it was made into a film starring Michael Caine. In the intervening years, Patterson has had two other bestsellers under the Higgins name—*Storm Warning* and *Solo*—the latter of which is perhaps the best book he's ever done (though too short), a stunner that shows he is *still* improving. Because of Jack Higgins's success, other publishers asked Patterson to do books under his own name. (Suddenly, *everyone* recognized his ability after so many years of overlooking it.) Stein and Day published the first novel under Patterson's real name; it was titled *The Valhalla Exchange,* and it became a bestseller. *To Catch a King,* the second Harry Patterson novel, was also a bestseller. Thus far, that is all there have been, but I'm certain there will be many more bestsellers under both the Higgins and the Patterson identities in the years to come. But why did Patterson have to write more than twenty superior thrillers before any publisher began to take him seriously?

The Higgins-Patterson story is not unique. In 1949, Ross Macdonald (whose real name is Kenneth Millar) wrote his first Lew Archer detective novel; during the following twenty years he wrote more than a dozen other Archer adventures, each of which transcended genre definitions. It wasn't until 1969, twenty years after that first Lew Archer tale, that Macdonald's publisher began to take him seriously enough to promote his work, and it was then that he finally had a bestseller, *The Goodbye Look,* the first of several big hits.

Another case in point is John Jakes. Mr. Jakes wrote a score or two of tightly plotted, sharply observed novels, mostly science fiction, but including a handful of superior historicals, none of which received anything in the way of advertising and promotion. Jakes was a good writer during those years in which he remained largely unknown and unsung; the hand of a master storyteller was always visible in his work, but no publisher ever seemed to take full notice of it. Finally, with *The Bastard*—and the other novels in his Bicentennial series—John Jakes became a bestselling novelist, not primarily because of the ad money that was spent, but because he was *good.* All he needed was a chance.

There are other stories like these, but a great many publishers never seem to learn from them. Some of today's most successful writers progressed slowly from modest books with small sales to middle-level bestsellers, to blockbusters, much to the benefit of their forward-thinking editors and publishers. John D. MacDonald is a case in point. So are Louis L'Amour, Kurt Vonnegut, and Frank Herbert. These one-step-at-a-time success stories and many others like them should encourage *every* editor to give the Wally Wordses of this world a second look. Publishing suffers a loss of revenue and even a spiritual loss every time a developing author is labeled "small-time" or "genre" and is consigned to a confining niche too early in his career.

So much for publishers' problems. Of course there are others: high interest rates, printing costs, paper costs, competition with television and films, et cetera. I have touched only on those I believe have as devastating an effect on writers as they do on publishers.

And finally, a few words about editors:

When your book fails to sell as many copies as you thought it would, when the movie deal falls through at the last minute, when the paperback rights are auctioned for only a fraction of what you had hoped, when the critics don't like you, when the book clubs turn you down, when the whole world seems to be going to Hell in a handbasket, you can still muddle through if you've got a good editor or two on your side. If writers are the blood of the publishing business, then editors are the arteries. A good editor can help a troubled author transform a weak manuscript into a triumphant bestseller. A bad editor, on the other hand, can weaken a strong book and utterly destroy a weak one. Over the years, I worked with some editors who were either lazy or incompetent or both; I couldn't walk away from them because I needed the money. Today, I am able to pick and choose, and I work *only* with editors I respect. Life is much easier because of that. A good editor is God's best handiwork. When you stumble across a good one, for God's sake, don't let go!

15.

**Read, read, read
or
Read, read, read.**

I have discussed, at some length, the need for a writer to be well-read. I now refer you to the following list of authors. If you have read novels by only one-fifth of them, your chances of writing successful popular mainstream fiction are very small indeed. If you have read half of these authors, you are beginning to form an idea of what modern popular fiction *is*, but you still have a lot to learn. If you have read at least 70 percent of these authors, and if you have any talent of your own, you are probably ready to write salable fiction. Works by the people listed below have *defined* modern popular fiction; if you are serious about wanting to be a writer, you not only should read these authors, but you will desperately *want* to read them in order to learn from them.

Warning! If you want to be a mystery novelist, that does not mean that you should read only mysteries. Regardless of the type of fiction you write (or wish to write), you should read every kind of popular fiction you can get your hands on, both mainstream and genre. The more you broaden your interests as a reader, the more you will simultaneously broaden your perspective and your talent *as a writer*. I know a few authors who read only one kind of fiction, the kind they write themselves; in every case, this provincialism is evident in the author's work, and none of these writers is very successful in the marketplace.

Warning! This list of recommended authors isn't complete by any means. I purposely have not mentioned classic wordsmiths like Dickens, Trollope, and Melville, for I assume that anyone who wishes to write popular fiction is aware of the need to familiarize himself with the work of authors who have proven themselves to be artists of lasting stature. The list mainly comprises the names of contemporary novelists. I have not listed authors who have published only one or two books, not even if those books were awfully good, for I have tried to direct you toward those writers who not only have published good material but have had an effect upon the development of modern popular fiction. Finally, the list is incomplete because I am bound to have overlooked a dozen or two names that should have been included. Once you have read the people I recommend, for God's sake don't stop! Your need to read some fiction every day should be almost like a drug dependency.

Read, read, read!

Richard Adams. *Watership Down, The Plague Dogs, The Girl in a Swing.* Adams is primarily a fantasist, uneven in his plotting from one book to another, but always a superb stylist. *Watership Down* is the one "must read" of his books; it is a tightly structured and emotionally involving saga unlike any other book you have ever read.

Catherine Aird. Aird is a superb mystery novelist whose work shows breakthrough potential. Her novels include *A Late Phoenix, The Religious Body, The Stately Home Murder, His Burial Too,* and *Some Die Eloquent.*

Brian Aldiss. Aldiss is primarily a science fiction writer, although he has published several mainstream novels, at least two of which have been major bestsellers in Britain and modestly successful over here. I recommend Aldiss because reading him is a sure way to stretch your imagination, get your idea pump working, and further your appreciation of well-polished, literate prose. Among Aldiss's many books are *The Dark Light Years, The Long Afternoon of Earth, Frankenstein Unbound, Greybeard, The Hand-Reared Boy,* and *An Island Called Moreau.*

Eric Ambler. Ambler, a stylish writer of espionage novels, made large contributions to the definition of the modern spy story. *A Coffin for Dimitrios, State of Siege,* and *Passage of Arms* are a few of his books.

Kingsley Amis. Amis is a one-of-a-kind writer who should be read because: 1) he knows how to tell a story; 2) he is a fine stylist; 3) he can teach you how to write with both humor and suspense at the same time. His books include *Lucky Jim, The Green Man,* and *I Want It Now.*

Poul Anderson. Anderson writes both historical novels and science fiction novels, primarily the latter, but he often combines the two forms. He is a fine adventure writer who, with better direction from a caring agent and an imaginative editor, might well have been an extremely popular author of mainstream historical novels. Some of his many books include *Brainwave, Tau Zero, Shield, The Corridors of Time,* and *The High Crusade.*

Isaac Asimov. Asimov has pretty much abandoned fiction in favor of nonfiction, but in his prime he wrote a few science fiction classics, including *The Naked Sun* and *The Caves of Steel,* that helped shape the field.

Desmond Bagley. Bagley is considerably more popular in the rest of the world than he is in the U.S., largely because his U.S. publishers have never done a very good job of packaging and promoting his books. He writes thrillers with a real flair, in a literate style that puts many thriller writers to shame. His books include *Running Blind, The Tightrope Men,* and the stunning *The Enemy,* which was a huge bestseller in many other countries.

Alfred Bester. Bester has had as much impact on the science fiction field as any writer, excluding Robert Heinlein. His two most famous novels—*The Demolished Man* and *The Stars My Destination*—are packed with more ideas and excitement than any dozen other novels, and they have had a great impact on other writers in the SF genre.

Ray Bradbury. The one and only. Bradbury's publishers—Doubleday, Knopf, Ballantine, Bantam—have always insisted on pinning the SCIENCE FICTION WRITER label on him. In reality, Bradbury is at times a fantasist, at times a grisly-horror writer, at times a fable-maker, at times a straight mainstream author, and only very seldom a science fiction writer. His one science fiction novel, *Fahrenheit 451,* is a classic in the field. His horror-fantasy novel, *Something Wicked This Way Comes*, is simply one of the ten best stories of its kind ever written. Bradbury's forte is the short story, and there are many collections of his short fiction in print: *Long After Midnight, The October Country, The Martian Chronicles, The Golden Apples of the Sun, R Is for Rocket, A Medicine for Melancholy, The Illustrated Man*, and several others.

Gary Brandner. His *The Howling* was the basis for one of the best horror movies ever made. *Walkers*, another horror novel, has several fresh ideas that any horror novelist would envy. He has great potential.

John Brunner. Brunner is a good, craftsmanlike science fiction writer who has published dozens of adventure novels in the field. Now and again, he outdoes himself and produces books that are as good as anything SF has to offer: *The Whole Man, The Squares of the City, Stand on Zanzibar*, and *The Long Result*.

W. R. Burnett. A few decades ago, Burnett helped to define hard-boiled fiction and created an archetype with novels like *Little Caesar*.

James M. Cain. Some time ago I decided to collect rare, first-edition novels by American writers who seemed, to me at least, to have written breakthrough books, artists who created forms and characters and stories that would last. I started with James M. Cain, who almost single-handedly created the hard, lean prose style that formed the basis of modern American writing. In novels like *The Postman Always Rings Twice, Double Indemnity, Serenade*, and *Mildred Pierce*, Cain painted a picture of certain American cultural groups, social strata, and psychological patterns that was revolutionary in his time; his work *still* stands as a vital and unique vision. For the most part he shaped his art in the form of *thrillers*.

Today, almost fifty years after it was first published, *The Postman Always Rings Twice* is as readable and poignant and relevant as it was when it first saw print. Indeed, *Postman* reads as if it were written last week! Cain was so in touch with the people about whom he wrote, so intimately familiar with the fears and desires of the masses in the 1920s and 1930s, that he seems to have known not only how the common man and woman talked and thought at that time, but also how they would talk and think for decades to come. I am not aware of another American writer of our century whose books have been so utterly untouched by the passage of so many years, as have Cain's.

When I started to collect first editions of Cain's work a couple of years ago, those books sold for just a few dollars, even in fine or mint condition with dust jacket, even in spite of their rarity. Although they now command prices three times that high, they are relatively cheap compared to what they will surely bring in ten or fifteen years. A large collection of Cain's letters and original manuscripts recently sold for more than $20,000, though the man who had put together the collection had spent less than $1,000 to do so. Cain's value as a novelist is clearly becoming generally recognized among those who love books enough to collect and cherish them.

The academic world has always shunned James M. Cain, but that has nothing to do with whether or not he will ultimately occupy a permanent shelf in the library of American literature. Yes, Cain wrote some thrillers—just as Mark Twain wrote some adventure stories, just as Poe wrote some horror stories—but within the framework of suspense fiction, Cain said something important about the way people of his time and place lived, thought, dreamed, and died. Cain has lasted this long and will last much longer because the masses still read him. He conned us with entertainment while he subtly made his thematic points. Today, all of Cain's works are available in paperback editions. At least three of his books are being made into movies as I write this. Nearly every writer I know has read and greatly admires Cain's books. Several years ago, James M. Cain died, but because of his wonderful novels, he is still very much alive and will continue to live for a long, long time to come.

I strongly recommend you read *all* of Cain to see how the simplest genre ideas can be transformed into fresh, compelling mainstream fiction.

Raymond Chandler. I also collect first-edition copies of Raymond Chandler's novels—*The Long Goodbye, The Big*

Sleep, The Lady in the Lake, The Little Sister, The High Window, Farewell My Lovely. Thus far, Chandler has been written off by the academic community as a mere detective story writer. In truth, no novelist of his period painted a better or more vivid picture of American culture, especially the sleazy and lonely aspects of it, than did Chandler. No writer has ever surpassed Chandler's evocation of Southern California. He made Los Angeles his, as surely as Dickens laid claim to London. Today, decades after his novels were written, they still sell very well indeed, year in and year out, because in addition to saying something important about the human condition, Raymond Chandler made an effort to *entertain.*

I recommend that you read every word Chandler wrote. His plotting is sometimes weak, but from reading him you will learn everything you need to know about pace, characterization, mood, background, and *style.* My God, what style!

Agatha Christie. I must admit I'm not a Christie fan. But she was one of the half dozen most important influences on the modern mystery novel, and you could do worse than to read her *Death on the Nile, And Then There Were None, Murder in the Calais Coach,* and *The Murder of Roger Ackroyd.*

Mary Higgins Clark. Clark's books often suffer from too many coincidences in the plots, and she is not a glittering stylist. However, *A Stranger Is Watching* and *The Cradle Will Fall* possess such marvelous, fast-paced, ambitiously complicated plots that the reader is willing to forgive her a few flaws.

James Clavell. Clavell is a consummate adventure novelist. He established himself with *King Rat,* took a giant step with *Tai-Pan* (his best book to date), and set sales records with *Shogun.* His latest, *Noble House,* will probably firmly establish him as one of the two or three bestselling authors of the decade.

Richard Condon. The one and only. He writes curious books that contain a large measure of suspense, an almost equally large measure of extremely dry humor, and a healthy dollop of social commentary. If you don't like Condon, you hate him. If you do like him, you *love* him. There is no middle ground. Some of his best novels are *The Manchurian Candidate, Any God Will Do, Mile High*, and *Winter Kills*.

Edwin Corley. I said that most of the people in this list helped to shape the direction of modern fiction. I cannot pretend that Corley has done anything of the sort. He has enjoyed his share of successes, but he has never been a top-of-the-list bestseller, and he has not really broken any important new ground with his fiction. But dammit, I *like* his stuff. He has one of those easy-reading styles that lifts you up and sweeps you along and . . . well . . . *delights* you. I recommend you read him with the idea of acquiring some of his smoothness. And while you're studying his style, he'll never fail to entertain you. Try *The Jesus Factor, Air Force One, Sargasso, Siege*, and *Long Shots*.

Michael Crichton. Crichton is unpredictable. He has written mainstream-science fiction—*The Andromeda Strain* and *The Terminal Man*—one mainstream-historical-caper novel titled *The Great Train Robbery*, one African adventure-science fiction piece titled *Congo*, and a slew of taut thrillers under the name "John Lange." He has proved to be a good screenwriter and an even better director—*Westworld, The Great Train Robbery*. The only thing that isn't unpredictable about him is the quality of his novels: They're always great fun. Crichton is a slick writer rather than a stylish one. His characters are too thinly drawn for mainstream. Yet he *is* a mainstream writer by virtue of his background, his heavy thematic structures, and his extremely fresh and inventive plots.

Samuel R. Delany. Delany burst upon the science fiction field in the early 1960s, dazzling fans and critics alike, and scooping up armsful of awards. Rightly so. His early books like *Babel-17, The Jewels of Aptor, The Einstein Intersection, Nova, Empire Star, Captives of the Flame, The Towers of Toron, The City of a Thousand Suns*, and *The Ballad of Beta-2* were beautifully intricate, crammed full of startling and memorable images, filled with characters who were sharply drawn yet as mysterious as the shadowy reflection one sees in a bronzed mirror. By reading

Delany's early works you can not only learn how to write the very best kind of science fiction, but you can also learn how to write, period. Recently, Delany seems to have forsaken the average reader in an attempt to cater to academe, and his latest novels are pedantic and sometimes unreadable. In his youth, he wrote better than anyone in his genre.

Philip K. Dick. The one and only. No one writes like Dick. His style is so personal, so different that it defies imitation. *The Eye in the Sky, The Three Stigmata of Palmer Eldritch, Do Androids Dream of Electric Sheep?* (recently retitled *Blade Runner*), *Clans of the Alphane Moon, The Martian Time-Slip, Solar Lottery, Now Wait for Last Year, The Man in the High Castle, A Scanner Darkly, Ubik,* and many other Philip K. Dick novels are one-of-a-kind, mind-expanding examples of the lengths to which popular fiction can be stretched while retaining its popularity. His 1962 novel *The Man in the High Castle* is certainly one of the dozen best science fiction novels ever written.

Gordon R. Dickson. He is a fine writer of science fiction and adventure. Try *None But Man, Dorsai, The Alien Way,* and *Timestorm.*

Thomas Disch. Disch began his career as a science fiction writer and still occasionally produces a novel in that field. He also does work outside of SF—such as *Black Alice* in collaboration with John Sladek and the bestselling *Clara Reeve* under a pseudonym. Disch's books are so cynical and downbeat that they are sometimes unintentionally amusing; but when he is good he is very, very good. His writing is literate and often dazzling. SF: *On Wings of Song, The Genocides,* and *Camp Concentration.*

Stanley Ellin. Ellin is a winner of many awards for his mystery fiction. His books are ingeniously plotted, and his characters are real. Try *House of Cards, The Eighth Circle,* and *The Big Night,* among others.

Harlan Ellison. Ellison is a short story writer, but I believe I should include him in this list. He may have won more Hugos and Nebula Awards than any other science fiction writer, and he is one of the few to cross genres and win an Edgar Award from the Mystery Writers of America as well. I find his work uneven, but it is also often brilliant, and it is never, ever boring. There are many collections of his short fiction on the market: *Alone Against Tomorrow, Deathbird Stories, Shatterday, The Beast That Shouted Love at the Heart of the World, Approaching Oblivion,* and others. He is a key figure in the SF-fantasy-horror fields.

Paul Erdman. Erdman isn't a stylist, and he isn't a creator of deep, thoroughly revealed characters. But he is one hell of a storyteller. He knows *exactly* how to shape a plot, and his imagination is so fertile that he is always two steps ahead of his readers. He also manages to take an often dull subject—international finance—and make it not only interesting but gripping. His well-deserved bestsellers—*The Billion-Dollar Sure Thing, The Silver Bears, The Crash of '79*—are superb examples of how background material should be integrated into a novel.

Philip José Farmer. Farmer is another key figure in the science fiction world and a marvelous adventure story writer. In his early days he shocked the SF field with his sexually daring—though never sexually explicit—stories. Later he created the "Riverworld" books, which embody one of the most intriguing backgrounds any SF writer has ever devised. His many books include *To Your Scattered Bodies Go, The Fabulous Riverboat, The Dark Design, Dare, The Maker of Universes, The Gates of Creation, A Private Cosmos, Behind the Walls of Terra, Inside-Out,* and *The Wind Whales of Ishmael.*

Edna Ferber. Her novels seem a bit dated now, but she is still worth reading if you want to know how American fiction got to its present state. Try *Show Boat, Giant,* and *Saratoga Trunk.* Winner of a Pulitzer Prize for fiction, Ferber was an excellent storyteller and had an admirable talent for in-depth characterization.

Dick Francis. For years Francis's U.S. publisher insisted on fixing the MYSTERY WRITER label to his books, thus condemning him to no better than modest sales. In fact, he ceased being a strictly genre writer at least sixteen or seventeen books ago. The quality of his characterizations and the richness of his backgrounds, which are always combined with sharply drawn thematic structures, put his books leagues above most mystery novels. He is very much in the mainstream, and his new American publisher, G. P. Putnam's Sons, seems at least somewhat aware of this, for they have given his latest novel, *Reflex*, bestseller promotion and advertising. A few of his other novels are *Bonecrack*, *High Stakes*, *Blood Sport*, *In the Frame*, *Enquiry*, *Slayride*, and *Whip Hand*.

William Goldman. Goldman is the famous screenwriter—*Butch Cassidy and the Sundance Kid*, *All the President's Men*, and many others—but he also has had quite a career as a novelist. His early books were solidly mainstream and of the highest quality. *The Temple of Gold*, *Soldier in the Rain*, and *Boys and Girls Together* are novels that virtually any writer would be delighted to have written. Later, he tried his hand at thrillers that he lifted into the mainstream largely by virtue of his splendid characterizations and his thematic purposes. *No Way To Treat a Lady* is a clever, gripping, and entirely successful little tour de force. His other thrillers are generally flawed but nevertheless well worth reading. Try *Magic* and *Marathon Man*.

Arthur Hailey. As I mentioned earlier, Hailey is a master of background. His characters are usually little more than adequately drawn, but his plots tick away like fine Swiss watches, and his backgrounds are splendidly drawn. You should read *Hotel*, *Airport*, *Wheels*, *The Moneychangers*, *The Final Diagnosis*, and *Overload*.

Adam Hall. This is the pen name for novelist Ellston Trevor. As "Adam Hall," Trevor has helped to shape the modern mainstream spy story in a long series of very well-crafted books including *The Quiller Memorandum*, *The Ninth Directive*, *The Tango Briefing*, and *The Cobra Manifesto*.

William Hallahan. Hallahan's first two books—*The Dead of Winter* and *The Ross Forgery*—were published as mysteries and pretty much sank without a trace. Then he produced *The Search for Joseph Tully*, which many believe to be one of the finest and most original occult novels of the past twenty years. I am one of those many. After

Tully, Hallahan gave us *Catch Me: Kill Me,* a thoughtful suspense novel which, for me at least, seemed uneven. Next came *The Keeper of the Children,* another occult novel with some wonderfully evocative scenes but with some less wonderful stuff at the end which gave it an uneven tone again. His latest, *The Trade,* is squarely on target, a mainstream thriller of real power. With *The Search for Joseph Tully,* Hallahan had a truly profound effect upon many authors of supernatural novels, and with each successive book, his colleagues have become increasingly sure that eventually he will go all the way to the top of the bestseller lists.

Dashiell Hammett. Hammett was perhaps the hardest of the hard-boiled writers working in the 1930s and 1940s. His prose is so spare, so completely trimmed of all fat, that it sometimes looks childishly simple. Be warned: His prose is *never* simple. It is stripped down, often cold, but it always carries an enormous load of meaning and purpose. Hammett is an American original, a one-of-a-kind writer who has inspired thousands of cheap imitations. As with James M. Cain and Raymond Chandler, there is an excellent chance that Hammett's novels will withstand the test of time and will be read long after most of us now living are dead and gone. You should read every one of Hammett's books: *Red Harvest, The Dain Curse, The Maltese Falcon, The Glass Key,* and *The Thin Man.*

Harry Harrison. Harrison is a fine craftsman who writes highly entertaining science fiction adventure stories like *Deathworld, Deathworld-2, Deathworld-3, The Plague from Space,* and *The Daleth Effect.* He also manages to pull off the difficult trick of writing hilariously funny science fiction like *Bill, the Galactic Hero.* And finally, he can be as serious and "meaningful" as any writer in the field, as witness his prophetic novel about overpopulation, *Make Room! Make Room!.*

Robert Heinlein. The one and only. If there is any single author who defines science fiction, it is Robert Heinlein. He is surely the most widely read science fiction author of all time, for his books long ago began to break out of the straight science fiction market to tap a vein of the mainstream audience. By virtue of his amazing skill at background, his fresh plotting, and his powerful thematic structures, his books have usually been solidly in the mainstream in spite of their futuristic settings and science fictional concerns. His characters are sometimes thinly drawn but always very colorful and memorable. And when he *does* give us well-rounded characters, they are as real and as fascinating as any fictional human beings can ever be. They are usually individualists, strong and clever and determined and *moral* people who know how to get things done; they are people you can respect, and their triumphs somehow stir and move you. There are other writers who are every bit as entertaining as Mr. Heinlein, and there are other writers who have written a greater number of fine books than he has, and there are other novelists who are better stylists than Heinlein. But there is no other writer whose work has *exhilarated* me as often and to such an extent as has Heinlein. His books are nearly always, at the core, about liberty, freedom, and the sanctity of the individual. His books have great spirit, and I recommend the following: *The Moon Is a Harsh Mistress, Stranger in a Strange Land, Orphans of the Sky, Farnham's Freehold, The Puppet Masters, Revolt in 2000, Starship Troopers, Methuselah's Children, Double Star, The Day After Tomorrow, Podkayne of Mars, The Unpleasant Profession of Jonathan Hoag, The Green Hills of Earth, Glory Road,* and *Assignment in Eternity.* Heinlein has also written the most successful series of SF novels for young adults ever produced, and all of them will entertain adults every bit as much as they entertain adolescents. Try *Citizen of the Galaxy, Red Planet, Tunnel in the Sky, The Star Beast,* and *Between Planets.* You should be warned that some of Heinlein's more recent works are burdened down by excess dialogue and sermonizing. Later books like *Time Enough for Love* and *The Number of the Beast* should be saved for last, after you have read all of his other marvelous novels.

Frank Herbert. Herbert is another science fiction writer who has broken out into the mainstream, in part because of his thematic vision and his care with background material. *Dune* is one of the most successful SF novels of all time. Try it and its sequels, *Dune Messiah, Children of Dune,* and *God-Emperor of Dune,* as well as non-Dune novels like *The Heaven Makers* and *Dragon in the Sea.*

James Herbert. Herbert is a much-underrated horror novelist who is good enough to lift his work into the mainstream. Try *The Spear, The Fog, The Dark,* and others.

Jack Higgins. I've already written about Higgins (actually Harry Patterson) in Chapter 14. Try some of the novels I listed in that discussion, but by all means read *Solo, The Eagle Has Landed,* and *Storm Warning.*

Patricia Highsmith. Her mystery novels have helped define the field, and her *Strangers on a Train* is a classic.

Evan Hunter. Hunter is one of the most underrated novelists of the past twenty-five years. His style is literate and as smooth as glass. He has written everything from serious and ambitious mainstream fiction like *The Blackboard Jungle* to comedy capers like *The Horse's Head* to seriocomic mysteries. For years his career was hampered, I believe, by poor agenting, but he seems to be on his way back to prominence with his most recent novel, *Love, Dad,* which is receiving bestseller promotion. Few writers are better at characterization than Hunter, and no writer I know of is equal to him in the creation of mood. Such books as *Last Summer, Come Winter,* and *Nobody Knew They Were There* are superb evocations of various moods, times, places, and psychological states. In addition to the books I've already mentioned, don't miss *Streets of Gold, Strangers When We Meet, Mothers and Daughters,* and *Sons.* (See the entry for "Ed McBain" later in this list.)

Hammond Innes. Innes's work helps to define the modern adventure story. He is a literate writer who never fails to entertain. I especially recommend *Gale Warning, Air Bridge, The Wreck of the Mary Deare,* and *The Naked Land.*

John Irving. Irving manages to write moving and very meaningful, ambitious novels without ever forgetting that readability is essential. He is embraced by academe but has not yet allowed it to corrupt him. Try *Setting Free the Bears* and especially *The World According to Garp.*

Shirley Jackson. Jackson was an elegant writer, and at least two of her works have had profound influence upon writers of mainstream supernatural fiction. Try *The Haunting of Hill House* and *We Have Always Lived in the Castle*.

Rona Jaffe. Let's get a couple of things straight: Jaffe is not a consummate stylist, and she is not a creator of tight and clever plots. But she *is* an excellent storyteller nonetheless. Her characters are real, modern, and sympathetic. Her books always have thematic purpose. She writes dialogue that rings true. She succeeds routinely where so many writers of "women's fiction" fail miserably. Try her ground-breaking *The Best of Everything* and *Class Reunion*.

John Jakes. I have written about John Jakes in Chapter 14. He started one of the biggest trends in recent publishing history with his American Bicentennial Series, including *The Bastard*, *The Rebels*, *The Furies*, and *The Americans*. He has scores of imitators hanging on his coattails.

Harry Kemelman. Kemelman's series of mysteries, all featuring Rabbi David Small as the lead character, manages to break out of the genre classification by virtue of characterization, background, and thematic purpose all far more richly developed than genre fiction requires. Try *Friday the Rabbi Slept Late* and all the other books in the series.

Stephen King. I have written at length about King throughout this book. It is vitally important that the new writer sample King's work. Even if he weren't as good as he is, he should be read because he probably sold more books during the past decade than any other novelist. Try *'Salem's Lot*, *The Shining*, *The Stand*, *The Dead Zone*, and *Firestarter*.

James Kirkwood. He is co-author of the smash Broadway hit, *A Chorus Line*, and other plays. His novels are unique, funny, suspenseful, and stylish. Try *P.S. Your Cat Is Dead*, *Some Kind of Hero*, *Hit Me with a Rainbow*, and *Good Times/Bad Times*.

C. M. Kornbluth. Kornbluth was a science fiction writer with a special, dark vision. Most of his best work is in short story and novelette length. His *The Syndic* is a fine novel, and his collaborations with Frederik Pohl are among the field's short list of genuine classics. Those collaborations include *Gladiator-at-Law* and *The Space Merchants*. Kornbluth's work has had a strong influence on many modern SF writers.

Louis L'Amour. If you want to write genre Westerns, or if you want to write mainstream novels with Western backgrounds, you must read L'Amour's Western novels. Try: *Shalako, Over on the Dry Side,* or any of his other eighty-plus novels.

Keith Laumer. Laumer is an excellent writer of science fiction adventure. He's not the most brilliant characterizer to put pen to paper, and there are a few other weaknesses in his work, but he *is* a master storyteller. *A Plague of Demons, The Other Side of Time, A Trace of Memory, The Monitors, Worlds of the Imperium,* and many of his other novels are solid entertainments. (Note: Retief is a series character appearing in a number of Laumer's books. These Retief stories, while popular, do not represent his best work.)

Fritz Leiber. He is a superb stylist, a literate writer whose prose has both color and clarity. He writes both science fiction and fantasy, though he is at his best when dealing with the latter. Try *The Big Time, The Wanderer, Our Lady of Darkness, Swords in the Mist, Swords Against Deviltry,* and *Conjure Wife* among others.

Elmore Leonard. Leonard has written some excellent Westerns, including *Valdez Is Coming* and *Hombre.* However, these days he is writing very tight, very tough contemporary thrillers, generally with Detroit settings. *Nobody* writes about street types better than Leonard. At his best, Leonard is sort of a cross between James M. Cain, Dashiell Hammett, and George Higgins, though the quality that makes him Elmore Leonard is something that resists comparison. By all means, read *Fifty-Two Pickup, Unknown Man No. 89, City Primeval, The Switch, Mr. Majestyk,* and his other novels. Someday, a smart publisher is going to go to Leonard's agent, offer an obscene amount of money, and ask for the *ultimate* novel about street types, small-time hoods, and big city corruption; the result is going to be a huge bestseller. At least that's what *should* happen; but remember, imaginative publishers are few and far between.

Ira Levin. The one and only. With a surprisingly short list of credits, Ira Levin has established himself as *the* writer of contemporary terror stories. *A Kiss Before Dying* is one of the most brilliantly plotted thrillers ever written. It contains several surprises, one of which is so startling that most readers are quite literally catapulted right up out of their chairs. That surprise, by the way, does not come at the end of the book, as you might expect, but at about the one-third mark, at the end of Part One. When you suddenly realize how Levin has been deceiving you, the rest of *A Kiss Before Dying* becomes unputdownable, for you can't wait to see what *else* he might be able to pull off. Of course *Rosemary's Baby* is the book that single-handedly revived the supernatural novel as a viable modern form. The prose in that book is so stylish and the plot is so exquisitely designed that I could easily spend fifty or sixty pages discussing it here; unfortunately, I do not have the space to do so. I can only say that *Rosemary's Baby* is a must-read book for anyone seriously attempting to write popular fiction of *any* kind. *The Stepford Wives,* while good, is far less successful than Levin's first two novels, and *This Perfect Day,* a science fiction story, is less than perfect. But with *The Boys from Brazil,* Levin gets back on track. This is another flawlessly plotted story from page one right down to the wonderfully chilling, one-page scene at the end. Levin is a playwright as well as a novelist— *Death Trap,* currently running on Broadway, has totted up the largest number of performances of any thriller ever produced in the New York Theater. When you read his novels, keep his playwriting career in mind, for you will see its effect on his transitions, on his dialogue, and on the sweet simplicity of his scene structure.

Robert Ludlum. No writer of recent years has made as much of a splash in the mainstream thriller market as Ludlum. His relentlessly fast-paced books often give short shrift to character development, but they are never short of thematic purpose and are rich in background detail. And most important of all, Ludlum never tries to write like anyone else; his style is very much his own and, like it or hate it, you must admire its individuality. I highly recommend that you read *The Scarlatti Inheritance*, *The Bourne Identity*, *The Matarese Circle*, and other Ludlum novels.

Gregory Mcdonald. When Mcdonald writes about his series character, Fletch, he is very good indeed. *Fletch*, and *Confess, Fletch*, and *Fletch's Fortune* are marvelous, and you ought to read them to see how the best dialogue is written. When Mcdonald writes about other characters, he does so with mixed results, so I suggest you stick to the Fletch books—and have one hell of a good time!

John D. MacDonald. The one and only. MacDonald is often called "the best suspense novelist of our time," but he is far, far more than *just* a suspense novelist. Personally, I would even go so far as to say that he is *the* best American writer of his generation, or that at least there is no one better, and I would not stand alone in making that assessment, either. MacDonald's best-known books—his series featuring Travis McGee—are superbly plotted, filled with brilliantly drawn characters and riveting action, enhanced by exceedingly well-rendered backgrounds, and infused with thematic purpose of the best sort. Nevertheless, the McGee books are in many ways less powerful and less fascinating than MacDonald's other work. A couple of dozen of his non-McGee novels—*The Damned; Cry Hard, Cry Fast; Slam the Big Door, Cancel All Our Vows; Where Is Janice Gentry?; One Monday We Killed Them All; April Evil; The Brass Cupcake; A Key to the Suite; The Last One Left; On the Run; The Girl, the Gold Watch & Everything; Deadly Welcome; A Bullet for Cinderella; Contrary Pleasure; The Crossroads*; and many others—are so good that they have become standards by which a great many writers measure their own work. I know of no writer more universally admired by other writers than is John D. MacDonald. Even the academic-literary crowd admits a sort of shame-faced fascination with MacDonald's fiction (shame-faced because really cultured, lit'ry folks aren't *supposed* to like that kind of stuff.) MacDonald is one of the few living American writers about whom I would say, unequivocally, "He will be widely read a hundred years from now." I have read every one of his novels at least twice, and I recommend that you do the same. If you are perceptive and talented, you will learn everything you need to know about writing fiction by studying his example. And you will be so well entertained in the process that you won't for a moment look upon that study as work. Virtually every book MacDonald wrote is a *must-read* title for the would-be novelist.

Ross Macdonald. He has influenced the modern detective story with his Lew Archer series, and he is one of the few mystery novelists to escape the genre trap after writing many novels that were consigned to that oblivion. He is now published as a mainstream author, and all of his old books have found a wider audience. You should read his crisply written, very atmospheric books, including *The Chill, The Ivory Grin, The Zebra-Striped Hearse,* and *The Moving Target.*

Helen MacInnes. She is one of the few women who can write major mainstream-thriller novels that appeal equally to men and women. Her greatest strengths are plotting and background. Try *The Double Image, While Still We Live, Agent in Place,* and others.

Alistair MacLean. No author has done more to define the modern mainstream adventure story than MacLean. By the time he had written just three novels, publishers were boldly using his name to promote lesser storytellers; bookstands were cluttered with novels bearing such banners as BETTER THAN ALISTAIR MACLEAN and MORE RIVETING THAN ALISTAIR MACLEAN and THIS BOOK MAKES THE NOVELS OF ALISTAIR MACLEAN SEEM DULL. Of course none of those claims was true. In his prime, MacLean was at the top of the heap; no one could touch him. For examples of how the adventure story can be lifted into the mainstream and sold to a wide audience, you could do no better than *The Guns of Navarone, Force 10 from Navarone, H.M.S. Ulysses, Where Eagles Dare, Ice Station Zebra, When Eight Bells Toll, South by Java Head, Fear Is the Key, The Secret Ways,* and others. I would suggest starting with those books I have named, for a number of MacLean's recent novels are considerably less successful as art and as entertainment.

Dan J. Marlowe. Marlowe has written some fine, tightly plotted suspense novels that have won him a couple of awards, and he is well worth your attention. You should read *One Endless Hour, Four for the Money,* and *Never Live Twice.* Most of Marlowe's work is, unfortunately, out of print, but I suspect it may be coming back into the bookstores soon, as publishers start seeking what they call "men's action fiction."

Richard Matheson. Matheson is a key figure in the fantasy-horror field. He is usually labeled SCIENCE FICTION WRITER, but most of his work doesn't really fit into that genre. Two of his novels have had great influence on modern mainstream-horror writers, and you should read both of them: *I Am Legend* and *The Shrinking Man.* (If you've seen the grotesque Lily Tomlin film in which Matheson's book is trashed, do not get the idea that you know what the story is about.) *The Shrinking Man* is a perfect example of how stylish prose, thematic purpose, and a well-drawn central character can lift a book out of the genre pit, into the mainstream.

Ed McBain. This is the pen name for Evan Hunter, who was discussed earlier in this list. Under the McBain pseudonym, Hunter has written a shelfful of police procedural novels with a continuing cast of characters. These mysteries include *Jigsaw, Shotgun, Fuzz, Ax, King's Ransom, See Them Die, Cophater,* and *Pusher* plus many others. Mystery-suspense aficionados consider these books—the 87th Precinct Series—to be among the best police procedurals ever written. Other McBain books, outside the 87th Precinct milieu, are worthy of carrying the Evan Hunter by-line. I strongly suggest you read *Guns* and *Goldilocks* after you've gone through the 87th Precinct line-up.

Robert Merle. This French author has struck big several times in the U.S. market and deservedly so. His works are stylish, well characterized and freshly plotted. Try *The Day of the Dolphin,* one of the first of a wave of techno-terror stories, and *Malevil.*

C. L. Moore. She's a much underrated science fiction writer. She was one of the first women to seize a piece of that male-dominated genre and make it her own. *Judgment Night* and *Doomsday Morning.*

Larry Niven. He is one of the better hard-science writers in the SF genre. His influence in the field has been greater than many of his colleagues realize. To fully understand modern SF, you should read Niven's work, including *Protector*, *Ringworld*, *Ringworld Engineers*, and *World of Ptaavs*. Niven enjoyed a major mainstream bestseller, *Lucifer's Hammer*, which was co-authored by another good hard-science SF author, Jerry Pournelle.

Andre Norton. Most of her science fiction novels were written for young adults, but they are suitable for grown-ups, too. I recommend sampling at least a couple of her books, so that you can see what most science fiction fans grew up reading and loving before they moved on to more ambitious authors. She does what she does quite well. Try *Moon of Three Rings*, *Star Gate*, *The Zero Stone*, *Lord of Thunder*, *Star Hunter*, *Victory on Janus*, or any of her other books.

Belva Plain. Just when everyone said that massive family saga novels had peaked and would be in disfavor with readers for a few years, Plain came along with *Evergreen* and confounded all of the experts. Her *Random Winds* was also a bestseller. Reading her will give you a feel for the current requirements of this kind of novel.

Frederik Pohl. He is a key figure in science fiction, both as an author and as an editor. His collaborations with C. M. Kornbluth (listed earlier) are classics in the field. His other books—notably *Gateway*, *The Age of the Pussyfoot*, *A Plague of Pythons*, and *Man Plus*—have won awards within the genre and are superior examples of science fiction storytelling.

Mario Puzo. As previously discussed, his *The Godfather* is a minor American classic, and his influence on the publishing industry has been enormous. He is a fine writer, and he is at his best when writing what he apparently thinks of as "strictly commercial" books.

Ayn Rand. Rand is not just a popular mainstream writer;

she is a major figure in American literature, a fact which will probably not be fully recognized for at least another twenty years. Her two most famous novels are *Atlas Shrugged* and *The Fountainhead,* which can best be described as "fiction of ideas," although that does not mean they are dull. Far from it! Rand's books read like thrillers, but they are crammed full of philosophy. This is an author to read if you have doubts about how to integrate thematic content into your story line. American critics have treated Rand with indifference and even hostility because her political assumptions are alien to them; her philosophy is libertarian, and her books stress the need for individual freedom at virtually any cost. But if current trends in politics and philosophy continue, Rand may eventually be seen as a prophet. In any event, she is a superior storyteller.

Willo Davis Roberts. She was one of the best Gothic novelists at the height of that craze. She wrote some good mysteries. She has done fine novels for young adults. Now she is on the verge of major mainstream success. Read *Destiny's Woman.*

Lawrence Sanders. Sanders has taken the detective story and lifted it out of the genre pit. In fact he hasn't merely lifted it out, he's *thrown* it with considerable force. In books like *The First Deadly Sin, The Second Deadly Sin,* and *The Sixth Commandment* he has shown a talent for characterization and a plotting skill that have put him on all the bestseller lists. His first novel, *The Anderson Tapes,* was a thriller told in an experimental style and is a true tour de force.

Dorothy Sayers. Here is an author who had a style so unique that imitating it would lead only to hilarity. She managed to blend suspense and humor in a fashion so stylish that she lifted the mystery novel to new heights. Most readers feel that she is an acquired taste, but once the taste is acquired, you will always be hungry for her books. Try *Clouds of Witness, The Unpleasantness at the Bellona Club, The Dawson Pedigree (Unnatural Death), Hangman's Holiday, Busman's Honeymoon,* and all her other titles. With the books of Dorothy Sayers, the mystery novel began to come of age; she is of historical importance to the genre. Besides, her stories are as much fun today as they were when she began writing them in the 1920s, and virtually all of them are still in print.

Irwin Shaw. His short stories are acclaimed in academe, and many of them are very good indeed. But it is in his novel-length fiction that he speaks to the average reader, and it is this work that I find worth recommending to you. (Of course the academic community dislikes Shaw's novels, for they are not elitist.) He is a very stylish writer who creates characters as real and believable as any others in modern American fiction. Try *Nightwork* and *Rich Man, Poor Man* and *The Young Lions* and *Top of the Hill.*

Nevil Shute. Here is another British author who helped to define the parameters of the modern adventure story. But Shute is much more than an adventure novelist; he is very good at background and characterization. A real find if you've never read his work. I suggest you try *Most Secret, The Rainbow and the Rose,* and *On the Beach,* among others.

Robert Silverberg. He is a major figure in the science fiction field. In his early days, he ground out a phenomenal number of novels—literally hundreds of them—and wisely invested his money. Later in his career, he began writing more ambitious books which, while working within the confines of the genre, were nevertheless dazzling and of lasting importance. A few of his books have transcended the science fiction genre, and all of the following are well worth your time: *Downward to the Earth, Dying Inside, The Book of Skulls, Up the Line, Nightwings, Thorns,* and *Lord Valentine's Castle.*

Clifford Simak. He's another science fiction writer whose work has defined the field. Try such classics as *City, Time and Again, They Walked Like Men,* and *All Flesh Is Grass.*

Maj Sjowall and Per Wahloo. I am listing this Swedish husband-and-wife team as a single entry, for their best and most famous work was written in collaboration. Their psychological mysteries are highly regarded and have enjoyed worldwide popularity. Their writing is crisp, moody, and enriched with strong thematic purpose. Try *The Laughing Policeman, The Abominable Man, Cop Killer,* and others.

Cordwainer Smith. This science fiction writer did not produce a large body of work, but his stories have had a lasting effect on the genre. He is so stylish that sometimes he risks seeming mannered, but never falls into that pit. Read *The Planet Buyers, The Underpeople,* and the short story collection titled *You Will Never Be the Same,* plus any other Cordwainer Smith works that you can get your hands on.

Richard Stark. This is Donald Westlake's pseudonym. The Stark books are among the most tightly structured, lightning-paced novels ever produced by an American writer. Most of them are built around the same anti-hero, a man known only as Parker. This is the hard-boiled school of writing, given a modern tone, brought into the America of the 1960s and 1970s. If you have never read the Stark novels, I envy you the hours of first-rate entertainment that lie ahead of you. Some of the Stark books are: *Slayground, Deadly Edge, Point Blank!, The Split, The Rare Coin Score, The Sour Lemon Score, The Black Ice Score, The Jugger,* and *Butcher's Moon.* Most of the Stark novels have been out of print too long, and I imagine that some enterprising publisher will finally remember them before too many more years go by. In the meantime, if you cannot find them in your bookstore, it is well worth haunting used-book emporiums and searching through stacks of mouldering paperbacks in order to put together a collection of these gems. Stark will teach you plotting and mood and the value of economy in language.

Rex Stout. Stout's long list of Nero Wolfe novels is a gold mine for anyone looking to be entertained. Furthermore, these are landmark novels in the mystery genre. The writing is economical. It is also some of the most highly polished prose anyone has ever produced inside the genre. Stout was also a fine characterizer, and his story people—especially Archie Goodwin, Nero Wolfe, and some of the other regulars in the series—are always sympathetic and convincing. A few of his many titles are *The Doorbell Rang, Death of a Doxy, The Father Hunt, The Mother*

Hunt, Too Many Clients, Triple Jeopardy, and *Where There's a Will.*

Theodore Sturgeon. The one and only. This man is truly an American original. His viewpoint is unique. His stories are unique. And his sensitivity is more than unique; it is devastating. Sturgeon is primarily a science fiction writer, if you would believe the publishers who routinely label him as such, but I think he easily qualifies as a mainstream author. The characters in his books are so real we can hear them talking while we read the page. More than most writers in the SF genre, Sturgeon is aware of the need for thematic structure. His concerns are not the hardware of most science fiction stories; he's not interested in space-ships and time machines and such stuff. Sturgeon's material is human emotion—love, hate, love, greed, love, jealousy, love, and love again—and he can translate *feeling* to the printed page better than anyone else in the genre and better than nine out of ten writers who *aren't* in the genre. You must read *More Than Human, The Dreaming Jewels, The Cosmic Rape,* and such story collections as *Caviar, E Pluribus Unicorn,* and *Sturgeon in Orbit.* This is not so much a writer who has defined modern fiction as a writer who has shown us what the genre could be if more of its writers cared enough and had enough talent to elevate it out of its pulp traditions. Sturgeon also wrote one of the finest psychological horror novels ever to see print. The title is *Some of Your Blood,* and it should have had the impact on the American public that Levin's *Rosemary's Baby* had. Find it, read it, enjoy.

Ross Thomas. Thomas is a fine mainstream thriller writer who is a favorite among aficionados of the form. His work is polished, erudite, and compelling. Try *The Cold War Swap, The Singapore Wink, The Mordida Man, A Chinaman's Chance, The Eighth Dwarf,* and others.

J.R.R. Tolkien. This is *the* writer of fantasy in our century. His magnificent *Lord of the Rings* trilogy has sold many millions of copies and is even more popular today than it was when it was first published. Tolkien's prose is so polished it shines. His characters are deeply drawn, and his backgrounds are so vividly detailed that they seem more real than the world in which we actually live. Tolkien is another author whose awareness of the need for thematic structure has elevated his work to the highest levels that fiction can attain.

Jack Vance. Vance has written both mysteries and science fiction novels, but it is his SF for which he is famous. He has won many awards in that genre, and virtually all of his many science fiction books are still in print. Try *The Dying Earth, Big Planet, Emphyrio,* and others.

A. E. van Vogt. He is another key figure in the science fiction field. Some of his work seems dated now, but most of it is still as readable, fascinating, and mysterious as it was when it first saw print. Van Vogt is not much of a stylist. He is not adept at characterization. But he plots like a demon, and he has an ability to create mood and delineate futuristic backgrounds that earns him a lasting place in the SF field. Try such classics as *The Weapons Shops of Isher, Slan, The Players of Null-A, The World of Null-A.*

Gore Vidal. His use of language is as close to faultless as anyone could reasonably expect a writer to get. He creates characters as real as those you meet on the street. (In fact, considering some of the people I've been meeting on the street lately, Vidal's characters are even more real than that!) He never sets pen to paper without a clear thematic purpose. And he is a storyteller first-class. Sometimes I find his political opinions to be distinctly elitist and perhaps even anti-human, but somehow that never gets in the way of his story. *Messiah* is one of the finest novels about religion and about Americans' attitudes toward death that I have ever read. *Burr, 1876,* and *Creation* are first-rate historical novels.

Kurt Vonnegut. Here is another American original. No one writes like Vonnegut, and no one should even try. Only Vonnegut can do what Vonnegut does so well. Nevertheless, because he is one of the most widely read of modern writers, you ought to be familiar with his work. Try *Player Piano, The Sirens of Titan, Slaughterhouse Five, Breakfast of Champions,* and others.

Joseph Wambaugh. Wambaugh is a police detective who eventually gave up his badge to be a full-time writer.

No one has ever written more realistically about the day-to-day lives of modern American police officers. Wambaugh is a born storyteller, and you would do well to study the ways in which he inserts large amounts of background material into a novel. Read *The New Centurions, The Blue Knight, The Black Marble,* and others. As an added bonus, Wambaugh can be quite funny.

Donald Westlake. Westlake stands alone as master of the comic suspense novel. His most recent books have been weak, but many of his others—*The Fugitive Pigeon, God Save the Mark, The Hot Rock, Adios Scheherazade, Cops and Robbers*—have never been equalled. Earlier in this list, I discussed Westlake's alter-ego, Richard Stark, and perhaps it is worth comparing the two sides of Westlake's talent. In my opinion, and in that of many other writers I know, even though the Donald Westlake books are wonderful, they are not quite as successful in artistic terms as the Stark novels. This might be because comedy seems inherently less important than serious fiction. Whatever the reason, when you read a Donald Westlake novel and then read a Richard Stark novel, you kind of wish that Westlake had spent more time on the hardboiled stuff. And *then* you start wishing that he set his sights even higher at some point in his career, for he is such a fine writer that he might well have become a major mainstream author if he had at some point made up his mind to break out of the genres.

Colin Wilson. This British author has written books of philosophy and some of the best studies of the occult ever done. He is also a novelist with a rather dense but uncannily affecting style. Just to broaden your horizons, I recommend you read *The Mind Parasites, Lingard,* and *The Glass Cage.*

Gene Wolfe. Wolfe is a science fiction writer and a fantasist who is gradually becoming one of the half-dozen most important writers in his field. He's a fine stylist. Try *The Fifth Head of Cerberus, The Shadow of the Torturer,* and *The Claw of the Conciliator.*

Cornell Woolrich. Although he apparently died believing that his life's work had been shallow and worthless, Woolrich has had enormous influence upon mystery and suspense writers. His style is usually slick and colorful, in spite of occasional slips into the melodramatic pulp tradition from which he originally came. His plotting is fresh. His characters are real, and his understanding of their psychology is always deep. He is historically important in his field. Try *The Bride Wore Black, The Black Angel,* and *Deadline at Dawn,* among others.

Herman Wouk. It is true that his prose seldom sings. Nevertheless, I am a great fan of Wouk's, for his characters come alive, and his work is brimming with compassion. He's no slouch at plotting, either! *The Caine Mutiny, The Winds of War, Marjorie Morningstar,* and *Youngblood Hawke* will grab and hold you from first page to last. Wouk is always acutely aware of the need for good fiction to go beyond entertainment, and the thematic structures of some of his books are complex and amazing to behold. Sometimes, in the middle of a Wouk novel, I wonder if the critical consensus—that he is a good pop novelist but little more—might be woefully wrong; perhaps he will turn out to be our Dickens. If he *does* last, it will be his keen eye for character and his compassion that will earn him immortality.

Roger Zelazny. Zelazny is a science fiction writer, but he clearly could have written anything he chose to write. In his early days he wrote such stylish, poetic novelettes and novellas as "The Keys to December," "A Rose for Ecclesiastes," "The Furies," "The Graveyard Heart," "For a Breath I Tarry," "This Moment of the Storm," "This Mortal Mountain," and "He Who Shapes." His earliest novels were also poetic, overflowing with brilliant imagery: *The Dream Master, This Immortal,* and *Lord of Light.* Many of his later books have been unpretentious adventure novels—such as the *Nine Princes in Amber* series. Other things—like *Doorways in the Sand, Today We Choose Faces,* and *Jack of Shadows*—are not so easily categorized within the subgenres of science fiction. I recommend that you read his early works first. He has had considerable influence upon his field.

Although I am sure I have inadvertently left out a dozen

or two dozen important authors, this should get you started on your quest toward being a writer. Perhaps your name will appear on the next list of this sort that I compose, in the revised edition of *How to Write Best-Selling Fiction*, five or ten years from now. I truly hope so. Good luck.

Index

Other Books of Interest

General Writing Books

Beginning Writer's Answer Book, edited by Polking and Bloss, $14.95

Getting the Words Right: How to Revise, Edit and Rewrite, by Theodore A. Rees Cheney $13.95

How to Become a Bestselling Author, by Stan Corwin, $14.95

How to Get Started in Writing, by Peggy Teeters $10.95

International Writers' & Artists' Yearbook, (paper) $10.95

Law and the Writer, edited by Polking and Meranus (paper) $7.95

Make Every Word Count, by Gary Provost (paper) $7.95

Teach Yourself to Write, by Evelyn A. Stenbock $12.95

Treasury of Tips for Writers, edited by Marvin Weisbord (paper) $6.95

Writer's Encyclopedia, edited by Kirk Polking $19.95

Writer's Market, edited by Bernadine Clark $18.95

Writer's Resource Guide, edited by Bernadine Clark $16.95

Writing for the Joy of It, by Leonard Knott $11.95

Writing From the Inside Out, by Charlotte Edwards (paper) $9.95

Magazine/News Writing

Complete Guide to Marketing Magazine Articles, by Duane Newcomb $9.95

Complete Guide to Writing Nonfiction, by the American Society of Journalists & Authors, edited by Glen Evans $24.95

Craft of Interviewing, by John Brady $9.95

Magazine Writing: The Inside Angle, by Art Spikol $12.95

Magazine Writing Today, by Jerome E. Kelley $10.95

Newsthinking: The Secret of Great Newswriting, by Bob Baker $11.95

1001 Article Ideas, by Frank A. Dickson $10.95

Stalking the Feature Story, by William Ruehlmann $9.95

Write On Target, by Connie Emerson $12.95

Writing and Selling Non-Fiction, by Hayes B. Jacobs $12.95

Fiction Writing

Creating Short Fiction, by Damon Knight $11.95

Fiction Is Folks: How to Create Unforgettable Characters, by Robert Newton Peck $11.95

Fiction Writer's Help Book, by Maxine Rock $12.95

Fiction Writer's Market, edited by Jean Fredette $17.95

Handbook of Short Story Writing, by Dickson and Smythe (paper) $6.95

How to Write Best-Selling Fiction, by Dean R. Koontz $13.95

How to Write Short Stories that Sell, by Louise Boggess (paper) $7.95

One Way to Write Your Novel, by Dick Perry (paper) $6.95

Secrets of Successful Fiction, by Robert Newton Peck $8.95

Writing Romance Fiction—For Love And Money, by Helene Schellenberg Barnhart $14.95

Writing the Novel: From Plot to Print, by Lawrence Block $10.95

Special Interest Writing Books

Cartoonist's & Gag Writer's Handbook, by Jack Markow (paper) $9.95

The Children's Picture Book: How to Write It, How to Sell It, by Ellen E. M. Roberts $17.95

Complete Book of Scriptwriting, by J. Michael Straczynski $14.95

Complete Guide to Greeting Card Writing, edited by Larry Sandman (paper) $7.95

Complete Guide to Writing Software User Manuals, by Brad McGehee (paper) $14.95

Confession Writer's Handbook, by Florence K. Palmer. Revised by Marguerite McClain $9.95

Guide to Greeting Card Writing, edited by Larry Sandman $10.95

How to Make Money Writing . . . Fillers, by Connie Emerson $12.95

How to Write a Cookbook and Get It Published, by Sara Pitzer, $15.95

How to Write a Play, by Raymond Hull $13.95

How to Write and Sell Your Personal Experiences, by Lois Duncan $10.95

How to Write and Sell (Your Sense of) Humor, by Gene Perret $12.95

How to Write "How-To" Books and Articles, by Raymond Hull (paper) $8.95

Mystery Writer's Handbook, edited by Lawrence Treat (paper) $8.95

Poet and the Poem, revised edition by Judson Jerome $13.95

Poet's Handbook, by Judson Jerome $11.95

Programmer's Market, edited by Brad McGehee (paper) $16.95

Sell Copy, by Webster Kuswa $11.95

Successful Outdoor Writing, by Jack Samson $11.95

Travel Writer's Handbook, by Louise Zobel (paper) $8.95

TV Scriptwriter's Handbook, by Alfred Brenner $12.95

Writing and Selling Science Fiction, by Science Fiction Writers of America (paper) $7.95

Writing for Children & Teenagers, by Lee Wyndham. Revised by Arnold Madison $11.95

Writing for Regional Publications, by Brian Vachon $11.95

Writing to Inspire, by Gentz, Roddy, et al $14.95

The Writing Business

Complete Handbook for Freelance Writers, by Kay Cassill $14.95

Freelance Jobs for Writers, edited by Kirk Polking (paper) $7.95

How to Be a Successful Housewife/Writer, by Elaine Fantle Shimberg $10.95

How You Can Make $20,000 a Year Writing, by Nancy Hanson (paper) $6.95

Profitable Part-time/Full-time Freelancing, by Clair Rees $10.95

The Writer's Survival Guide: How to Cope with Rejection, Success and 99 Other Hang-Ups of the Writing Life, by Jean and Veryl Rosenbaum $12.95

To order directly from the publisher, include $1.50 postage and handling for 1 book and 50¢ for each additional book. Allow 30 days for delivery.

Writer's Digest Books, Department B
9933 Alliance Road, Cincinnati OH 45242
Prices subject to change without notice.